Why Institutions Matter

The New Institutionalism in Political Science

**Vivien Lowndes
and
Mark Roberts**

palgrave
macmillan

First published 2013 by
PALGRAVE MACMILLAN

Palgrave Macmillan in the UK is an imprint of Macmillan Publishers Limited, registered in England, company number 785998, of Houndmills, Basingstoke, Hampshire RG21 6XS.

Palgrave Macmillan in the US is a division of St Martin's Press LLC, 175 Fifth Avenue, New York, NY 10010.

Palgrave Macmillan is the global academic imprint of the above companies and has companies and representatives throughout the world.

Palgrave® and Macmillan® are registered trademarks in the United States, the United Kingdom, Europe and other countries

ISBN 978-0-333-92955-1 hardback
ISBN 978-0-333-92954-4 paperback

This book is printed on paper suitable for recycling and made from fully managed and sustained forest sources. Logging, pulping and manufacturing processes are expected to conform to the environmental regulations of the country of origin.

A catalogue record for this book is available from the British Library.

A catalog record for this book is available from the Library of Congress.

10 9 8 7 6 5 4 3 2 1
22 21 20 19 18 17 16 15 14 13

Printed in China

Contents

List of Illustrative Material

Boxes

Figure

Tables

Acknowledgements

Our interest in politics and institutions was nurtured (albeit in slightly different timeframes) at the Institute of Local Government Studies (INLOGOV) at the University of Birmingham, and in the Department of Public Policy at De Montfort University, Leicester. Both settings provided a rather special type of academic environment that challenged conventional disciplinary boundaries and theory/practice divides.

Whatever insights we have been able to articulate in this book are as much a product of the informal discussions, debates and (occasional) arguments we enjoyed with colleagues at Birmingham and Leicester as they are of the more formal processes of theoretical analysis and empirical research. We would like to thank the colleagues who have influenced our thinking over the years, sometimes helping us down the road upon which we were already travelling, and sometimes disrupting our path dependence and sending us off into previously unknown territory. From our time at the University of Birmingham, we would like to thank John Stewart, Helen Sullivan, Chris Skelcher, Steven Griggs, Janet Newman and Teresa Payne, and acknowledge the contribution of the late Kieron Walsh. From De Montfort, we would like to thank Lawrence Pratchett, David Wilson, Steve Leach, Melvin Wingfield, Jonathan Davies, Rachael Chapman, Catherine Durose, Ismael Blanco, Rabia Karakaya Polat and Valeria Guarneros. Many of these colleagues have moved on to new challenges elsewhere, but we continue to share a common commitment to interdisciplinary scholarship that is both theoretically robust and policy-relevant.

Now at the University of Nottingham, Vivien would like to thank Paul Heywood, Mat Humphrey, Lucy Sargisson, Sue Pryce, Phil Cowley, Jan Meyer-Sahling, Maria Wade, Harald Decker and Despoina Grigoriadou. Thanks are also due to Francesca Gains (Manchester), Peter John (University College London) and Michael Saward (Warwick) for advice and support over many years.

We would like to thank Steven Kennedy at Palgrave Macmillan for his patience, encouragement and practical support, including his suggestion that we present and debate our emerging arguments on neutral ground. Out of this suggestion came our engagement with the Department of Politics at the University of Sheffield. We would like to thank Simon Bulmer, Colin Hay, Martin Smith and Georgina Waylen for their input, and the MA/PhD students who acted as a highly effective testing ground for our initial thoughts.

Also at Palgrave Macmillan, we would like to thank Helen Caunce for her advice and assistance throughout the production process, and the series editors Gerry Stoker, John Pierre and Guy Peters. We would particularly like to thank Gerry Stoker and Rod Rhodes (now both at the University of Southampton but who also cut their teeth at INLO-GOV, Birmingham) for believing that this book would really happen over what turned out to be a very long gestation period!

Away from work we have both enjoyed the fantastic support of family and friends. Vivien would like to thank Stuart, Alastair, Hope and Rory Douglas, Richard, Barbara and Phil Lowndes, Julia Buchanan, Penelope Gorman, Elizabeth May, Sara Gowen, Audrey Zemiro, Jackie West and Sharon Squires. Mark would like to thank Sylvia, Graham, Kim, Sam, Yasmin and Lucia, and also Harry Roberts and Jan Didrichsen.

VIVIEN LOWNDES
MARK ROBERTS

Chapter 1

Why Study Institutions?

Institutions are central to the subject matter of political analysis. Indeed, up until the 1950s, institutionalism *was* political science, in the sense that the discipline concentrated upon the study of constitutions and the organizational arrangements of representation and government. Political scientists compared executive and legislatures, or parties and electoral systems, across countries and over time. Legal and historical methods dominated, alongside a descriptive idiom and a set of assumptions about what constituted a 'good political system'.

The behavioural revolution made its challenge to institutionalism from the late 1950s onwards, questioning what lay beneath the formalisms of politics and using empirical investigation to find out 'who (really) governs' in different contexts (Sanders, 2010). A generation later, rational choice theorists sought to explain politics in terms of the interplay of individuals' self-interest (Hindmoor, 2010). From another direction, neo-Marxists focused upon the role of 'systemic power' (deriving from capital/labour relations) in shaping politics (Maguire, 2010). Political scientists of all colours seemed intent upon debunking the institutionalist certainties of their forebears. The clear message was that there was much, much more to politics than the formal arrangements for representation, decision making and policy implementation.

What happened to the institutionalists who got left behind, as these powerful currents took the discipline in new directions? Many continued to practice their art in the conviction that 'You only need to sit still, it all comes "round again"' (Rhodes, 1995: 57). Others were provoked to defend their 'common sense' assumptions and methods – notably in sub-fields like public administration and constitutional studies. In fact, by the end of the 1980s, institutionalism had 'come round again' as the internal limitations of the new paradigms became clear. A 'new institutionalism' emerged as a response to the 'undersocialized' character of dominant approaches in the discipline, in which institutions were, at best, seen as no more than the simple aggregation of individual preferences.

'New institutionalists' asserted simply that 'the organization of political life makes a difference' (March and Olsen, 1984: 747). Political scientists from different corners of the discipline flocked to the banner of new institutionalism. Historical and comparative scholars brought with them ideas about the institutional shaping of policy choices in areas like welfare and taxation (Steinmo *et al.*, 1992). Rational choice scholars drew attention to the role of institutional factors in structuring individuals' choices (Weingast, 1996; Ostrom, 2005). Neo-Marxists developed 'regulation' and 'regime' theories to analyse the institutional variation that was played down by the structuralists of the 1970s (Painter, 1995; Stoker, 1995). Reflecting this upsurge of interest, Goodin and Klingemann (1996: 25) described the new institutionalism as 'the next revolution' in political science. Rather than returning to the descriptive and atheoretical style of an earlier generation of institutionalists, new institutionalists developed a more expansive definition of their subject matter (to include informal conventions as well as formal rules) and operated with more explicit (if diverse) theoretical frameworks. Historical, rational choice and sociological institutionalism were developed as distinct analytical approaches (Peters, 2005).

In this book, we tell the story of the new institutionalist 'revolution' and give our assessment of its contributions, positive and negative, to political science. But we also identify another set of less spectacular, but equally important, changes taking place. If the 'old' institutionalism was the first phase of the intellectual trajectory and the 'new' institutionalism the second, then we see in clear relief the emergence of a third phase. This development is characterized by a growing consensus across the (previously fragmented) schools of institutionalism around core concepts and key dilemmas.

As institutional theory has been changing rapidly over the last thirty years, so have institutions themselves. For this reason the book is not only concerned with new institutionalism as a way of understanding politics, but also with the development and spread of new institutions, which are structuring politics in new ways across the world. In fact, the two concerns are linked. As the organization of politics and government becomes more complex and fragmented, political scientists need access to more sophisticated theoretical and methodological tools. At the same time, the availability of these tools illuminates phenomena that might otherwise go unnoticed.

Some commentators have referred to the 'de-institutionalization' of politics and government, with the break-up of large scale bureaucracies and the growth of 'soft' processes like networking, collaboration or 'steering' (Rhodes, 1997; Sullivan and Skelcher, 2002). But political institutions have not become any less important; rather, they have changed. Institutionalist theory provides a good set of conceptual tools for analysing contemporary governance precisely because it does not equate institutions with organizations, nor assume that politics is determined by formal structures and frameworks alone. Institutionalists embrace institutional differentiation in political life, for instance the increasing role of markets and networks alongside hierarchy and bureaucracy. And they expect hybridity, anticipating that existing and emerging institutions will overlap and recombine in context-dependent ways. Moreover, they recognize that informal conventions can be as binding as formal constitutions, and can be particularly resistant to change. Most importantly, second, and now third, phase institutionalists underline the 'double life' of institutions, in which institutions constrain actors, but are also human creations (Grafstein, 1988: 517–18). The burgeoning political institutions we see around us have not landed from another planet; rather, they are the products of political action and the outcomes of political struggles.

What are institutions – and what is an institutionalist explanation?

The dictionary defines 'institution' as 'established law, custom or practice'. From the sixteenth century, the term has had a particular association with the practices and customs of government. Today, 'institution' also refers more generally to forms of social organization (Williams, 1983: 169). It is a multi-faceted term which is used to refer to social phenomena at many different levels – informal codes of conduct, written contracts, complex organizations. It also hints at some evaluation of these phenomena. Institutions are somehow 'more' than they appear: they are 'special' procedures and practices (Lowndes, 1996). Moreover, they show resilience over time, producing 'stable, valued and recurring patterns of behaviour' (Huntington, 1968).

As we live our lives, we play our part in both reinforcing and undermining the institutions around us. Institutions exist in every sphere of our lives, the social, economic and political. Marriage, markets, mosques, media... these can all be described as 'institutions'. They all create 'patterned interactions that are predictable' (Peters, 2005: 18).

While the sources of institutional regularities are diverse, they are also overlapping. We know that expectations regarding male and female roles in politics are shaped by the institutions of marriage and the family, the influence of which is not confined to the domestic sphere. The institutions of the market (prices, contracts, competition) increasingly penetrate the public realm as social activities become more commercialized and many state services are privatized. Religious institutions are no longer a 'private' matter as they come to shape political conflicts, whether in the USA, the Middle East or Europe.

But what does it mean to describe an institution as 'political'? We can follow Adrian Leftwich's (Held and Leftwich, 1984: 144) definition of politics:

> politics is about power; about the forces which influence and reflect its distribution and use; and about the effect of this on resource use and distribution; it is about the 'transformatory' capacity of social agents, agencies and institutions; it is not about government or government alone.

It follows that, in understanding political institutions, we are as much concerned with what 'ordinary people' can and cannot do as with the capacities of government and the actors who directly inhabit the political arena. Political institutions shape the opportunities that all of us have as citizens to make our voices heard, to participate in decision making, and to access public services. Institutions like electoral systems, political parties, social movements and human rights legislation all affect what we can and cannot do politically (and the costs, risks and potential benefits involved). The way in which government is organized provides opportunities for citizens to make contact with their representatives and decision makers – through institutional mechanisms such as consultations, complaints systems or question and answer sessions, as well as traditional routes like voting. Whether citizens take up these opportunities is conditioned by other, less obvious aspects of the institutional configuration – such as the timing and location of public meetings – and by informal conventions about the way in which issues are discussed and decisions made. Institutional opportunities and constraints may operate differentially for particular groups of citizens: parents may not be able to attend an evening meeting, young people may be put off by traditional committee procedures, new migrants may need translation or interpretation facilities.

While a bottom-up perspective is important, it is also true that the formal institutional architecture of the state sets parameters as to what is possible and impossible (and desirable/undesirable) for politicians and the civil servants who work for them. For example, whether a country has a proportional or majoritarian electoral system makes coalition government more or less likely, which in turn affects both the relationship between parties and the conduct of politicians towards their electorates. A prime ministerial system allows parties more influence over the executive than a presidential one. Equally in countries where state assets or services have been privatized, there is a reduction in the political influence of public sector workers, but new investment opportunities for business (and new incentives for business to lobby politicians or build alliances with consumer groups).

The influence of institutions over the conduct of politics is manifold, encompassing both the 'dignified' and the 'efficient' parts of the constitution (Bagehot, 1867), and reaching from matters of state to the day-to-day operation of local government. Informal institutions can be as powerful as formal ones – the debating conventions which are observed in a parliamentary assembly are not usually specified in writing but have a profound effect on the nature of that country's politics. The 'glass ceiling' in public life has no formal status but remains effective in shaping women's opportunities. The public service ethos that shapes the conduct of health or education workers in many social democratic states is sustained chiefly through informal processes and is part of a powerful legitimizing narrative about the role of public servants *vis-à-vis* their counterparts in the private sector.

Moreover, political institutions do not stand still. The familiar institutional landscape is being transformed as the international movement of people, goods and information gains pace. The technological revolution is both part of this phenomenon and a driver of it. Indeed, at the present time, many of our familiar political institutions are responding to these and other demands for change:

- Political parties have been challenged by new interest groups and social movements that reflect the fracturing and internationalization of political identities. Politicians assess electoral outcomes in the context of new mechanisms for gauging public opinion (polls, direct action, talk shows, blogs, tweets and e-petitions).
- Politicians and civil servants find themselves operating in an ever-more complex system of multi-level governance, in which they are constrained by transnational institutional frameworks – e.g. the

European Union and also global agreements on climate change and trade, as well as more familiar military and defensive alliances.
- Pressures to reduce the scope of central state intervention have also increased the importance of 'lower' levels of governance – devolved assemblies, regional bodies and (on some matters) local councils.
- The drive for efficiency and competition has driven the break-up of state bureaucracies though privatization and marketization, and the formation of multi-sector partnerships involving public, private and civil society actors.
- Pressures to greater transparency are uncovering the continued significance (and ongoing adaptation) of informal institutions – like patronage, corruption and clientelism – in the interstices of seemingly accountable formal structures.

Our approach has the flexibility to extend its purchase beyond the Western liberal democracies with which we are most familiar. Unlike the 'old institutionalists' (see Chapter 2), we do not make any assumptions about the shape of political institutions or the values they embody. New institutionalism is just as interested in the ways in which political behaviour and identities are shaped (or more harshly delimited) by institutions of dictatorship, tribalism, militarism, one-party states or religious republics. The conduct of international politics (whether in relation to trade, migration, security or peacekeeping) across such very different institutional orders presents both politicians and researchers with formidable challenges.

So we have established the varied and dynamic nature of political institutions and introduced some of the ways in which they shape political behaviour. But what explanatory purchase does *institutionalism* give us over political phenomena that we may be missing when using other approaches? Guy Peters (2005: 164) summarizes the core proposition:

> The fundamental issue holding all these various approaches... together is simply that they consider institutions the central component of political life. In these theories institutions are the variable that explain political life in the most direct and parsimonious manner, and they are also the factors that themselves require explanation. The basic argument is that institutions *do* matter, and that they matter more than anything else that could be used to explain political decisions.

Box 1.1 Comparing institutionalist and non-institutionalist accounts

Case A: The UK MPs' expenses scandal

The United Kingdom Parliamentary expenses scandal resulted in a large number of resignations, sackings, de-selections and retirement announcements, together with public apologies and the repayment of expenses, after *The Daily Telegraph* newspaper obtained a leaked full copy of the expenses records and began publishing details in daily instalments from 8 May 2009. These disclosures dominated the British media for weeks, and appeared to show flagrant and gross misuse of the expenses system for personal gain by many MPs, including Government ministers, and across all parties. The popular analysis of the scandal focused on the agency of individual actors and on their self-maximising conduct in relation to 'public money'. The institutional perspective brings out the following additional points of significance:

- The rules for claiming expenses were only very loosely drawn and, when opportunities to tighten the rules were apparent, party leaders had not shown the political will to do so.
- The Parliamentary Fees Office failed to police claims and, in fact, encouraged MPs to claim for items which were later deemed to be outside the rules.
- At the extreme, some MPs intentionally maximized their pecuniary self-interest, but the majority of MPs believed that they were working within a set of practices which was explicitly endorsed by parliamentary officials and implicitly accepted by their party leaders.
- As the scandal unravelled, many were forced to repay expenses 'legitimately' claimed in previous years and MPs' resistance to reform and expressions of grievance at 'rough justice' hardened the public and media perception of their conduct.

The self-maximising approach ignores how the rules were drafted, enforced and retrospectively reinterpreted, and as such, only explains why some MPs began to 'fiddle' the system. It does not explain why others claimed very little, or no expenses at all, or why politicians continued to contest the public view to the point where they were clearly damaging their interests, individually and as a professional group.

Institutionalists contend that the greatest theoretical leverage is to be gained by studying the institutional frameworks within which political actors operate. In short, political behaviour and political outcomes are best understood by studying the rules and practices that characterize institutions, and the ways in which actors relate to them (whether they are politicians, public servants, citizens or social movements). The

8

Box 1.2   Comparing institutionalist and non-institutionalist accounts

Case B: Policy development in the European Union

Policy development in the European Union (EU) relies heavily on agreement being reached between its member states. In this context, realist perspectives in international relations, and the news media more widely, have tended to focus on EU 'summits' as the arena in which crucial policy developments are progressed as a result of diplomacy and bargaining between autonomous state actors. Since France and Germany possess the most political and economic 'clout' within the member states it is commonly assumed that most policy outcomes directly reflect the interests of those powerful states. By taking a longer-term view, the institutional approach highlights a number of significant policy initiatives which do not fit this pattern, and, indeed, have not been within the direct control of member states, as individuals or groups:

- Over the decades the EU has assumed a key role in the development of gender equality, but this was not a direct expression of the strategic intent of member states, but instead an unintended by-product of the inclusion of Article 119 in the original Treaty of Rome.
- The EU has intervened extensively in the field of health and safety at work, and has developed policies which exceed the standards required by most individual states. But here politicians have played only a loose supervisory role and 'technocrats' have pieced together best practice from many states to produce a whole which is greater than the sum of the individual parts.
- The EU Social Protocol was a summit outcome, but not one which key actors, including France and Germany, expected. Locked in a battle with an intransigent UK government, these states put forward a 'deluxe' version of the protocol which they expected to have to water down to bring the UK on board. In the event John Major's government rejected all compromise, and, as a result, all other member states were locked into a much more ambitious and wide-ranging policy than any individual actor had proposed.

The international relations approach, therefore, tells half of the story in its accounts of the battles between high-profile actors in summits. However, it neglects a range of effects which generate from the nature of the policies themselves, and are influential in the lengthy 'valleys' between peaks. These include the unintended consequences of legislation, gaps in fit which allow lower-profile actors to shape policy below the surface, and pressures imposed by deadlines for agreement.

Box 1.3   Comparing institutionalist and non-institutionalist accounts

Case C: The 'global' financial crisis

The series of shocks which hit a number of national economies in 2009 was narrated as a 'global' financial crisis. In fact, the greatest effects were felt by the USA and Europe and, within these countries, both the causes and impacts were shaped by the specific political and social context. An institutional analysis enables us to examine the interconnections between economies in terms of regulations and practices, but also challenges the 'globalization thesis' by focusing down on the fine grain of institutional change in each specific country and the responsibility of actors at various levels within that economy.

In the case of UK, the institutional approach brings out the following points of significance:

- During the 1970s and 80s, the UK lost much of its manufacturing industry and developed 'service' industries and financial products. The removal of regulations, which were seen to inhibit this shift, was a key policy initiative of the Conservative governments at the time, which was continued when New Labour came to power in 1997.
- For many years, banking in the UK had had its own formal code of ethics which constrained the conduct of employees in creating and selling products to customers.
- The developing process of deregulation at the national level weakened these constraints with the result that, at company level, actors were free to introduce 'self-certification', which was designed to allow applicants to receive mortgages on property without any checks on the truthfulness of their statements.
- The extra flow of capital into the housing market from these self-certified mortgages over several years created a bubble effect which lead to the collapse of previously stable and highly regarded banks such as the Halifax Bank of Scotland (HBOS) Group.

And so while the 'globalization thesis' tends to disguise the difference between countries in terms of their financial policies and approach to regulation, the institutional perspective allows us to examine how actors at all levels played their part in generating a shock and how differences in impacts as well as causes can be better understood.

sorts of questions we might ask include: What are the formal 'rules of the game' within a particular political arena? What are the dominant practices that are not actually written down? Are there gaps between the formal rules and the way things 'really work'? Are there frequently rehearsed 'stories' that explain why people act one way rather than another? What do actors think will happen if they do not follow rules or observe dominant practices? How do actors circumvent, or seek to adapt, rules and practices? Do different actors relate to rules differently? Are there alternative rules and practices 'bubbling under'? Are new stories emerging about how things *could* work in the future? How do actors react to those who want to change the rules?

As Peters (2005) has cautioned, institutionalism runs the risk of 'conceptual stretching' as it develops a more expansive definition of what constitutes a political institution. To guard against this charge, we need to be clear about what *is not* an institutionalist explanation, as well as what is. Quite simply, an institutionalist explanation puts political institutions first, and is different from (say) a structuralist, or an idealist or a behaviourist, approach, which prioritizes respectively the role of social and economic structures, political ideas or the observable behaviour of individual actors. Boxes 1.1, 1.2 and 1.3 take a series of short vignettes and illustrate the difference between institutionalist and non-institutionalist accounts of the same political phenomena.

The contribution of the book

Many valuable contributions have been made to evaluating the impact of institutionalism on political theory and research since the millennium. Hay's (2002) *Political Analysis* is a seminal text of its genre, dealing not only with institutionalism but the full range of political theory from a broadly dispassionate stance. Peters' *New Institutionalism* (2005) is an encyclopaedic account of (what we call in this book) first and second phase institutionalism, describing and categorizing particularly those varieties of institutionalism which have emerged during the second phase. The *Oxford Handbook of Political Institutions*, edited by Rhodes, Binder and Rockman (2006), is a collection of writings from distinguished scholars of institutionalism which, as a compendium, is not intended to have a central theme beyond the presence of institutions themselves.

Our approach differs from these contributions in taking an unashamedly 'engaged' approach. By this we mean three things. First, we are practitioners of, and indeed enthusiasts for, institutionalism: we have used institutionalist theory extensively in our own research and believe that it 'works' theoretically, methodologically and in the field. Second, and following from this, we believe that institutionalism offers us vital insights into crucial political issues such as power, inequality and the continuing conflicts between groups and individuals in society and across nations. Institutionalism allows us not just to understand better how political institutions work, but also to generate strategies for resistance and reform, designed to prioritize new interests and values. Third, we use the term 'engaged' to refer to a 'value-critical' perspective not only on political conduct and outcomes but also on the development of institutionalism itself. As reflexive human beings and scholars, we not only argue that institutionalism 'works' but also stand back and ask where the theory may be found wanting and how it might be improved in the future. We wish to distance ourselves from the sectarian defence of any particular scholarly niche.

The book argues that there is a credible and compelling story to be told about the development of institutionalism which makes sense of the changes we see over time. The story begins with a relatively narrow fixation by 'old' institutionalists on the formality of laws and constitutions. Institutionalism then becomes lost for a while beneath rival theories, only to be rediscovered in many different and apparently disconnected forms. Centripetal trajectories have subsequently emerged in which the various strands of institutionalism are being brought together by the agency of boundary spanning scholars and the enduring interconnections between the ideas in question. We do not, of course, reach the end of the story here, because, as we write, the intellectual trajectory continues. Our aim is to provide the reader with a rich and detailed account of where institutionalism has come from while also contributing to its future development. In short, our book has the following objectives:

- to identify the common core of concepts at the heart of institutionalism;
- to explain institutionalism's relationship with key dilemmas around agency and power, time and space, and change and stability;
- to demonstrate the contribution which institutionalism as a coherent body of work has made to empirical research in political science;
- to examine the range of methodological approaches (and challenges) associated with institutionalism;
- to investigate its potential to inform the design of public policy now and in the future;
- and finally to contribute to the development of institutionalism as an engaged and value-critical theory.

Our core argument is that, beneath the apparent diversity and fragmentation of scholarly endeavour, there is a single, coherent institutionalism emerging from the central core of concepts which has been in place since institutions were first recognized for what they are. What sort of claim is this? We are not simply talking about a distinctively 'institutionalist way of thinking' (Heclo, 2006) or a broad slogan asserting that 'institutions matter'. Rather we are talking about an integrating theory which takes the concerns and dilemmas posed by the various strands of institutionalism and brings them together to produce convincing explanations of political conduct and outcomes. At the same time, we are not describing an integration which is complete at this time or will ever be perfectly constructed. To pretend so would be both to overstate the case for convergence, and run the risk of inconsistency in terms of how we characterize the imperfection of institutions and human agency throughout our text.

The biggest obstacle to our project is a hesitancy on the part of many institutionalists to combine insights from rational choice theory and sociological approaches. Such hesitancy ranges from a squeamishness about engaging with 'the other side' to a principled objection on ontological grounds. Colin Hay and Daniel Wincott (1998: 953) famously argued that there existed 'an intractable divide between two contending and incompatible approaches to institutional analysis', counselling against the 'cobbling together of institutional insights from differently informed institutionalisms'. In contrast, Vivien Schmidt (2006: 117) suggests that a way ahead can be found only if institutionalists 'begin exploring areas of mutual compatibility along their borders'. In a more confident vein, Colin Crouch (2005: 4–10) observes that 'intellectual recombination' is already a characteristic of institutionalism, concluding that such differences as remain 'should not be taken too seriously as authors can easily move away from the obvious limits of each of these "schools"'.

Our own ontological position can be broadly typified as constructivist. Constructivism is based on the premise that the world is constructed by individuals in different ways and people act on what they believe to be the case (as guided by their different constructions). Moreover, one and the same individual might construct the same or a very similar set of circumstances in a different way at a later point in time and as a consequence take action which is different from that which they took on the first occasion (Parsons, 2010). But, as Hay (2002: 126–34) argues, human actors are capable of rather more than this, being additionally 'conscious, reflexive and strategic'.

Consequently, we are entitled to ask: what if actors are capable of constructing the same immediate set of circumstances in different ways *simultaneously*? When an individual is faced by a set of circumstances which she believes demand action on her part, she is simultaneously and reflexively able to work out a course, or courses of action, which accommodate in some way what she sees as the needs of her family, the wider groups to which she belongs (including, for example, her political allegiances), and her 'selfish' desires to advance or simply protect her own position. As Garret Hardin (1968) observed, 'We can never do merely one thing.'

In some cases the courses of action which she attempts to bring together will conflict with one another too much to be reconciled, and some fudge or compromise will be the result. But in others she will be able to construct a 'squaring of the circle' which serves to achieve the perceived benefits for her family, the wider societal groups of which she is a member, and for herself. The particular theoretical insight we gain from conceptualizing the capabilities of actors in this way is that their strategic intent is not simply defined by a single construction of their place in the world, but by a number of different ontological positions which create mixed motivations. Strategic intent from this perspective is more about an actor's attempts to reconcile these competing demands, rather than simply achieving one of the objectives in mind.

If this type of simultaneous 'mixed motivational' construction is prevalent, then from a distinctively institutional perspective it will follow that we are born into a world where the institutions that impinge upon us are themselves the outcome of mixed motivational construction (Schickler, 2001: 4). Furthermore, if we accept that actors are engaged in a dialectic relationship with institutions, then what we most frequently observe in politics are the interactions between actors who are attempting to 'square the circle' of contemporary mixed motivational demands, and institutions which themselves contain legacies of different mixed motivational demands from the past. This way of thinking contains quite profound implications for institutional theory, because it suggests that it is not so much a matter of whether it is desirable to develop a 'multi-theoretic' (Rhodes, 1995: 56) perspective from the various strands, but more that it is essential to do so. Without examining the full range of possibilities for actors' motivation, the political analyst not only fails to understand the strategic intent of the actors themselves, but also fails to understand the core business of institutionalism – institutions themselves.

Box 1.4   Reforming US health care

In 2010, the USA saw a large and significant change in its arrangements for the health care of its citizens. In the first year of his presidency, Barack Obama had called for Congress to pass legislation reforming health care in the United States, as a key campaign promise and a top legislative goal. He proposed an expansion of health insurance coverage to cover the uninsured, to cap premium increases, and to allow workers to retain their coverage when they leave or change jobs. His proposal was to spend $900 billion over 10 years and include a government insurance plan, also known as 'the public option', to compete with the corporate insurance sector as a main component to lowering costs and improving quality of health care. It would make it illegal for insurers to drop sick people or deny them coverage for pre-existing conditions, and require every American to carry health cover. The plan also included medical spending cuts and taxes on insurance companies that offer expensive plans.

On 14 July 2009, House Democratic leaders introduced a 1,017-page plan for overhauling the US health care system, which Obama wanted Congress to approve by the end of 2009. After much public debate during the Congressional summer recess of 2009, Obama delivered a speech to a joint session of Congress on 9 September where he addressed concerns over his administration's proposals. On 7 November 2009, a health care bill featuring the public option was passed in the House. On 24 December 2009, the Senate passed its own bill – without a public option – on a party-

$\rightarrow$

But is it possible to operationalize such a multi-theoretic approach, and does it offer any significant epistemological gain? This question will be addressed fully in the chapters that follow, illustrated by numerous case studies from research in a range of different countries. For the time being, we can consider the case of changes in US health care, which serves to illustrate the benefits of a multi-theoretic approach which surfaces mixed motivations (see Box 1.4). It is clear that explanations based on different motivations are not mutually exclusive. President Barak Obama constructed a self-reinforcing and emboldening explanation for what he was doing which combined the need to help the poor, the need to save his presidency, and the need to honour and realize a historic Democratic commitment. On its own, each of these explanations is necessary but not sufficient; that is to say each is essential to a credible explanation but none is complete in isolation. Hence, for example, it is difficult to construct a credible explanation without taking account of Obama's desire to save his presidency from ridicule, but at the same time it is difficult to believe that there was no value based or historical context to his determination to keep pushing

line vote of 60 to 39. On 21 March 2010, the health care bill passed by the Senate in December was passed in the House by a vote of 219 to 212. Obama signed the bill into law on 23 March 2010.

There are a number of remarkable features about this exercise in institutional change, most of which relate to the fact that it happened at all. First, many previous presidents, including Republicans such as Theodore Roosevelt and Richard Nixon, had tried and failed to bring the issue to Congress in an acceptable form. Second, at the time he forced through the legislation, Obama himself was at one of the lowest points in his popularity, and opposition to the bill from the Republican Party and those representing 'American values' was ferocious and personally targeted the President. However, instead of backing off from the legislation when it seemed it would fail, as others had done before him, he chose to play 'hard ball' with his opponents, in a gamble which would make or break his presidency. Finally, even when Obama announced it as one of his top legislative goals, few believed it would be possible to overturn the existing health care arrangements because of the formidable institutionalization of these in the US welfare system. These sceptics included national and international politicians and journalists, but their doubts were also foreshadowed by political analysts such as Hacker (1998) who defined path dependence in the American system as the main blockage to reform, and Pierson (2004: 77) who looking back on attempts at health care reform up to 2004 declared: 'In a fundamental sense these reformers were too late.'

the controversial reforms. All three explanations are required, working in concert, to bring together a satisfactory account of why Obama persisted with the bill.

We are not claiming that the convergence and consolidation of institutionalist strands is complete or that multi-theoretic approaches are ubiquitous. But, like the political actors we study, political scientists are themselves reflexive agents. Labels or no labels, many scholars are working across theoretical boundaries and are continually attempting to bring different constructions of the political world together, simultaneously, in order to expand knowledge. Concluding that such an approach is both theoretically respectable and empirically practical should not, however, lead us down the road of mix-and-match methodologies which pay no heed to transparency or justification. The complexity implied by our theoretical stance demands a rigorous approach to key questions about how institutions are constituted, how they constrain actors' behaviour, and how they change and develop over time.

The structure of the book

Our objective in the next chapter is to identify the common core of concepts at the heart of institutionalism. We show how institutionalism developed from its 'old' to 'new' forms by moving along a series of analytical continua. These moves lead towards a conception of institutions that admits informal as well as formal elements, recognizes dynamism as well as stability, and assumes differentiation and contingency rather than functional efficiency in the ways institutions work (given power struggles and changing contexts). From these points of departure, we argue that institutionalism is now entering its third, consolidating phase, having previously passed through its first, exploratory phase and its second, fragmented phase.

In Chapter 3 we consider the central question of how institutions do their work. We propose that institutions constrain actors in three different ways: through rules, practices and narratives. How these modes of constraint are combined (or not), is an empirical rather than an ontological matter. Separating out the different modes is important, not just analytically but methodologically, providing a guide as to what to look for in research on political institutions. Chapter 4 is concerned with questions of power and agency, as the flipside to structure and constraint. We examine how institutions directly empower some actors through visible, recorded mechanisms such as laws, rights and licences; how they indirectly empower through informal and unwritten mechanisms such as gendered norms or privileges associated with nepotism or patronage; and how the narrative accounts of individual and group actors legitimize their authority and pre-empt challenge. We consider the wider rehabilitation of concepts of agency within institutionalism, as scholars from different perspectives seek to explain institutional diversity and dynamics. We propose our own distinctively institutionalist approach to power and agency.

Chapters 5, 6 and 7 look at how institutions change, and are changed. These are the dilemmas at the heart of third phase institutionalism. Chapter 5 critically evaluates theories of institutional change. While first phase institutionalism focused on explaining stability in politics, second phase institutionalism conceptualized change in stop/go terms, identifying critical junctures (or 'punctuations') followed by long periods of 'path dependence'. But with the arrival of third phase institutionalism, interest switched towards the significance of gradual (but potentially transformative) change and to the role of internal as well as external drivers. We argue that institutions' apparent stability over time is actually the outcome of a contested process of institutional maintenance, reflecting shifting power relationships and an ongoing 'war of position' over ideas and values. Chapter 6 shows how these dynamics generate variety within the institutional landscape, across space and over time. Political institutions are often combinations of disparate elements, with tight connections to institutions in the broader social and economic domains. The 'generative' theories of third phase institutionalism are contrasted with earlier 'reproductive' accounts which explored tendencies towards institutional convergence.

Chapter 7 asks whether institutions can be designed in any meaningful sense, given the ongoing and contested nature of institutional change. While highly unlikely to achieve all they set out to do, attempts at institutional design are inevitable as political actors seek to make their ideas and values 'stick' through institutional mechanisms. Such action does not only include heroic foundational moments (new constitutions, for instance) or fundamental reform programmes, but also many small acts of adjustment undertaken by strategic actors on the ground. We explore, in this context, what constitutes a 'good' process of institutional design, proposing twin criteria of 'revisability' and 'robustness'. In the final chapter of the book we look back at what we have learned about theory and practice, and consider the progress to date of third phase institutionalism and the challenges to come.

Chapter 2

Three Phases of Institutionalism

Our principal objective in this chapter is to identify the common core of concepts at the heart of institutionalism. We start by exploring what we mean by a theory in relation to political analysis and institutionalism in particular, specifically considering the limits on knowledge claims. In this sense, theory continually evolves and is never complete in the sense of having located a pure and unmovable truth. The chapter goes on to look at how institutionalism has developed through two phases and has now entered a third stage. In the first phase, from the 1930s to the 1970s, we find a process of *exploration and rediscovery* which combines the so-called 'old' institutionalism, its challenge from rational choice theory and behaviouralism, and its subsequent rediscovery as the 'new' institutionalism. In the second phase, from the early 1980s to the late 1990s, we track trajectories of *divergence and division* which see the new institutionalism growing rapidly in many different directions. We detect a new phase of institutionalist scholarship and research emerging from around 2000, which is characterized by *convergence and consolidation*, evidenced in a growing consensus around key concepts and significant dilemmas.

Institutionalism as theory

What use is theory to the political scientist? Surely political science is simply about observing politicians and politics and drawing conclusions from what you see? Such scepticism about the value of theory in political analysis is by no means unusual (Blyth, 2002a), and indeed is embedded within a tradition which can be traced back to both the 'old' institutionalism and to early behaviouralism (Sanders, 2010: 32). From this perspective, what you see is what you get, and our carefully collected observations of politics guide us smoothly down the path to 'evidence based' policy in practice (Davies *et al.*, 2000).

Such an approach can be characterized as 'inductive' because it relies on *drawing in* knowledge from the outside world. In contrast, there are well-rehearsed arguments about the bias which we, as political analysts, inevitably build into our observations of our world and its politics. From this perspective, what we observe and the way we make sense of our observations are conditioned by what we believe about the world and how we think it should be. In this way our beliefs and values act as filters between our senses and the outside world and we cannot trust our observations of politicians and politics to be simply 'objective'.

One way of approaching this problem is to establish a theoretical position which serves to focus and fix the analyst's view of the world (an 'ontology'), seeking to reduce unwelcome outside interference and the complexity which accompanies it. Having established a bounded and relatively simple world view, the analyst can then model how political actors might conduct themselves in this world and test out propositions derived from these models in real-life research. The evidence emerging from the inquiry is fed back through the lens of the analyst's world view and (in principle at least) enriches the theoretical base.

These approaches are termed 'deductive' because they rely on *drawing down* from the internally held beliefs of the analyst him or herself, rather than through immediate reference to the outside world. But these perspectives themselves have come under sustained criticism, not least because in focusing and fixing their viewpoint, they may simply be reinforcing some of the filtering processes they seek to neutralize. Hence while the purely inductive position is too 'open', in the sense of exposing the analyst to anything the world can throw at him or her, the purely deductive position can be said to be too 'closed' in only allowing an opening onto one predefined aspect of the political terrain and forcing any data collected back through that same window.

In looking for a more nuanced approach, we can envisage a continuum of attitudes to the role of theory in political analysis. Here there are two fixed poles and, between these, gradations of those attitudes, the complexions of which are clearly discernible but which blend into each other at the points where they meet. The two poles of the continuum represent fixed positions which are purely deductive and *theoretically driven*, on the one hand, and purely inductive and *empirically driven*, on the other. In the modern history of political analysis, classical Marxism is a good example of the former, while early behaviouralism or simple empiricism is illustrative of the latter.

For the researcher working on or close to the left-hand pole, theory is firmly established as both the driving force for enquiry, and its ultimate beneficiary. From a purely deductive perspective, theory is *the point* of political analysis. For the researcher working at or near to the right-hand pole, the reverse is the case. Here political science can only begin with observation of the 'real world', from which the researcher hopes to generalize empirical findings into a set of broadly stated laws which govern politics. Theory's position holds firm only as long the researcher's observations continue to endorse these laws; it is 'only as good as its last result' and vulnerable to revision each time it is confronted with evidence gathered in the field. Theory is then simply a staging post on the loop around to the next observation of realpolitik.

However the real value of imagining a continuum lies in indicating that there is a wide terrain between these two extremes. Indeed, since the 'rediscovery of institutions' by March and Olsen in 1989, institutionalists have sought to explore this very territory, seeking to escape from the dichotomy of deductive versus inductive approaches, of either empirically driven or theoretically driven work. Ranging across the continuum, institutionalists have been notable for their efforts to produce work which, to differing degrees, is both theoretically *informed* and empirically *informed*. The iteration between theory and empirics, which is at the heart of institutionalism, is nicely captured by Hay (2002: 46–7):

> theory is about simplifying a complex external reality, but not as a means of modelling it, nor of drawing predictive inferences on the basis of observed regularities. Rather theory is a guide to empirical exploration, a means of reflecting more or less abstractly upon complex processes of institutional evolution and transformation in order to highlight the key periods or phases of change which warrant closer empirical scrutiny. Theory sensitises the analyst to the causal processes being elucidated, selecting from the rich complexity of events the underlying mechanisms and processes of change.

Institutionalism escapes from the fixed poles described above and, instead, 'worries' backwards and forwards between theory and empirical exploration in an iterative fashion. Such a project requires the researcher to reflect at regular intervals on the relationship between the two and respond sensitively to what they are finding in any particular context. While a dialogue between theory and evidence is not the exclusive property of institutionalism, it is a distinctive characteristic of the approach. Avoiding deductive and inductive extremes also helps guard against tendencies to decontextualization, and drives institutionalists' growing concern with temporal and spatial dynamics (see Chapter 6).

This determination to draw on the best of both worlds brings with it costs as well as benefits. Crucially, it puts limits on knowledge claims. By moving a significant distance away from both poles of the continuum, institutionalists also move away from the credible application of the classical methods of the physical sciences to the political world. In this respect, Hay's (2002) 'political analysis' may be a better term than 'political science'. In political *analysis* there are no absolute certainties and end points, either in relation to the theory itself, or what it produces in application. In this way a theory like institutionalism continues to evolve and is never complete in the sense of having located a pure and unmovable truth.

The lack of anchorage at either the deductive or inductive pole also builds in a range of tensions within institutionalism, which are exemplified in its apparent lack of predictive power. Does a theory which boldly states that 'rules matter', seeing the world in terms of regularities of conduct, afford any leverage in predicting what political actors will do in the future, particularly as contexts change? Is the approach no more than intellectual opportunism, exploiting the spaces across the continuum? Might it be based not on a rigorous dialogue between the theory evidence at all, but on a concern to keep all options open and a tendency to change horses in mid-enquiry as the situation demands?

To evaluate these criticisms, and better evaluate institutionalism as a theory, we must first understand where institutionalism has come from, its recent development and ongoing trajectory. The provenance of new institutionalism is often narrated in terms of what it is not, in particular its departure from the dominant behaviouralist and purist rational choice approaches of the 1960s and 70s (Hay, 2002: 46). But this is to begin the story of institutionalism rather too late in the day and to underplay the importance of long-standing social science legacies. We offer instead an account based upon three phases of development:

- *Phase 1 – Exploration and Rediscovery,* which combines the reappraisal of insights from the so-called 'old institutionalism' (in the wake of the rational choice theory and behaviouralist tides) and the subsequent 'successful counter-reformation' (Peters, 2005: 1) in the form of the 'new institutionalism'.

- *Phase 2 – Divergence and Division,* which sees the new institution-alism growing rapidly in many different directions, notably via the three schools of rational choice, sociological and historical institutionalism, but also yielding newcomers such as discursive and feminist institutionalisms.
- *Phase 3 – Convergence and Consolidation,* which sees a coming together across the different schools of institutionalism around core concepts and key dilemmas in political analysis, while recognizing that theory is always evolving, incomplete and contested.

We now consider each phase in turn.

Phase 1: Exploration and rediscovery (1930s to 1970s)

The emergence of a common core of institutionalist concepts relates to the way in which several different social science disciplines have responded to the same challenges. Responding in similar ways, different disciplines have frequently borrowed concepts and strategies from one another along the way. We start with a brief account of how the potential of institutionalism was explored in economics and organization theory in the first half of the twentieth century and rediscovered in the second. We then go on to look in more detail at a similar pattern of exploration and rediscovery in political science itself.

In *economics,* the dominant neo-classical approach took institutional contexts as given, fixed and exogenous. This tradition was challenged in the early decades of the twentieth century by 'institutional' economists like Veblen, Myrdal and Commons who criticized the neo-classical reliance on simplifying theoretical and mathematical models. Arguing that political and social structures could block and distort 'normal' economic processes, they proposed an interdisciplinary approach to economic problems, drawing on insights from sociology, politics and law.

Interest in institutions reached a low point after the Second World War, only reviving after the 1960s with the work of economic and business historians (North and Thomas, 1973; Chandler, 1977) and organizational economists, notably Williamson (1985). The new institutionalist economics departs from the earlier institutional tradition in its claim that institutions can be analysed within the mainstream equilibrium-oriented neo-classical approach. The task, explains

Williamson (1985: 1), is to develop a 'micro-analytical approach to the study of economic organization'.

While accepting assumptions of individuals' utility-maximizing behaviour, the new institutional economics highlights the emergence and persistence of institutions in the face of cognitive limits, incomplete information, and difficulties in monitoring and enforcing agreements. The fundamental hypothesis is that institutions exist where their benefits exceed the costs involved in creating and maintaining them. As we shall see, rational choice scholars in political analysis borrowed from these insights as they started to turn their attention towards the institutional contexts of political action.

In *organization theory*, institutionalism takes a rather different starting point. The new institutional economics sees institutions as the deliberate creations of instrumentally oriented individuals. But organization theorists argue that while institutions arise out of human activity, they are not necessarily the products of conscious design (DiMaggio and Powell, 1991a: 8). Such an approach is rooted in long traditions in organization theory. In the 1950s, Selznick (1957) came up with his classic distinction between 'administration' and 'institutionalization'. Pure administration is rational, means-oriented and guided by concerns of efficiency; institutionalization is value-laden, adaptive and responsive, reflecting the values of internal groups and external society (Perrow, 1987: 167).

The new institutionalism in organization theory dates from the late 1970s. The old and new approaches have much in common: both approaches are concerned with the way in which particular organizational forms become 'legitimated', inscribed with cultural value over and above an instrumental concern with efficiency or even material outcomes. They differ however in the locus of their attention. While the old approach studied the way in which individual organizations become 'institutionalized', the new approach locates the process of institutionalization in the wider environment. While Selznick and his followers saw organizations as responding to the values and culture of their local communities and internal members, the new institutionalists argue that organizations adapt to 'institutional templates' or 'myths' present in the wider organizational field (Meyer and Rowan, 1977). These themes have also been taken up in political analysis, especially among political sociologists and discourse theorists.

In *political science*, the 'old institutionalism' has been described as the 'historic heart' of the discipline (Rhodes, 1997: 5). Maybe for this reason it has been most vigorously attacked. But it is important to distinguish between the more vulgar versions of the old institutionalism, and those more sophisticated treatments which have provided important foundations for the new institutionalism. Rod Rhodes (1988, 1995, 1997) has stalwartly defended the institutional approach in the study of government and politics. He describes it as 'part of the toolkit of every political scientist' (1997: 64). Rhodes seeks to tease out the main elements of traditional institutional analysis as applied, for instance, by Finer and Robson in the early part of the century and, in the 1970s and 1980s, by scholars like Johnson and Ridley:

> the institutional approach is a subject matter covering the rules, procedures and formal organizations of government. It employs the tools of the lawyer and the historian to explain the constraints on both political behaviour and democratic effectiveness, and it fosters the Westminster model of representative democracy. (Rhodes, 1997: 68)

Eckstein (1979: 2) notes that practitioners of this approach 'were almost entirely silent about all of their suppositions'. Peters (1999: 2) characterizes their methodology as 'that of the intelligent observer attempting to describe and understand the political world around him or her in non-abstract terms'. The silence regarding theory and methods actually tells us something about the approach – that it was generally unreflective on issues of theory and method, took 'facts' (and values) for granted, and flourished as a kind of 'common sense' within political analysis.

Critics of traditional institutionalism point to its limitations in terms of both scope and method. It was concerned (of course) with the institutions of government, and yet operated with a restricted understanding of its subject matter. The focus was upon formal rules and organizations rather than informal conventions; and upon official structures of government rather than broader institutional constraints on governance (outside as well as within the state). Critics have sought to 'out' the assumptions that lurked behind the descriptive method and disdain for theory. Peters (1999: 6–11) characterizes the 'proto-theory' of old institutionalism as: normative (concerned with 'good government'); structuralist (structures determine political behaviour); historicist (the central influence of history); legalist (law plays a major role in governing); and holistic (concerned with describing and comparing whole systems of government). John (1998: 40–1) points to a strong functionalist tendency: the assumption that particular institutions are the 'manifestations of the functions of political life', or 'necessary for a

---

Box 2.1   'Old institutionalism': contrasting examples

- Looking at political institutions in the US, Britain, France and Germany, Finer (1932) eschewed a country-by-country analysis (more typical of his time) and instead compared institution-by-institution (e.g. parties, electorates, civil service, judiciaries) across countries. Representing an enlightened version of the traditional approach, he grounded his analysis in an understanding of the state as the 'monopoly of coercive power'.
- Woodrow Wilson (1956), himself an early President of the United States, studied the problems of 'divided government' that were beginning to affect the presidential system, and analysed the possibilities presented by parliamentary government as an alternative.
- Studying the emergence and functioning of nationalized industries in Britain, Robson (1960) provided a comprehensive account of all aspects of the organization and management of public corporations. Despite the critical climate of the time, Robson was determined to defend the public corporations as 'an outstanding contribution to public administration', and provided prescriptions as to their future reform.
- Polsby's (1975) famous essay on legislatures was typical of the reductionist strain of institutionalist analysis; it focused upon 'how a peculiar form, the legislature, embeds itself in a variety of environmental settings'.

Sources: Rothstein (1996); Rhodes (1997); Peters (1999).

democracy'. For the modern reader, the old institutionalists' claims of objectivity and 'science' often sit uneasily alongside their polemical idiom and desire to foster the 'Westminster model'.

Box 2.1 provides some examples of more and less sophisticated work within the institutionalist tradition. Rhodes (1995: 49) counsels against erecting a 'straw man'. Many of the old institutionalists adopted a far more nuanced form of analysis than their critics imply. Herman Finer in the 1930s went out of his way to show that the study of constitutions extended far beyond written documents (Finer, 1932). Nevil Johnson's work in the 1970s reveals a concern with procedural norms as well as formal structures (Johnson, 1975). Exponents of the historical-comparative method from Woodrow Wilson onwards understood that the values underlying one system become clearer when contrasted with another.

Moreover, as we shall see in Chapter 3, traditional institutional approaches are not something out of the dark ages to be patronized from a position of hindsight. They have, in fact, continued to serve political analysis well in sub-fields like constitutional studies and public administration. But the limitations of the traditional approach became increasingly clear in the context of empirical changes in the workings of politics and governance. The 'tools of the lawyer and the historian' were proving increasingly inadequate as the formal hierarchies of government came under pressure in many countries. How could traditional institutionalists explain governance through networks and coalitions, the growing interpenetration of markets and bureaucracies, or the withering of political parties as mass organizations? How could a form of analysis that focused upon stability and regularity make sense of the contested dynamics of rapid institutional change?

For a substantial period, between the decline in influence of the 'old' and the rediscovery of the 'new' institutionalism, these questions remained unanswered. By the 1950s, behaviouralism had established a strong position alongside institutionalism in political analysis in the USA and UK and through the 1960s and 1970s it eclipsed its rival. Throughout this period behaviouralists insisted that, '(a) *observable* behaviour, whether it is at the level of the individual or the social aggregate, should be the focus of analysis; and (b) any explanation of that behaviour should be susceptible to empirical testing' (Sanders, 2010: 23, original emphasis). And in doing so, they aligned their version of 'political science' with Karl Popper's principle of falsifiability and the model of enquiry used in the physical sciences ('positivism'). However, having come under sustained attack in subsequent decades for a remorseless adherence to Popper's tenets and a 'tendency towards mindless empiricism', many early behaviourists have now moved to a 'post-behaviourist' position in which 'theory not only generates testable hypotheses, but also provides guidelines and signposts as to the sort of empirical evidence to be gathered in the first place' (Sanders, 2010: 30 and 40). As institutionalism was rediscovered and reformed, behaviouralism adapted to place itself closer to the mainstream deductive–inductive mix; but, unlike rational choice theory (considered below), fashioned no overlap with institutionalism, largely because of its continuing staunch adherence to the principle of falsifiability and the 'scientific method'.

As behaviouralism's pervasive influence gradually began to wane and before the rediscovery of institutionalism, rational choice theory established its own dominant position in political analysis. Emerging through the 1950, 1960s and 1970s, but particularly influential in the 1980s and the decades since, the theory's central ambition is summarized by Hay (2002: 8) as 'to construct stylised (and often mathematical) models of political conduct by assuming that individuals are rational and behave *as if* they engage in a cost-benefit analysis of each and every choice available to them before plumping for the option most likely to maximise their material self-interest'. In following the individualist turn, while behaviouralism drew on psychology or sociology for its knowledge base, rational choice theory drew on economics.

Nevertheless, like the behaviouralists before them (and indeed the institutionalists themselves), after decades of criticism and internal disagreement, many rational choice theorists have modified their original ambitions and theoretical positions. Ward (2002: 88), for example, argues that while rational choice offers 'a valuable set of tools' to political science, 'methodological individualism and fully reductive explanations are impractical. Its status is more akin to that of statistical techniques which are appropriate for certain types of data; it is not a stand-alone paradigm for understanding the whole of the political sphere'.

A more eclectic generation of rational choice theorists has brought insights to the new institutionalism as it has developed, making substantial contributions to our understanding of key dilemmas. Patrick Dunleavy (1991) explores the ways in which interpretations of self-interest are institutionally shaped; Elinor Ostrom (2005) considers the wide variety of institutional solutions to collective action problems; Riker (1980) models institutional change, and Pierson (2004) considers the temporal dynamics of institutional design and development. So while behaviouralists have modified their stance while maintaining their distance from institutionalism, many rational choice theorists have sought inspiration from institutionalism and, indeed, helped to fashion its leading edge.

The new institutionalism which surfaced in the 1980s reasserted many of the old institutionalist principles in a determination to upset the dominance of 'under-socialized' and reductionist accounts of social, economic and political conduct. In their seminal article, March and Olsen (1984: 747) argued that 'the organisation of political life makes a difference', and asserted a more autonomous role for institutions in shaping political conduct. While institutionalism had never really gone away, by the 1980s it was perceived as being outside the political science mainstream. As we have seen, behaviouralists saw institutions as emerging simply from the aggregation of individual roles, statuses and learned responses; and for pure rational choice theorists, institutions were no more than an accumulation of individual choices based on utility-maximizing preferences (Shepsle 1989: 134). March and Olsen (1984: 747) asserted that political institutions played a more autonomous role in shaping political outcomes:

> The bureaucratic agency, the legislative committee, the appellate court are arenas for contending social forces, but they are also collections of standard operating procedures and structures that define and defend interests. They are political actors in their own right. (March and Olsen, 1984: 738)

Considering the future of the institutional approach eleven years on, Rod Rhodes argued that:

> The focus on institutions and the methods of the historian and the lawyer remain relevant... [but] Implicit assumptions must give way to an explicit theory within which to locate the study of institutions. (Rhodes 1995: 50)

This is precisely the challenge that the 'new institutionalists' embraced.

Phase 2: Divergence and division (early 1980s to late 1990s)

The new institutionalist perspectives, which emerged in political analysis, sought to build on the best foundations of the traditional approaches. Indeed, they reasserted the key tenet of the earlier institutional tradition: political structures shape political conduct, and are normatively and historically embedded. But they sought to break open the restricted definitions and implicit theory of their predecessors. New institutionalists have operated since the 1980s with a more expansive (yet more sophisticated) definition of their subject matter, and with more explicit (if diverse) theoretical frameworks. Consequently this new institutionalism can be differentiated from its older sister in three important respects:

- Beginning with formal rules and structures, the new institutionalism expanded its concern to include the informal conventions and coalitions that shape political conduct.
- Refusing to take political institutions at face value, it took instead a critical look at the way in which they embody values and power relationships.

- Rejecting the determinism of earlier approaches, it asserted institutions constrain individual conduct but are also human creations that change and evolve through the agency of actors.

If new institutionalism was built around this common core, why was it that different 'schools' emerged so rapidly and the academic discourse around institutionalism became so combative (Schmidt, 2006: 117)? To answer this question we need to consider the intellectual and political environment into which institutionalism resurfaced in the 1980s and 1990s. At this time there was an onus on institutionalist scholars to respond convincingly to a series of both internal and externally based challenges. Looking outwards, institutionalists took on the task of making the case against the individualism of behaviouralist and rational choice perspectives and showing that there were pre-existing structures in society which both constrained and empowered actors on a collective basis. Looking inwards, institutionalists sought to develop the theory to respond to the now well-embedded criticisms of the 'old' institutionalism. The 'successful counter-reformation' (Peters, 2005: 1) embraced a critical perspective on theory which in itself encouraged divergence of thought and the formation of different 'camps' of institutionalism.

This critical turn was developed within a body of theory which was already influenced by, and borrowing from, several academic disciplines. In this sense, a degree of divergence of thought was already established within new institutionalism from its origins; divisions which were to reassert themselves in the intellectual struggles which followed its rediscovery. The wider political and intellectual environment was also creating a wave of displaced scholars who were looking for an intellectual home, and in many cases turned to new institutionalism. Events of the 1980s and 1990s tested the credibility of perspectives associated with first the left and then the right wing of politics. The fall of the Berlin Wall and the subsequent exposure of state socialism's failings raised fundamental doubts about classical Marxist theory (Marsh, 2002: 153). Against this backdrop, the relative stability of markets cast doubt on the tenets of first-phase rational choice theory, with its prediction of constant fluctuation reflecting the aggregation of individual actors' choices (Blyth, 2002a: 292–310).

As these factors came together, scholars from a number of different intellectual traditions, with a variety of purposes in mind, converged upon new institutionalism. Hence they came with different interpretations of core concepts, and the uses to which they could be put. They positioned themselves variously along the deductive–inductive continuum and, for the most part, defined their theoretical stance by how far they were prepared to tolerate the influence of the rational choice interlopers on the one hand, and neo-Marxists on the other. They sought to defend their positions and signal their allegiances by applying labels to their particular interpretation of institutionalism (Crouch, 2005: 9). In 1996 Hall and Taylor identified three variants, by 1999 Guy Peters had discovered seven, and Box 2.2 outlines nine versions.

We give this brief account of the positioning of these nine institutionalisms for the sake of completeness, to show some of the provenance of and interconnections between the strands. However, we do not accord a similar significance to each variant within the institutionalist canon. Instead, we concur with the majority of writers on institutionalism who have settled on a schema in which three main strands dominate this second phase (e.g. Scott, 2001; Gorges, 2001; Hall, 2009) – sociological, historical and rational choice institutionalism. Table 2.1 provides a summary of their main features.

Sociological institutionalism emerged from the 'old' institutionalist influence in organization theory, which we noted above. Institutions are viewed as constraining, or offering opportunities to, actors within a particular organizational context (DiMaggio and Powell,1991a; 1991b). This world, with its complex relationships between institutions, organizations and actors, is also typified by irrationality in the sense that actors have forgotten, or never been told, the reasons why the rules of the game are as they are. These 'logics of appropriateness' (March and Olsen's, 2004: 3) are 'followed because they are seen as natural, rightful, expected and legitimate'. Actors 'seek to fulfil the obligations encapsulated in a role, an identity, a membership in a political community or group, and the ethos, practices and expectations of its institutions'.

Sociological institutionalism not only endorses 'the power of public ideas' (Reich, 1990) but takes their theorization a stage further. In essence, it defines the process of institutionalization as one of perception rather than evaluation. In doing so, it proposes that actors are constrained by cultural conventions, norms and cognitive frames of reference which privilege a certain way of thinking about a policy problem and ensure that other perspectives remain submerged from view. Premfors (2004: 16) suggests that the sociological institutionalist approach is based on three related ideas. First, human action is strongly dependent on the social context in which it takes place. Hence agency is more context-driven than goal-driven and particularly influ-

Box 2.2   Different strands of new institutionalism

- *Normative institutionalists* study how the norms and values embodied in political institutions shape the behaviour of individuals (see the seminal work of March and Olsen, 1984 and 1989).
- *Rational choice institutionalists* argue that political institutions are systems of rules and inducements within which individuals attempt to maximize their utilities (see Weingast 1996 for a review of rational choice approaches).
- *Historical institutionalists* look at how choices made about the institutional design of government systems influence the future decision-making of individuals (see Hall and Taylor 1996 for a review).
- *Empirical institutionalists*, who most closely resemble the 'traditional' approach, classify different institutional types and analyse their practical impact upon government performance (see Peters 1996 for a review).
- *International institutionalists* show that the behaviour of states is steered by the structural constraints (formal and informal) of international political life (for an accessible example, see Rittberger, 1993).
- *Sociological institutionalists* study the way in which institutions create meaning for individuals, providing important theoretical building blocks for normative institutionalism within political science (see Meyer and Rowan 1977, for the classic statement).
- *Network institutionalists* show how regularized, but often informal, patterns of interaction between individuals and groups shape political behaviour (see Marsh and Rhodes' 1992 edited collection).
- *Constructivist or discursive institutionalism* sees institutions as shaping behaviour through frames of meaning – the ideas and narratives that are used to explain, deliberate or legitimize political action (see Hay, 2006a and Schmidt, 2006). 'Post-structuralist institutionalists' go further in arguing that institutions actually construct political subjectivities and identities (Moon, 2012; Sørensen and Torfing, 2008).
- *Feminist institutionalism* studies how gender norms operate within institutions and how institutional processes construct and maintain gendered power dynamics (see Krook and Mackay, 2011; Kenny, 2007 and Chappell, 2006). Revealing further fragmentation, a 'feminist historical institutionalism' (Waylen, 2011) and 'feminist discursive institutionalism' (Freidenvall and Krook, 2011) have also been identified.

enced by cultural logics. Second, 'such contexts are often heavily institutionalized' – that is to say that institutions are not only influential within their immediate sphere, or 'field', as sociologists tend to term this, but spread their interconnections and make their impacts felt

Table 2.1   *The three main strands of institutionalism:*
key characteristics

	Sociological institutionalism	Rational choice institutionalism	Historical institutionalism
Definition of institution	Cultural conventions, norms, cognitive frames, practices (Scott, 2008).	'The rules of the game in a society' (North, 1990).	'Formal and informal procedures, routines, norms and conventions' (Hall, 1986).
Key objects of study	Organizational fields, social movements, diffusion of institutions.	Individual choices and outcomes, collective action problems, games scenarios.	National policy and power elites, the divergent paths and 'varieties of capitalism'.
Theoretical focus	The institutional and cultural context for, and shaping of, agency.	Institutions to create stability and curb the worst excesses of agency.	The institutional and historical context for, and shaping of, agency.
Theoretical assumptions	Actors follow norms and conventions or 'logics of appropriateness' (March and Olsen, 1989).	Actors calculate best course of action to pursue their interests, within institutional framework (Ostrom, 1986).	A combination of cultural and calculus logics (Hall and Taylor, 1998).

$\rightarrow$

across society. Finally, institutions also operate at a sub-conscious level through which they provide a sort of taken-for-granted 'cultural infrastructure' in society. Such theories find it hard to explain change, rather than stability, within institutions. Institutionalization is seen as an ongoing process, involving adaptation to changes in the external environment (e.g. Peters and Hogwood, 1991). When change is initiated by actors themselves, this is often about the borrowing, sharing, and remembering of ideas, producing outcomes that are 'recombinant' (Crouch, 2005) rather than transformational. Elsewhere, we have examined the paradox of 'how institutions change (and stay the same)' (Lowndes, 2005: 291).

	Sociological institutionalism	Rational choice institutionalism	Historical institutionalism
Common methods	Case studies, 'thick' description, interpretive methodologies.	Testing models, use of quantitative data, laboratory and field experiments.	Historical cases, process tracing, cross national comparative analysis.
Time horizons	The recent past and the future.	The present and the immediate future.	Long-term in the past.
Views on change	Change as 'institutionaliz-ation' (Scott, 2008), including imitation, adaptation and the re-use of existing institutions.	Change willed by actors, emphasis on conscious design, rational adjustment, bargaining and 'gaming'.	Change as highly context-specific, focus on formative moments and path dependence (punctuated equilibrium).
The meaning of engagement	Relatively powerless groups mobilize within an institutional environment shaped by public and private sector organizations.	Small community and business groups design their own institutions without the help of central government actors.	Large groups and coalitions of empowered actors block or promote institutional reform in their own interests.

In their empirical work, sociological institutionalists undertake case studies of specific organizational 'fields' in the public, private and third sectors of society. Researchers in this tradition typically use interpretive methodologies to produce 'thick' descriptions of subtle and dynamic processes, which are not usually easily apprehended and articulated by their subjects. Thus the detailed history of the institutionalization of specific ideas or norms in organizational settings is a common object of study in this strand. Klijn (2001), for example, shows how institutions form the context for decision making within two social housing networks in Rotterdam and the Hague in the Netherlands. In particular, he shows how the different sets of rules in the two case studies lead to distinctly different outcomes. In the US, Schneiberg and Lounsbury (2008: 648) review studies on social movements 'which share an interest in contestation and collective mobilization processes – how groups coalesce to make claims for and against certain practices or actors in order to create or resist new institutional arrangements or transform existing ones'. These include the registration of black voters in the 1960s (McAdam, 1988), the mobilization of farmers, women and workers to make claims on the state (Clemens, 1997), shareholder contestation of managerial control over corporations (Davis and Thompson, 1994), the growth of peace, gay and lesbian and environmental movements (Laraña, Johnson and Gusfield, 1994), and the rise of transnational pressure groups (Keck and Sikkink, 1998).

In sociological institutionalism we see a distinctive stance but also some well developed overlaps with the other two main institutionalisms. In particular, concepts of institutionalization assume time horizons which, while not as long term as those of historical institutionalism, take account of extended temporal dynamics. In addition we see the development of an 'actor-centred institutionalism' (Mayntz and Sharpf, 1995) where actors hold perceptions of self-interest in a way that overlaps with rational choice assumptions. Sociological institutionalists are typically 'engaged' theorists to the extent that they foreground issues of power and disadvantage, and the continuing conflicts between groups in society. Institutions are seen as expressing power settlements, whereby constraints and opportunities are unevenly distributed, and likely to be subject to both resistance and defence.

There is a tendency among many scholars to present *rational choice institutionalism* as something of the 'cuckoo in the nest' of institutionalism – that is to say a child adopted under false pretences and bent on the destruction of those with whom it is in competition for nourishment. From our 'engaged' stance, we sympathize with the critique that rational choice has been 'politically destructive' (Hindmoor, 2010: 56–7), when it has asserted, for example, that what cannot be measured does not exist, suggesting 'there is no such thing as society' (to borrow Margaret Thatcher's famous phrase). We lay much of the blame for the persistence of this line of criticism at the door of rational choice theory itself, which has sought radically to simplify its world view and 'model of man' (Premfors, 2004), and has consequently laid itself, and its offspring, wide open to attack.

However, we also take the view that the agency of scholars does not let theory rest. Rather, over time, theory becomes blurred at the edges, making it progressively harder to pigeonhole the different strands of institutionalism. In a similar vein, we see a tendency on the part of some hostile reviewers of rational choice *institutionalism* to see it as interchangeable with rational choice theory in its original and purist form, or to freeze rational choice institutionalism in its first phase manifestations. To counterbalance this tendency, we show in Chapter 3 how rational choice institutionalists, very much against the sceptical grain, have acknowledged the role of norms and ideas in explaining institutions (e.g. Aoki, 2001, 2010). Rational choice scholars have also embraced institutionalism's preference for 'engagement', through work on the cooperative institutions for the management of 'common pool resources', such as forests or fisheries (Ostrom, 2007), and how protest groups have become institutionalized in the USA (Lichbach, 1998).

With these caveats, we broadly agree with Premfors' (2004: 17) depiction of rational choice institutionalists' position:

> First ... they single out the self-centred, strategic, rational behaviour on the part of individuals as the prime form of social causality, and although institutions do affect the contents of the utility calculus of individual actors their impact will not transform people into anything else but utility-maximizers. Second, and in a similar vein, preference formation is essentially viewed as exogenous – institutions affect means, not goals. Finally, rational choice institutionalists harbour ideals about the nature of social scientific work that stand in sharp contrast to those of sociological (and most historical) institutionalists – thus theories should above all be parsimonious and only (or at least mainly) be judged on the basis of their predictive capability, and the preferred criteria of assessing empirical evidence should be those of traditional positivist empiricism.

Indeed, for some rational choice institutionalists, even as we approach the third phase of institutionalism, their theoretical and methodological approaches have not changed a great deal. In this fragmented universe of remorseless individualism, each actor pursues his or her self-interest in the context of a rational calculation of what is the best course of action to achieve that strategic intent. Equally, institutions themselves are parsimoniously theorized and consequently are quite simple to apprehend – they are the conspicuous rules of the game which are obvious to all actors and designed to maximize returns. In this world, the key purpose of politics is to aggregate the self-maximizing choices made by individuals into public choice outcomes and to put in place institutions which will detect and deal with cheating on the part of delinquents.

In empirical work, this simple ontology allows researchers to attempt to predict behaviour from their parsimonious theoretical modelling of life understood as a series of bargaining games. Here the individual is constantly asking the consequential question 'what action would produce the highest utility for me?', in a context where institutional rules place some constraints on subsequent behaviour. In this way, a particular aspect of life, such as bargaining, can be analysed within the laboratory, with the ways actors respond to different rule sets measured using mathematical formulae and through quantitative testing. Within this approach actors' horizons are typically short term, with changes to the rules likely to be precipitated by the conscious design of the actors themselves, and those wishing to constrain them. But even within this methodology, there are rational choice innovators. For example, Ostrom (2007: 1) debunks two core assumptions used in designing rules to govern common pool resources:

> (1) resource users are norm-free maximizers of immediate gains who will not cooperate to overcome the commons dilemmas they face, and (2) government officials, on the other hand, have the information and motivation to design efficient and effective rules to sustain the use of common pool resources over the long run.

Ostrom summarizes 'findings from carefully controlled laboratory experiments that challenge the first assumption and lead one to have to assume that humans are fallible and boundedly rational. Depending on the context of the situation, individuals may add normative payoffs (positive and negative) to their preference function'. She then discusses 'the complexity of using rules as tools to change the structure of commons dilemmas, drawing on extensive research on rules in field settings'. Ostrom concludes that 'those dependent on small to medium-size common pool resources are *not* forever trapped in situations that will only get worse over time, we need to recognize that governance is frequently an adaptive process involving multiple actors at diverse levels. Such systems look terribly messy and hard to understand' (Ostrom, 2007: 21, original emphasis).

Here, then, the three basic tenets we took from Premfors are enhanced by layers of complexity which, in sum, suggest a much more socialized view of actors and institutions. Actors, for example, make mistakes and are influenced by the norms of their society. Rules have also become more complicated, insofar as they are now 'tools' to achieve certain objectives in particular contexts, or 'rules-in-use' (Ostrom, 1999). Laboratory experiments are used to construct models, which are then tested in complex environments where life and death issues are at stake (e.g. the control of irrigation systems). From an engaged perspective, Ostrom's research suggests that 'those dependent on small to medium-size common pool resources' (including small community-based groups of disadvantaged individuals) are able to devise rules to cooperate around scarce resources, which operate far more effectively than those imposed from above by central government. These characteristics in turn suggest that actors' horizons cannot only be short term, because individuals are necessarily making some projection of how rules-in-use will operate in the future. It seems that bargaining games typically involve high levels of imagination, anticipation and expectation. The fragmented world of isolated individuals has become significantly more coherent as groups are formed around collective action problems, albeit still with personal advantage in mind.

Whereas sociological institutionalism emerged from organization theory and rational choice institutionalism from economics, *historical institutionalism's* lineage is not quite so easy to pin down. But we can identify three common concerns which historical institutionalists have shared. First, historical institutionalists have been interested in politics on a grand geographical scale, that is to say with a whole country's institutional apparatus and national-level building blocks such as employment rights and welfare provision. Such scaling contrasts with sociological institutionalism which tends to look at the organizational level, and rational choice institutionalism which builds its theoretical approach up from the individual actor. Second, historical institutionalists are concerned with the long-term development of institutions and thus the associated temporal effects. Third, most, but not all, of the work of historical institutionalists contains some attempt to critique and develop classical Marxism in the light of the theoretical splits of the 1970s (Hay, 2002: 115–16) and the experience of the collapse of the Soviet bloc in 1980s. A 'calculus' approach allows scholars to build on insights from rational choice theory to explain how self-interested groups of actors comply with and maintain the institutional configurations of capitalism. A 'cultural' perspective embraces the power of ideas and, in particular, Gramscian explanations of why capitalism has been able to survive for so long and in several different institutional forms.

This mixed approach leads to a broad definition, captured in Hall and Taylor's (1996: 947) definition of a political institution: 'Not just formal rules, procedures or norms, but the symbol systems, cognitive scripts, and moral templates that provide the 'frames of meaning' guiding human action.' In their empirical work, historical institutionalists undertake case studies, generally on the national scale and over significant time frames, examining the unfolding relationships between the formation and implementation of public policy and the large collective bodies (employers' organizations, trades unions, political parties, and pressure groups) which form the power constellations within that particular country. Researchers in this tradition typically use techniques known as 'process tracing' (Thelen, 2004) to track how actors have influenced institutions over time, and vice versa.

The 'Varieties of Capitalism' school is a good example of the historical institutionalists' concern with collecting comparative data on how institutions associated with the same policy problems have developed in different ways across different countries, and the extent of their stability over time. Comparativists working in the late 1970s are credited with 'bringing the state back in', and effectively launching the historical institutionalist project (for example, Katzenstein, 1978; Skocpol, 1979; Krasner, 1980; Skowronek, 1982). Following this, Peter Hall's (1989) study of Keynesian economics across nations is widely regarded as a classic text of historical institutionalism, not least because it deals with large scale institutions which exercise influence across long periods of time and with variable comparative outcomes across the globe. Hall considers Keynesianism as a set of ideas which, for much of the period after 1945, provided a handy template of rules, procedures and cognitive scripts to apply to economic policy problems, until the rise of monetarism in the 1970s.

The influence of rational choice approaches in historical institutionalism can be illustrated via Immergut's (1992) classic study of healthcare reform in different countries, which explains the transnational differences she uncovers in terms of how each nation's medical community acted in a calculated manner to block institutional reform which may harm their interests. Pierson's (2004) *Politics in Time* develops the notion of a rationally motivated actor assailed by contingent effects generated by 'invisible and slow moving' institutions, and by the behaviour of other actors who have little regard for or knowledge of the impact of their actions. Kathleen Thelen's (2004) comparative study of training regimes in Britain, Germany, Japan and the US over the last 100 years shows how the gradual evolution of institutions is accompanied by actors' formation (and frequent abandonment) of coalitions in pursuit of their perceived interests. Hence we can view historical institutionalism as a distinctive strand of institutionalism (particularly in its links to Marxist critique), but also one which has borrowed extensively from the other two main institutionalisms. Historical institutionalism has a typically 'engaged' character in its focus upon the ways in which powerful coalitions block institutional reform which would benefit the disadvantaged (for example, Immergut, 1992; Schmidt, 2009).

Through most of its development, historical institutionalism has tended to rely on a concept of 'path dependence'. The basic idea is that, once policy makers have started down a particular path (however arbitrary the initial choice), the costs of changing direction are high. Path dependency rests upon a conception of increasing returns or positive feedback. As Paul Pierson (2000: 252) explains:

> In an increasing returns process, the probability of further steps along the same path increases with each move down that path. This is because the relative benefits of the current activity compared with other possible options increase over time. To put it a different way, the costs of exit – or switching to some previously plausible alternative – rise.

Path dependency, it is argued, creates a powerful cycle of self-reinforcing activity. The cycle, however, may be virtuous or vicious. There is no reason to assume that the option which becomes 'locked in' is superior to the alternatives that were foregone. In fact, over time, this becomes progressively less likely, given the barriers that are produced to innovation and to adaptation to changing environments. The classic case in the history of technology concerns the QWERTY keyboard, which was designed to slow down typists and prevent the tangling of mechanical keys. Today it persists despite its inefficiency, purely because the costs of changing the industry standard are too high (David, 1985).

Reliance on this concept has made it particularly difficult for historical institutionalists to explain institutional change, as opposed to institutional stability. Explaining change has tended to rely on 'stop-go' models, notably through the concept of 'punctuated equilibrium' (originally from Krasner, 1988). While path dependency persists during 'normal' times, critical junctures emerge at moments of political upheaval which are typically stimulated by external shocks; during such periods, the costs of change versus continuity are reduced, and actors are able radically to reform the existing institutional framework (for example Collier and Collier, 1991). The stop-go approach has, however, come under sustained critique (as we shall see in the next section) for its inability to theorize endogenous forces for institutional change and the potentially transformative impact of small, evolutionary adjustments over time (Streeck and Thelen,2005; Mahoney and Thelen, 2010).

Phase 3: Convergence and consolidation (early 2000s to date)

So, in the first phase of institutionalism, the disciplines of economics, organization theory and political science each explored the potential of institutional theory. Then, for a period of time across these disciplines, and others within the social sciences, the 'under-socialized' accounts of rational choice and behaviourism pushed thoughts of institutions, and how society was structured, into the background. The rediscovery of institutions in the 1980s was based on the legacy of the 'old' institutionalism and recreated some of its previous academic divisions. But it was further enriched, and complicated, by the arrival of (amongst others) Marxist and rational choice scholars, seeking a home in the 'new' institutionalism. As phase two progressed, it became clear that, out of the many claims on the 'brand', three main new institutionalisms were discernible. Although having distinct characteristics in their own right, each of the three institutionalisms contained significant theoretical overlaps with one another, which went well beyond the simple assertion that 'institutions matter' in political life.

Consistent with our view of institutionalism as a 'living' body of theory which continues to evolve, we recognize that there remains plenty of room for disagreement between the different strands of institutionalism. We do, however, believe that a process of convergence and consolidation, which began slowly in the second phase, has now gained significant momentum over the first ten years of the third phase. For, just as we observe boundary-spanning agency in political action, so we see similar patterns of conduct on the part of institutionalist scholars. We observe a tendency of scholars to attach a label to their work and then confound such categorization by borrowing and sharing ideas with other strands. The labels often seem more like 'flags of convenience' (securing access to particular journals, conference panels or research groups) or even defensive identity statements (signifying more what a scholar is not, than what they actually stand for). Leaving the labels aside, we actually see a convergence in the work of leading institutionalist scholars around a number of 'wicked issues' which have troubled institutionalism for some time (agency, power, time and space). In turn we see growing consolidation around a number of core concepts (rules, practices, narratives, change), many of which have been drawn from first and second phase institutionalism and which now form the foundations of third phase institutionalism.

In subsequent chapters we explore these 'wicked issues' and core concepts in some detail. But we finish this chapter by establishing the main characteristics of political institutions, as understood by third phase scholars:

Institutions – formal and informal

As we outlined in the introductory chapter to this book, institutionalists have always been interested in rules as the 'hardware' of politics. Second phase institutionalists broadened the definition of an institution from formal written rules which are consciously designed and clearly specified (like contracts, job descriptions, committee terms of reference, budget systems) to include practices and unwritten conventions (concerning, for instance, the role of the party group in decision making or the relations between parties in a 'hung' administration). Early in second phase institutionalism, therefore, it became widely accepted that both rules and practices were the objects of study for institutionalists and indeed some argued that practices (or rules-in-use) may in fact be more powerful (Ostrom, 1999: 37). At the same time, as we shall show in Chapter 3, theorists across the three main strands have become interested in what part ideas, beliefs and values play in institutional dynamics. This concern has drawn on discourse theory, narrative methodologies and studies of political rhetoric (e.g. Feldman *et al.*, 2004; Jackson, 2006; Jessop, 2010) to look at the ways in which institutions take the form of collections of stories about 'the way we do things around here'. In short, we see a convergence within third phase institutionalism around the existence of, and interaction between, three different modes of constraint – rules, practices and narratives.

Institutions – stable and dynamic

Stability has always been theorized as an essential characteristic of institutions: in the first phase of institutionalism, Huntington (1968) defined political institutions as 'stable, valued and recurring patterns of behaviour'. Rediscovering institutions, March and Olsen (1989: 16) saw institutions as 'creating and sustaining islands of imperfect and temporary organisation in potentially inchoate political worlds'. But together these conceptualizations reveal key institutional dilemmas. If institutions are theorized as stable structures, then why and how do institutions change, in some circumstances quite rapidly? And, if they are theorized as 'temporary', in what sense are they institutions? Addressing these questions during the second and third phases, institutionalists have been concerned to explore the *processes* by which institutional stability is accomplished, on the basis that these may also give answers to the ways in which change is effected. In this way theorists have converged on two particular sets of explanations which account for institutional stability and destabilization as part of the same mechanism. The first is based on the nature of institutions themselves and suggests that no institution stands alone, but is interconnected with a range of other institutions which reinforce its effects, or complement them (Ostrom, 1986: 7–8). From this perspective, an institution is destabilized when change occurs in the institutional environment, particularly when the institutions with which it is connected are destabilized. The second type of explanation involves a search for endogenous rather than exogenous drivers for stability and change, and maintains that institutions are 'continuously established, restored, redefined and defended against all sorts of disorganising forces' (Streek, 2001: 31). This approach therefore emphasizes the importance of human agency in creating and sustaining stability, and the continuous vulnerability of institutions both to neglect and attack by political actors. The convergence we detect here is in terms of seeing institutions as only 'relatively' stable, in so far as their stability is conditional on the continuing presence of particular forms of support.

Institutions – power and critique

As we saw earlier, the 'old' institutionalism was accused (sometimes unfairly) of having an explicit concern with 'good government', and an implicit commitment to a particular set of values and model of government. Power and the uses to which it was put by government or individual citizens were not generally considered to be an issue worthy of protracted discussion. Second phase institutionalists sought to identify the various ways in which institutions embody and shape societal values, which may themselves be contested and in flux. March and Olsen (1989: 17) expose how seemingly neutral procedures and arrangements embody particular values, interests and identities, hence conferring power on some actors at the expense of others. Institutionalists from all three main strands have developed an 'engaged' approach to the study of institutions in terms of power and disadvantage, inequality and continuing conflict. Third phase scholars such as Schneiberg, Ostrom and Thelen show that, while disadvantaged groups in society are marginalized by existing institutional configurations, in certain circumstances they can use these or other institutions to, in Hay's (1997: 50) words, 'redefine the parameters of what is socially, politically and economically possible'. Here then we see a convergence around the idea that although institutions constrain and oppress certain groups of actors, resistance is always possible and usually present.

Institutions – messy and differentiated

From the early years of the second phase of institutionalism, historical institutionalists built on the 'old' institutionalist tendency to deal with the grand sweep of their subject, in terms of time, geography and size. As such they were vulnerable to John's (1998) criticism of failing to appreciate the 'fine grain' of institutional power, both in terms of a disregard for human agency, but also in terms of their assumption that institutions could be treated as internally consistent and homogenous. In response, we have seen second and third phase institutionalists, including many from the historical strand, theorizing the 'messiness' of institutions, both in terms of the wide variety of 'fields' of political activity they cover (for example electoral systems, tax and benefit systems, cabinet decision making, budgeting, policy making, or intergovernmental relationships), and in terms of the different modes through which they constrain political behaviour (not just rules but practices and narratives too). We see convergence towards an understanding of institutions as 'differentiated': first, in the sense that they do not necessarily 'fit' together to form a whole, or represent functionally desirable solutions (Orren and Skowronek, 2002: 747); second, in that they 'embody, preserve, and impart differential power resources with respect to different individuals and groups' (Goodin, 1996: 20); and third, in that institutions are never fully 'closed' or complete, with gaps or slippages existing between constraints and actual behaviour (March and Olsen, 1989: 16).

Institutions – determinant and contingent

Institutionalists must, however, grant institutions some capacity to determine, or at least shape, certain outcomes in political life. For if rules, practices and narratives do not produce significant impacts on political conduct, then they cannot be convincingly defined as institutions, as we understand the term. But in their disaggregated forms, they also evolve in unpredictable ways, producing contingent effects as actors seek to make sense of new or ambiguous situations, ignore or even contravene existing rules, or try to adapt them to favour their own beliefs and perceived interests. How then have third phase institutionalists accounted for the paradox of institutional determinacy and contingency? What we see is convergence around the importance of two sources of contingency. First, understanding how any one political institution operates requires that we locate it within its wider institutional context (or 'configuration', as Ostrom puts it), and study its two-way linkages with other institutions – political and non-political, at the same and different spatial scales, and across the passage of time. Second, understanding institutional dynamics requires an appreciation of the mutually constitutive character of agents and institutions, given the 'Janus face' we described earlier. For any particular political institution, contingent effects arise from the specific contextual interplay with other institutions and with actors in their environment.

Institutions – structure and agency

Indeed, a key dilemma for institutionalists is the degree of freedom to act that they allow individual actors. In the second phase of institutionalism all three main strands suffered from the criticism that real human beings were either badly drawn or absent from their explanations of institutional dynamics. In sociological institutionalism, logics of appropriateness trapped actors within dominant norms and beliefs leaving them little scope for agency; in rational choice institutionalism, actors were required to follow the single course which would maximize their self-interest; and in the historical strand, path dependency dictated that actors must continue to pursue traditional policy preferences. Responses to this dilemma have converged towards a common conception of agency in institutionalism. The three strands have formed a broad consensus that their actors must have some reflexive and strategic capacities. To some extent at least, actors are able to look back and learn from past experience (not always accurately of course), and can look forward and attempt to influence events in the future (again not always successfully). Following from this we see the three strands converging on the middle of the structure–agency continuum. As we saw earlier, rational choice institutionalists such as Ostrom have socialized their actors' environment, while sociological and historical institutionalists have each sought to 'bring the actor back in'. In this book we seek to develop a distinctively institutionalist conception of agency.

Conclusion

Our principal objective in this chapter has been to identify the common core of concepts at the heart of institutionalism. We began by exploring what we mean by a theory and what limits exist on knowledge claims. We insisted that theory evolves and is never complete in the sense of having located a pure and unmovable truth. Next we took the reader through the three phases of institutionalism concluding with the current phase. Building on 'old' institutionalist foundations (Phase 1), in political science and other disciplines, the new institutionalism fractured into numerous variants, with some coherence around three main schools (Phase 2). However, theoretical and methodological borrowing between the schools, alongside a common 'engaged' stance, has led to growing convergence around core concepts and key dilemmas. Through a series of consolidatory moves, a shared picture is emerging of how political institutions work: they shape actors' behaviour through informal as well as formal means; they exhibit dynamism as well as stability; they distribute power and are inevitably contested; they take a messy and differentiated form; and are mutually constitutive with the political actors whom they influence, and by whom they are influenced.

We do not, however, see convergence around these core concepts as universal or in any way complete. We seek to provide an account of institutionalism that is questioning of, rather than constrained by, sectarian quarrels between competing schools and factions. We will fill out our sketch in the remaining chapters of the book, taking each of the points of convergence in turn. In doing so, we continue the work of building a theoretically robust, but empirically provocative, institutionalist position. In the next chapter, Chapter 3, we focus on fundamentals. How would we recognize a political institution when we saw one? And how is it that institutions do their work?

Chapter 3

Rules, Practices and Narratives

How do political institutions actually shape actors' behaviour? In this chapter we specify and explore three modes of institutional constraint: rules, practices and narratives. In each case we review insights from rational choice, historical institutionalist and sociological scholars, but seek to establish points of convergence and consolidation, as well as identifying key dilemmas and forward research agendas. The existence of rules, practices and narratives does not, however, guarantee compliance, so we take a critical look at enforcement strategies, showing how resistance to constraint is inevitable and can prove a potent source of institutional change.

But, prior to this, we are mindful of the fact that many students and postgraduate researchers struggle to pin down the actual institutions that they wish to study. And in the work of many established scholars, the operationalization of institutionalist concepts can be frustratingly vague or surprisingly flexible. Consequently we start with the vexed question of what institutions look like on the ground (would you know one if you saw one?), and consider the analytical and methodological strategies we might use to find out more about them.

What do institutions look like – and how can we find out about them

Institutionalists are agreed that political institutions are 'the rules of the game'. But what should be included in the category of rules? By including informal conventions as well as formal procedures, new institutionalists are able to build a more fine-grained, and realistic, picture of what *really* constrains political behaviour and decision-making. An expanded definition of 'institution' runs the risk, however, of 'conceptual stretching' (Peters, 1996: 216) – its meaning and impact diluted as it comes to include everything that guides individual behaviour. North (1990: 83) goes as far as to include tradition, custom, culture and habit as informal 'institutions', and for March and Olsen (1989: 17) there seems to be no clear distinction between institutions and norms in general. As Rothstein (1996: 145) notes, if the concept of institution 'means everything, then it means nothing' – how can political institutions be distinguished from other social phenomena? John (1998: 64) argues that the new institutionalists 'include too many aspects of political life under one category... [which] disguises the variety of interactions and causal mechanisms that occur'.

On a practical level, how can political scientists recognize (and measure) an institution when they see one? On a theoretical level, how can they avoid the traps of reductionism and tautology? Peter Hall's (1986) concept of 'standard operating procedures'(SOP) offers a helpful way forward: the researcher's aim should be to identify the specific rules of behaviour that are agreed upon and (in general) followed by agents, whether explicitly or tacitly agreed (see Rothstein, 1996: 146). Informal institutional rules – or what we call 'practices' – are therefore distinct from personal habits or 'rules of thumb': they are specific to a particular political or governmental setting, they are recognized by actors (if not always adhered to), have a collective (rather than personal) effect, and can be described and explained to the researcher. The style and form of questioning in a government committee, for example, may not be set down in writing; however, it is clearly identifiable as a 'standard operating procedure' that structures political behaviour, while expressing particular values and power relationships. This 'SOP' can be described, evaluated, and compared with alternative arrangements for scrutiny. In contrast, the way that a committee member organizes his or her papers (however regularly and systematically) is a matter of personal habit or routine, and does not qualify as an informal institution or SOP.

Standard operating procedures may be circumvented or manipulated by certain individuals or groups of actors, but actors in general are still able to identify, and reflect upon, the nature of such rules and practices. At the same time, new rules may be formally agreed upon but take time to acquire the status of a standard operating procedure. In politics, as elsewhere, rules exist to be broken as well as to be obeyed! Peters' (1999: 144) charge of tautology only really applies to those rational choice perspectives that *define* institutions by the creation of regularity, that is, by the acceptance of rules of behaviour. If we accept that rules may be resisted or subject to adaptation over time, and that there may exist gaps between formal rules and informal practices, we establish a research agenda in which, (a) institutions can be studied separately from political behaviour itself, and (b) the active and reflective relationship between individuals and institutions becomes an object of analysis.

Box 3.1   Institutionalist methodologies

- *Mathematical modelling* – Crouch (2005) uses modelling to show that institutional heterogeneity facilitates innovation in economic policy, by presenting new opportunities when existing 'paths' are blocked, and by allowing for new combinations of elements from existing paths.
- *Game theory* – Dunleavy (1991) uses game theory to develop his theory of 'bureau shaping' as an alternative to conventional 'budget maximising' assumptions in explaining how self-interested bureaucrats seek to influence the institutions they work through.
- *Experimental methods* – Ostrom *et al.* (1994) work both in the laboratory and through field experiments to investigate the institutional and physical variables that affect whether cooperation can be achieved (and over-exploitation avoided) in the use of 'common pool resources' like forests or grazing lands.
- *Ethnography* – Douglas (1987) uses anthropological and ethnographic methods to develop her theory of 'how institutions think', differentially structuring categories of thought across cultures, whether in law, religion or science.
- *Country case studies* – Streeck and Thelen (2005) analyse macroeconomic trends and policy development to compare the different ways in which incremental change leads to institutional transformation in contemporary capitalism.
- *Practice case studies* – Lowndes *et al.* (2006) collect micro-level data via semi-structured interviews and focus groups to analyse the 'rules-in-use' that shape citizen participation in a sample of English cities (see Box 3.2).
- *Narrative analysis* – Freidenvall and Krook (2011) analyse the phrasing, imagery and layout of official documents (manifestos, legal decisions, technical guidance) associated with the introduction of gender quotas in different countries, looking also at the ways in which they articulate with discourses in popular culture.

The notion of standard operating procedures offers an example of how institutionalists can combine a concern for formal rules and informal practices, and yet distinguish political institutions from broader customs and habits. Elinor Ostrom (1999: 38) helpfully distinguishes between 'rules in form' and 'rules in use' (which include informal practices). Ostrom neatly defines rules in use as the distinctive ensemble of 'dos and don'ts that one learns on the ground'. But the job of identifying and measuring rules in use is not so easy. Peters (1999: 145) is right to remind institutionalists of the 'need for more rigour in conceptualisation and then measurement of the phenomena that are assumed to make up institutions'. Part of the difficulty here is the different spatial and temporal scales at which institutionalists operate. As we saw in Chapter 2, researchers inspired by rational choice frames often work on the micro-level analysis of decision-making, while those of a more sociological bent look to characterize a whole arena of activity (the legal system or parliamentary politics, for example) and historically oriented scholars will concern themselves with the development of, for instance, tax and insurance systems over several decades. Box 3.1 shows the broad repertoire of methodological techniques that institutionalists are developing, which range from ethnography and narrative analysis to laboratory studies and game theory. Historical, comparative and case study methods (not so very different from those of the better 'traditionalists') still dominate, but investigation now tends to proceed from theoretically generated propositions.

How do institutions do their work?

It is all very well to say that institutions constrain or shape actors' behaviour, but *how* does this happen? Through what processes do actors understand what is expected of them, and why do they bother to respond to these signals? While Hall's concept of SOPs has offered us a valuable first cut, we need to take a more detailed look at how institutions do their work.

As we saw in the last chapter, sociological institutionalists have argued that political institutions influence behaviour by shaping individuals' 'values, norms, interests, identities and beliefs' (March and Olsen, 1989: 17). Rational choice scholars argue that, while institutional factors do not 'produce behaviour', they do affect 'the structure of a situation' in which actions are selected, primarily through influencing incentives and information flows (Ostrom, 1986: 5–7). More recently, discursive or constructivist institutionalism has pointed to the way in which institutions shape behaviour through frames of meaning – the ideas and narratives that are used to explain, deliberate or legitimize political action (Schmidt, 2006: 99)

Do we need to choose between these accounts? While some commentators have insisted that these positions express fundamentally different ontological positions (Hay and Wincott, 1998: 953), we side with those who see the distance between competing variants as small and decreasing. What we term third phase institutionalism actually holds out the promise of a 'rapprochement' between traditionally warring factions of political science (Goodin and Klingemann, 1996: 11). This development is not just about academics being nice to each other; rather, it reflects an important theoretical point. The special character of institutions lies precisely in the fact that they are 'over-determined' (Scott, 2001: 51). In robust institutional arrangements, regulative, normative and discursive mechanisms work together to shape behaviour. This is what makes institutions 'more than' organizations, and explains why institutions endure over time and are valued in themselves (and struggled against by those who hold different values).

Vivien Schmidt (2006: 116) reminds us that 'problem-oriented scholars tend to mix approaches all the time, using whichever approaches seem the most appropriate to explaining their object of study'. As we explained in Chapter 1, political actors and institutional designers are themselves subject to mixed motivations, reflecting the artificial nature of 'pure' ontological constructs. Rather than trying to win an argument about what counts most, our argument is that institutions work through three modes of constraint – rules, practices and narratives. The real agenda for institutionalism is to better understand how these distinctive modes of constraint interrelate in practice, and to establish what this means for ongoing processes of institutional change and prospects for institutional resistance and reform.

Specifying different modes of constraint is an important theoretical task, which also provides methodological guidance as to what to look for in studying political institutions. As Huntington (1968) explained more than 40 years ago, institutions are 'stable, valued and recurring patterns of behaviour': to understand how these patterns emerge we need to identify the means by which actors know what is expected of them. From a sociological perspective, Scott refers to institutional 'carriers'; from a rational choice slant, Elinor Ostrom (1999) talks about the 'prescriptions' that define what actions (or outcomes) are 'required, prohibited or permitted', and the sanctions authorized if the rules are not followed. Such prescriptions are embodied in rules, practices and narratives. The ways in which these are articulated in different political settings is an empirical rather than an ontological question, albeit one with considerable political significance – for those seeking to resist or undermine dominant institutions, and for those charged with designing new institutions or reforming existing ones.

Before we discuss the three modes of constraint in more detail, we need to consider the issue of enforcement. It is not necessary to prove that rules are always followed to show that they exist, or are important. But the important point about breaking institutional rules, formal or informal, is that actors *know* they are doing it. In this way the action is different from the other daily choices that individuals make in going about their business. Institutional rules, practices and narratives are not only recognized by actors, they are also subject to some type of 'third party' enforcement. Put simply, this means that someone (or some set of interests) cares whether or not institutional rules and practices are adhered to. Moreover, they have put in place enforcement mechanisms to secure (or at least encourage) compliance, and punish (or at least deter) transgression. Claus Offe (1996: 203) argues that a defining characteristic of institutions is that they are 'triadic' – that is, 'established and enforced by "third parties" who are not part of the institutionalised interaction'. (In contrast, organizations are 'diadic', and pure conventions are self-enforcing.) Indeed, it is the opportunity to bind actors into the future to particular courses of action that makes institutional design and reform such important political matters.

While our formulation has a whiff of voluntarism about it, in reality the 'enforcing' agent may be lost in the mists of time, and replaced by some symbolic artefact: the constitutional document that underpins the institutions of democracy, the coronation crown that represents the institution of the monarchy, the dreaming spires that look over the institution of academia. But there are also active enforcers at work – the professional association that upholds legal standards or medical ethics, the quality assurance body that watches over teaching practices, the health and safety commission that polices manufacturing processes, the ombudsman who hears complaints and issues guidance, and the 'standards watchdogs' that audit the ever more diffuse agencies of government and public service delivery. Globalization creates a new cast of transnational enforcers, seeking to secure the rules (or at least 'best practice') in radically different contexts – think climate change protocols, international criminal law, trade agreements, or human rights.

Table 3.1 **Modes of institutional constraint: key characteristics**

	Rules	Practices	Narratives
How we recognize them	Formally constructed and recorded	Demonstrated through conduct	Expressed through the spoken word
Empirical examples	Clauses in a constitution, terms of reference, national and international laws	How elected members conduct themselves in parliaments, assemblies, or local councils	Speeches by politicians explaining the need for change; the collections of stories in an organization which justify the status quo
Enactment by actors through	Writing and formal interpretation – e.g. law to policy documents to guidance	The consistent rehearsal of 'the ways in which we do things around here'	The linking together and spoken expression of ideas into explanation and persuasion
Impact on actors through	Reading representations and interpretations of rules (e.g. speed limit signs, procedure manuals)	Observing the routinized actions of members of the group and seeking to recreate those actions	Hearing familiar stories and recognizing shared understandings to the point where the normative implications are taken for granted

$\rightarrow$

While third party enforcement is a characteristic of institutions *vis-à-vis* other organizational arrangements, this does not mean that it always takes a particular form, or is 'successful' in the sense of securing compliance. Enforcement refers simply to 'arguments as to why an institutionalised status order is to be held valid and hence deserves to be adhered to' (Offe 1996: 204). And, as Bob Goodin (1996: 41) explains, the most effective enforcement mechanisms may be those that cultivate trust and embody 'a direct appeal to moral principles', rather than those that seek simply to control the behaviour of actors assumed to be self-interested and prone to 'defection'. He points out: 'by "designing institutions for knaves" such mechanical solutions risk making knaves of potentially more honourable actors'. Enforcement

	Rules	Practices	Narratives
Sanctioned by	Coercive action through formal rewards and punishments	Displays of disapproval, social isolation, and threats of violence	Incomprehension and ridicule, and attempts to undermine the reputation and credibility of non-conformists
Interconnections between modes	Narratives are often used to justify the existence of rules; rules often formalize well-established practices	Practices often form the basis of narrative; rules may specify the practices through which actors must enact the rules	The case for changing the rules is usually made in narrative form; narrative accounts can present prevalent practices in a positive or negative light
Indicative research methodologies	Documentary analysis, laboratory studies including the use of games, mathematical modelling	Observation of conduct in formal meetings and behind the scenes, ethnographic approaches	Interviewing actors and recording their stories, seeking verbalized explanations for policies, narrative analysis of speeches and interviews

may rest as much upon the 'institutional software' of persuasive arguments and convincing narratives, as upon the 'hardware' of rules, rights and operating procedures. Table 3.1 outlines in summary form the three modes of constraint and their mechanisms of enforcement.

Rules: formal and recorded

Institutions constrain actors through rules that are formally constructed and written down, whether as clauses in a constitution, terms of reference for an assembly, national and international laws, and a vast panoply of standards, regulations, protocols and policies. As we saw in Chapter 2, it was the study of formal rules that dominated the first phase of institutionalism, and called for 'the tools of the lawyer and the historian to explain the constraints on both political behaviour and democratic effectiveness' (Rhodes,1997: 68). Peters (2005: 6–7) points to the importance of law making and enforcement for understanding politics:

> law is the essential element of governance for most Continental countries, and certainly plays a significant role in Anglo-American thinking about the public sector. Law constitutes both the framework of the public sector itself and a major way in which government can affect the behaviour of its citizens... Therefore, to be concerned with political institutions was [and is] to be concerned with law.

The association between formal rules and structures and the 'old' institutionalism should not, however, obscure their continuing importance, in both theory and practice. Comparative politics, as a sub-discipline, remains preoccupied with the effects of differing political systems upon policy outcomes, and the ways in which the development of formal structures relates to historical trajectories and cultural traditions. Arend Lijphart's classic *Patterns of Democracy* (1999) investigates the distinction between 'majoritarian' democracies, which concentrate political power, and 'consensus' democracies in which power is dispersed and limited. Lijphart compares formal institutions in each, analysing the effects of (for instance) single party versus coalition systems, unitary versus federal arrangements, unicameral versus bicameral legislatures, flexible versus rigid constitutions, and dependent versus independent central banks. There is also a rich literature comparing policy-specific institutions, for example welfare states, regulatory regimes, or economic and financial intermediaries (see Cairney, 2012: 72–3). International relations, as a sub-discipline, also concerns itself with the formal detail of treaties, protocols and conventions, and prospects for the design and re-design of multilateral institutions (the United Nations, the European Union, the International Criminal Court, and so on).

Research on formal rules has actually gained new energy in the context of democratic transitions, whether associated with the break-up of the USSR and its satellite states, or the collapse of authoritarian regimes in Latin America or South Africa. Designing new constitutions presents liberation movements with a massive opportunity to inscribe their values into the structures that will shape (however imperfectly) future political conduct and policy outcomes. Formal rules are needed to encode responses to such fundamental questions as: who will vote, who will make laws, who will dispense justice, who will tax, who will receive welfare services, and who will defend new-found independence? And for each 'who' question, there is a 'how' (by what system) question attached. Such challenges are faced also by international actors involved in post-conflict state building, for instance in Iraq and Afghanistan (see Carey, 2006).

Constitutional matters excite especial political interest in settled democracies too, given their status as the rules that govern the rules. In the USA, for instance, appealing to the articles of the constitution, or deeming a policy proposal 'unconstitutional', can be a killer blow in political debate. And, in most democracies, the rules of the constitution are subject to particular protection, as with the 'super majorities' required by legislatures wishing to make constitutional changes (e.g. devolution within the United Kingdom). As we shall see in Chapter 7, the challenges of constitutional design and reform are vast, given historical legacies, resource limitations, information deficits, competing political demands and ongoing power struggles within and without the state.

Although 'softer' forms of constraint, through practices and narratives, have been increasingly highlighted during the second phase of institutionalism, the enduring importance of formal rules in structuring political behaviour remains. There is a tendency among some second and third phase institutionalists to imply that such rules are a distraction from understanding what really happens on the ground, and to write them off as a mere formalism or epiphenomenon. This kind of approach is associated with a deep scepticism regarding the scope for projects of intentional institutional design. Our argument, in contrast, is that the proper subject matter of third phase institutionalism is the specific *combination* of formal and informal mechanisms that constrain political behaviour in different settings, and which may be both the object and the subject of attempts at change (however imperfect).

So how do formal rules work to constrain political actors? On the rational choice wing of institutionalism, Riker (1980) and Shepsle (1986) develop Arrow's (1951) theorization of 'decision rules' which produce a stability in political systems (or equilibrium) which otherwise would not exist. Visible and transparent rules are vital characteristics of this type of institution, allowing actors to know what they are agreeing to when they participate in a 'game', including whether they can make up for 'losses' in any one 'round' when they engage in subsequent iterations. As Peters (2005: 53) notes: 'From this perspective, institutions provide a stable means of making choices in what would otherwise be an extremely contentious political environment.' Similarly, both North (1990) and Eggertsson (1996) are concerned with how property rights regimes, as sets of formal and visible rules, allow markets to function.

The principal–agent model, developed originally by Heclo and Wildavsky (1974), has become the dominant approach to questions of institutional design in which a hierarchically superior actor is concerned to ensure that an inferior fulfils his contractual obligations, without engaging in the different forms of cheating available to rational actors (e.g. Lupia and McCubbins, 1994). Rational choice scholars have further developed this concept as 'design for compliance' by theorizing the problem in terms of a series of games played between those developing and implementing laws and those seeking to reinterpret these for their own purposes (Calvert, 1995; Scharpf, 1997).

Historical institutionalists, particularly those who had found a home in institutionalism from classical Marxism, have sought to 'bring the state back in' to political analysis in its role 'as rule maker, referee, and enforcer' (Scott, 2001: 54). In what we might call their historical institutionalist manifesto, Thelen and Steinmo (1992) developed a conception of institutions to include structures of government, laws and policies, and much broader categories such as social class. Seeking to hold together a concern with formal rules and informal practices has become a hallmark of the work of this group of scholars. As Hall and Thelen (2008: 9) explain:

> we conceptualize institutions as sets of regularized practices with a rule-like quality in the sense that the actors expect the practices to be observed; and which, in some but not all, cases are supported by formal sanctions. They can range from regulations backed by the force of law or organizational procedure, such as the rules that apply when a worker is laid off, to more informal practices that have a conventional character, such as the expectation that firms will offer a certain number of apprenticeships.

They add a footnote to indicate that rules and practices often complement each other in practice:

> While analytically distinct, it is worth noting that the more formal and the more informal or conventional dimensions of institutions

are often linked. For example, the convention that large firms supply apprenticeship slots is supported, albeit at slight remove, by a number of formal institutions – e.g. compulsory membership in employer chambers, strong unions pushing firms up-market, and relatively centralized wage bargaining institutions that compress wages and allow firms to earn rents on training.

On the sociological wing of new institutionalism, March and Olsen (1989: 21–6) stress the interrelated nature of what they call 'rules and routines' which come as a package in the empirical setting. Analytically, however, they distinguish between routines, which are stable patterns of behaviour governed by an institution-specific 'logic of appropriateness', and rules which constitute the 'formalization' of that logic (Peters, 2005: 32). Taking issue with crude rational choice premises, March and Olsen (1989: 38) argue that 'a calculus of identity and appropriateness' is more important to political actors than 'a calculus of political costs and benefits'.

Richard Scott (2008) has taken the sociological school forward through his conception of the 'three pillars of institutionalism', working respectively through regulative, normative and cognitive mechanisms. In his account of the regulative pillar, he shows how formal rules secure compliance via coercive means, on the basis of expedience. Institutions are designed in such a way to make it easier to comply with the rule or law than to break it. As Scott (2008: 52) summarizes: 'regulatory processes involve the capacity to establish rules, inspect others' conformity to them, and, as necessary, manipulate sanctions – rewards or punishments – in an attempt to influence future behaviour'. It is possible, however, that the means of sanction may be informal as well as formal, including 'folkways such as shaming or shunning activities, or they may be highly formalized and assigned to specialized actors, such as the police and courts' (Scott, 2008: 52).

Practices: informal and demonstrated

The second way in which institutions constrain is via practices. Unlike rules, these are not formally recorded or officially sanctioned. Their mode of transmission is, rather, through demonstration: actors understand how they are supposed to behave through observing the routinized actions of others and seeking to recreate those actions. As

Helmke and Levitsky (2006: 1) explain, these ways of doing things are 'created, communicated, and enforced outside officially sanctioned channels'. This does not make them any less influential in relation to constraint or compliance.

Practices may support 'positive' patterns of behaviour, like accountability or probity or a 'public service ethos'; equally they may underpin 'negative' frameworks like patronage, paternalism or sexism. In a well-established institutional set-up, practices may simply reinforce formal arrangements; but in periods of transition, they may prove especially tenacious and resistant to change, existing in parallel – or even direct contradiction – to formal rules. New rules and structures can be effectively incorporated into 'the old ways', leaving customary practices intact – neutering or subverting the intended changes in values and/or power relationships. Helmke and Levitsky (2006) develop a typology of four ways in which formal and informal institutions typically interact: complementary, accommodating, competing, and substitutive.

Neglecting these 'informal rules of the game' may lead us to miss many of the most important incentives and constraints that underlie political conduct. To take an example, Langston (2006: 143–59) focuses on 'dedazo' in Mexico, which can be loosely translated as 'pointing the finger', and was, as such, a practice which allowed sitting presidents through much of the twentieth century to 'handpick' their own successor, by ensuring that stronger candidates were excluded and the preferred candidate was given a 'clear run' through the selection process. As Langston points out, an important point here is that, from the formal perspective, the successor has in fact been elected according the rules of the constitution, but of course the intention and mechanics of the law have been subverted by the coexistence of a competing set of practices.

Practices can, however, be a resource for institutional design as well as a barrier to certain forms of intervention. Actors on the ground are involved in a constant process of matching situations to rules and, as formal rules and wider contexts change, informal practices may be modified to fit new circumstances (March and Olsen, 1989: 34). Practices provide resources for actors seeking to respond to change, and often form the foundation upon which more formal arrangements are subsequently developed (Knight, 1992: 172). Because any existing institutional settlement embodies a specific set of power relationships, defending traditional practices (or minimizing disruption to them) may be a way for particular actors to pursue their sectional interests. Indeed, rational choice theorists like Elinor Ostrom are very clear that 'rules in use' comprise informal elements alongside those formal rules that *actually* constrain, rather than exist on paper only. The case study in Box 3.2 shows how looking at formal rules and informal practices together can help answer important political questions.

For sociological institutionalists, there is an abundance of literature on institutions as practices which goes back over a hundred years. Scott (2001: 9–19) demonstrates how early institutional theory in sociology prepared the ground for the 'new' institutionalists' interest in practices, described variously as 'folkways' (Sumner, 1906), 'mores' (Hughes, 1936), and 'norms' (Parsons, 1951). Getting closer to the 'rediscovery' of institutions in the 1980s, Garfinkel's (1974) ethnomethodology was concerned to uncover 'the 'common-sense knowledge' of how to operate within some social arena, developed and acquired by its participants' (Scott, 2001: 41). At the same time, Giddens (1979) was developing a line of argument in sociology, begun by Selznick (1949), which saw institutions as systems of meaning which convey a sense of how actors should behave and habituate actors 'to accepting the norms and values of their organisation' (Peters, 2005: 118).

Influenced by this type of theory, March and Olsen brought institutions back onto centre stage for a new generation of political scientists, defining their subject matter thus:

> An institution is a relatively stable collection of rules and practices, embedded in structures of *resources* that make action possible – organizational, financial and staff capabilities, and structures of *meaning* that explain and justify behavior – roles, identities and belongings, common purposes, and causal and normative beliefs. (March and Olsen,1989, original emphasis)

On returning to their key concept of the 'logic of appropriateness' in 2009, March and Olsen reiterated the importance of institutions as demonstrated practices:

> Actors use criteria of similarity and congruence, rather than likelihood and value. To act appropriately is to proceed according to the institutionalized practices of a collectivity, based on mutual, and often tacit, understandings of what is true, reasonable, natural, right, and good. (March and Olsen 2009: 4)

Richard Scott (2008) locates practices as underpinning the 'normative pillar' of institutionalism: 'Norms specify how things should be done; they define legitimate means to pursue valued ends'. The basis of

> **Box 3.2   Rules and practices working together: explaining local differences in political participation in English cities**
>
> In England, as elsewhere, socio-economic status accounts for most of the variation in political participation between localities. However, there are localities that are out of sync with their predicted level of participation. What are the factors that determine why some wealthy areas have unusually low levels of participation, and some disadvantaged areas have vibrant local polities? Can an understanding of these 'deviant' cases contribute to the development of urban political participation?
>
> To investigate this phenomenon, four pairs of English local authorities were examined (Lowndes, Pratchett and Stoker, 2006). Each pair had a similar socio-economic profile but differed in terms of participation, taking into account both electoral and non-electoral activities aimed at influencing local decision-making. The research considered the proposition from social capital theory that norms of trust and high levels of associational activity were associated with political participation (Putnam, 2000). But, within the sample there were localities with high social capital and low participation, and low social capital and high participation. It was the institutional frameworks within which citizen participation took place (or did not) that turned out to be most important. Although formal structures were similar in most localities, the way in which these were elaborated and embedded in 'rules-in-use' (Ostrom, 1999) made a big difference to citizens' willingness to participate. Indeed, skills and capacities for participation associated with both socio-economic status and social capital remained 'latent' where rules-in-use were not conducive, but were activated in those localities where rules enabled and made attractive practices of citizen participation.
>
> →

compliance is social obligation. Actors are constrained by their knowledge of a logic of appropriateness which tells them which practices they should follow in any given situation, and third party enforcement is via the 'binding expectations' of other actors in the immediate context. For those who do not adopt accepted practices this may include attempts to formally outlaw the conduct but will also range from expressions of disproval, to social isolation of the offenders, to in extreme cases verbal intimidation and threats of violence.

The recognition of the significance of informal practices was central to the 'rediscovery' of institutions. But the key challenge for third phase institutionalism is to consider formal rules and informal practices alongside each other. Indeed, it is helpful to think of a continuum from highly formal to highly informal, with many places in between. We need to study the specific combination of formal and

Three different rule sets were found to be particularly important. In the party political domain, rules-in-use that favoured strong party competition and regular leadership changes were linked to more active citizen participation. In public management, the formal rules and informal conventions governing interactions between citizens and front-line staff engaged in service delivery were as important as the availability of specialist bodies and forums for participation. Rules-in-use relating to public service delivery affected citizens' perception of the accessibility and responsiveness of the local authority at a general level. Finally, in the civic domain, it was important whether there were formal and informal mechanisms to link different local organizations and their activities (networks, umbrella bodies), and whether there were channels for direct communication with local policy makers (forums, scrutiny).

As well as throwing light upon the reasons behind differences in citizen participation, the research had a positive message for policy makers and practitioners. By framing and sustaining rules-in-use, public bodies can provide additional and malleable incentives for participation (beyond socio-economic status and social capital, which are notoriously difficult for policy makers to influence). They can also seek to establish a normative context in which participation is seen as 'appropriate' behaviour (by citizens and decision makers alike). Shaping the institutional framework, while not easy, also provides a more attractive route for policy makers than seeking to dislodge longstanding socio-economic cleavages or social capital deficits.

Source: Lowndes *et al.* (2006).

informal elements through which particular institutions shape behaviour, how this shifts over time (and varies between cases), and the extent to which formal and informal elements reinforce one another or exist in tension. The gaps that often open up between formal and informal elements create spaces for change and are also a reflection of processes of institutional evolution. The communication and enforcement of *the same institutions* may shift between the formal and informal domains, reflecting the strategic considerations of dominant political actors. It is helpful, therefore, to look for processes of formalization and informalization, through which the character of institutional constraint changes over time. As we have already argued, institutions are best understood as processes rather than things – processes of constraint and empowerment that create 'stable, recurring patterns of behaviour' (Goodin, 1996).

An emerging school of 'feminist institutionalism' has been particularly active in evaluating the interaction between formal and informal institutional constraints (McKay and Krook, 2011). Research shows how informal gendered norms and expectations shape formal institutions, but may also contradict or undermine formal rules, operating to frustrate or dilute the impact of gender equality reforms (Freidenvall and Krook, 2011; Kenny and Lowndes, 2011). The interplay between formal rules and informal practices is conceived as a dynamic process that changes over time; there is evidence, for instance, of ways in which male-dominated political elites have shifted the locus of power from formal to informal mechanisms in order to counteract women's increased access and presence in formal decision-making sites (Kathlene, 1995; Hawkesworth, 2005).

Another challenge for third phase institutionalism is to address the frequent conceptual slippages between the notion of practices, or informal rules, and broader ideas of norms, culture, beliefs and values. One way ahead is to remember that practices share the core characteristics of other modes of institutional constraints – they are, in Ostrom's words, prescriptions as to possible and/or desirable behaviour and the sanctions for non-compliance. Practices are specific to a particular political setting, recognized and shared among actors within that setting, and are enforceable. As such, they are distinct from actors' personal values or broader cultural or normative tendencies within society. Actors' orientation to, and interpretation of, specific practices will, however, be influenced by these other elements. And, as Ostrom (2005: 27) explains:

> when all participants share a common set of values... the probabilities of their developing adequate rules and norms to govern repetitive relationships are much greater... If participants in a situation come from many different cultures... the costs of devising and sustaining effective rules are substantially increased.

With the growth of multi-level and transnational institutions, and of more culturally differentiated and plural societies, the challenge of securing institutional constraint can only become more challenging. Recognizing the role played by informal practices, alongside formal rules, is vital for both interpreting institutional dynamics and developing robust approaches to institutional design and reform. Practices should not be confused with values or culture, but a proper focus of study within third phase institutionalism is the way in which political institutions are articulated with institutional arrangements within society and economic relations more broadly – we return to this question in Chapter 6.

Narratives: semi-formal and spoken

The third way in which institutions constrain action is via narrative. Although the least developed of the three modes, it has actually been present in institutionalist thought for some time, including in rational choice (e.g. Riker, 1982), historical institutionalist (e.g. Weir and Skocpol, 1983), and sociological scholarship (e.g. Silverman, 1971). We show how narratives shape behaviour, constraining some actors and empowering others: the most effective political institutions are characterized by resonant stories. Although governments will always pass laws and seek to shape practices, a great deal of politics is about more subtle processes of explanation and persuasion.

A narrative can be defined as 'a sequence of events, experiences, or actions with a plot that ties together different parts into a meaningful whole' (Feldman *et al.*, 2004). A narrative comprises several embedded stories, so that while a narrative is an account of a 'grand conception', a story is a specific contextualized exemplar which supports and enriches our appreciation of that conception. Narratives embody values, ideas and power: 'Through telling their stories, people distil and reflect a particular understanding of social and political relations' (Feldman *et al.*, 2004). In an institutional sense, we have seen how rules are conveyed through documents and legislation and how practices are modelled by actors. Narratives, in contrast, are transmitted via the spoken word (literally, the telling of stories) or relayed in symbolic form or what Scott calls 'scripts' – in speeches, mission statements, logos, design or style. Music or pictures, even, can act as institutional narratives. Think, for example, of the ways in which diverse national anthems express and reinforce the ruling conventions of a specific state, how the orchestral music of the nineteenth century encapsulates the institutional legacies of European empires, or how art and architecture narrated, for instance, the expectations of state socialism. From the stories around the water cooler that serve as part of the induction of new office-based public servants to the elaborate rituals and ceremonies that characterize military life, the symbolic architecture of institutions acts to guide and constrain actors as much as formal rules.

Narratives are especially important modes of institutional constraint to the extent that they provide an account not just of *how* we do things around here, but also *why* we do things the way we do. As Ringen (2005) argues, 'It does not help governments to be able to give orders... they need to be able to *persuade* ... Regulating is not enough. Governments in addition depend on *speaking*. They need to explain, to "sell" their policies, to make themselves trusted.' In similar vein, Claus Offe (2009) suggests that a wide range of government policies 'rely on the successful activation of the cognitive and moral resources of citizens through signals and appeals that educate and remind people of what is "the right thing to do"'. Paul Sabatier (1988: 152) stresses the importance of establishing narrative as well as regulative modes of constraint: political systems cannot operate effectively 'through the raw exercise of power' but have to be 'convincing' in terms of the definition of problems and the elaboration of policies. While rules rely on expedience as the basis of compliance, practices rest upon binding expectations and a sense of social obligation, and narratives, on the other hand, secure compliance by establishing as 'taken-for-granted' certain framing devices, explanatory categories and normative understandings.

Narratives play an important part in securing institutional stability over time. In the UK, for example, there has been a long-running and deeply embedded political narrative about the National Health Service (NHS) which extols its virtues and concludes with the moral imperative that it is political suicide to attempt to attack this 'religion' or 'national treasure' (note the symbolic language). In the UK General Election of 2010 it was accepted by all major political parties that draconian cuts to public services were required to reduce the national debt 'crisis'. But even in this fevered atmosphere of fiscal disaster, voters were assured by the same parties at the hustings that the NHS would be protected, and this remained the policy of the Coalition government once it was elected, even though this is at the cost of more severe and politically difficult cuts in other fields of government. The government's ongoing attempt to introduce further market-based reforms to the NHS continues to run up against the constraints of the narrative.

Even rational choice scholars have identified the role played by forms of cognitive framing. Ward (2002: 77–8) cites Riker's early (1982) work showing how politicians 'may destabilize majorities by inserting extra issue dimensions into the debate and may solidify majorities by encouraging the separate consideration of issues'. The context for strategic action is structured by the 'organizing in' or 'organizing out' of certain arguments. Goldstein and Keohane's (1993) work is a key referent in rational choice institutionalism's attempts to account for ideas in the form of beliefs. Here 'principled beliefs are seen as the normative bases and justifications for particular decisions, while causal beliefs tell agents about means-ends relationships' (Blyth, 2002b: 303). Paul Pierson (2004: 39) highlights the significance of symbolic constraints in building a rational model of path dependency:

> Every time we shake hands, the strength of the norm is reinforced... The same argument can be applied with considerable force to collective understandings – of how the world works, what is to be valued, what an individual's interests might be, and who that individual's friends and enemies might be.

Echoing Pierson's call for more historical and sociological input to rational choice institutionalism, Mark Lichbach's work has examined what makes rational actors engage in collective dissent for over three decades. What Scott calls cultural-cognitive elements are held central: 'To understand protest in America, one must understand protest and one must understand America' (Lichbach, 1998: 402). In a similar cross-over, Masahiko Aoki (2001: 10) defines an institution as 'a self-sustaining system of shared beliefs about a salient way in which the game is repeatedly played'. Through recourse to what Scott (2008: 51) calls shared 'constitutive schema', Aoki seeks to explain why actors cooperate in situations which other theorists have assumed would lead only to competitive behaviour, and emphasizes the diversity of the institutional arrangements which emerge.

In historical institutionalism, Weir and Skocpol's (1983) study of divergent policy responses of states during the Great Depression stimulated wider work on how emerging political ideas are constrained within a particular country's current institutional architecture. Unless new ideas are in some way congruent with existing rules, practices and narratives, they are unlikely to be championed in the first place, and in the event they are brought forward, will be forcefully resisted by state and other powerful actors. In similar vein, Peter Hall's (1989) work on the influence of ideas on policy seeks to explain the impact of first Keynesianism and then monetarism on international politics. As Peters (2005: 75) points out, 'These ideas are the functional equivalents of the logic of appropriateness ... they constrain the limits of acceptable action by government.' (Richard Scott, 2008: 51, refers to this as the 'logic of orthodoxy'.) Hence, in a similar way to Skocpol and Weir's formulation, new economic ideas may be aligned with existing institutions in such a way that they strengthen the position of ruling state actors. But they need also to be 'actionable' in the sense that actors can see how new ideas can be operationalized within given institutional frameworks. In effect, Hall is drawing attention to the interconnected character of narratives, rules and practices, and the challenge of changing just one element of an institutional configuration.

The conceptualization of 'discursive institutionalism' by Vivien Schmidt moves the debate on further. For Schmidt (2006: 110) ideas are actually 'constitutive of institutions, even if shaped by them'. In later work, she explains that:

> political actors' ideas serve to (re)conceptualise interests and values as well as (re)shape institutions. Such ideas can be specific policy ideas, such as varying state responses to neo-Keynesianism... They may be more general programmatic ideas, such as states' radical paradigm shift from neo-Keynesianism to neo-liberalism... but they may instead be underlying public philosophies. These could be foundational political ideas about the role of the state... or collective memories that are generated at critical moments. (Schmidt, 2009: 530–1)

Schmidt argues that ideas are transmitted by a 'coordinative discourse' and a 'communicative discourse'. Coordinative discourse involves those 'individuals and groups at the centre of policy construction who are involved in the creation, elaboration, and justification of policy and programmatic ideas'. Communicative discourse, on the other hand, involves,

> political actors engaged in a mass process of public persuasion, in which political leaders, government spokespeople, party activists, spin doctors and others communicate the ideas developed in the coordinative discourse to the public for discussion, deliberation, and modification of the ideas in question. (Schmidt, 2009: 532)

Colin Hay (2006a) describes his 'constructivist institutionalism' as 'a work in progress'. But, like Schmidt, ideas seem to trump institutions as the key explanatory factors in accounting for political behaviour. Institutions essentially become a vehicle for transmitting the ideas that constrain (and empower) actors. Rules and practices are secondary to narratives; they derive from the ideational, rather than forming part of an 'over-determining' matrix. Hay (2006a: 59) defines institutions as 'codified systems of ideas'. It is questionable whether Schmidt and Hay's approach are 'institutionalist' at all. In their theorizations, it is ideas that drive political behaviour, mediated by institutions which are understood as historical crystallizations of dominant ideas.

To complete our account of the narrative mode of constraint, we need to consider the contribution of sociological institutionalism, with its constructivist tradition covering both normative (value based) and cognitive (knowledge based) narrations of the social world. In their seminal work on organizations, Meyer and Rowan (1977) analysed the 'rationalization' of beliefs, by which beliefs translated into procedures to achieve certain organizational aims; Zucker (1977: 726) shows how 'social knowledge, once institutionalized, exists as a fact, as part of objective reality, and can be transmitted directly on that basis'. DiMaggio and Powell (1991b) identified three mechanisms through which institutional effects are 'diffused' through an organization – coercive, normative and mimetic – which map nicely on to our three modes of constraint. In the latter case, as Strang and Meyer (1993: 489) observe, 'diffusion processes often look more like complex exercises in the social construction of identity than like the mechanistic spread of information'.

With their tradition of detailed case study analysis, sociological institutionalists also point to the methodological advantages of looking at narratives to understand the 'work' done by institutions. Box 3.3 provides a case study from US business. As Linde (2001: 163), its author, observes:

> Stories provide a bridge between the tacit and the explicit, allowing tacit social knowledge to be demonstrated and learned, without the need to propositionalize ethics, specify in detail appropriate behaviour, or demonstrate why particular heroes of the past are relevant today. The reason for this is that stories do not only recount past events. They also convey the speaker's moral attitude towards these events: the protagonist of the story acted well, acted badly, is to be praised or blamed, can be taken as a model for the hearer's own behaviour. These evaluations are sometimes explicitly stated within the story, but more often are suggested through the use of a single word or phrase.

For the narrative mode of constraint, the bases for compliance are frequently rehearsed shared understandings which lead to 'taken-for-

Box 3.3   Narrative institutions shaping conduct: story-telling at MidWest Insurance, USA

The attempts by big corporations such as Microsoft to produce meaningful, one line mission statements ('almost invariably vacuous failures') can be compared with the storytelling that goes on within organizations, which invites the listener to draw their own conclusions about the types of behaviour that are expected, required, or condemned. Linde (2001) studies this process in an insurance company she names 'MidWest'. Here, stories were invariably constructed around four points:

- The founder was charismatic, honest, hard-working and a brilliant salesman, who had a new vision for insurance sales. His defining idea was that farmers of good moral character should be charged lower rates for auto insurance, since they ran lower risks than city drivers.
- The American rural and small town origins of the founder and of the company were central to their values and identity. This was passionately promoted even by company members who had spent their entire lives in large cities.
- The development of the company represented an ever-expanding commercial and ethical success, as evidenced by the expansion from auto insurance into life and health insurance too.
- The company was itself a family, operating according to family values. The firm comprised directly employed managers, agents with the status of independent contractors, and, of course, the founder and owner.

Agents told stories about their early days, and how they built their own portfolio within the MidWest way of doing things. Managers told stories about their careers, and those of exemplary agents from whom others should learn, and about significant changes in the company that they had lived through. And everyone told stories about the founder. These stories formed a tightly linked system of first and third person narratives, in which entrepreneurship was always cited as the founder's major virtue. Reproducing and reinforcing this narrative, agents described their efforts in terms of the activities of independent businessmen, willing to 'back themselves' in terms of customers and income, rather than 'desk jockeys' relying on a monthly salary. Following the story of the founder, they attributed their success to hard work and a good product, rather than to risk taking or 'sharp practice'.

Source: Linde (2001).

grantedness'. Sanctions in response to non-compliance to shared logics of action, or to developing opposing narratives, may include recourse to law in extreme cases (e.g. inciting racial hatred) and the mobilization of normative sanctions (disapproval), but will be largely based on incomprehension, ridicule of the narrator and his or her argument, and attempts to undermine the reputation and credibility of the offenders.

How modes of constraint work together (or not)

There is considerable theoretical and methodological value in separating out rules, practices and narratives in the way we have done above. Theoretically, we have greater leverage on how institutions do their work – the means by which they shape actors' behaviour and the ways in which compliance is sought. Methodologically, we have a clear strategy for finding out about, in Ostrom's words, 'how things are done around here'. If we want to research political institutions and their effects, we should study rules, observe practices, and interpret narratives. We need to establish with actors their recognition and understanding of modes of constraint, but we do not assume compliance; in fact, we expect resistance, disruption and the promulgation of institutional alternatives. But this analytical deconstruction of institutions, while essential, is not sufficient. We also need to engage in a reconstruction, which considers how modes of constraint combine to produce institutional stability over time, and also how gaps and fissures open up to create instability – and possibilities for change.

If we look again at the MidWest example above from Linde (2001), we can see how employees newly inducted into the firm are likely to quickly succumb to the normative expectations that they should expect a level of income related to the business they can bring in rather than a regular salary, and will be inclined to work hard and extol the virtues of the company's products, without resorting to unnecessary risk taking. These richly detailed and frequently rehearsed stories about how we do things around here will shape how these employers see their role within the firm, and how they conduct themselves. Linde (2001: 164) raises the question of how these might interact with the shaping effects of practices and regulations but does not supply us with any answers in her empirical account. If we were to go back to MidWest, we could study the practices of experienced and respected employees to look at the extent to which they 'modelled' the prescriptions of hard work and self-reliance that were embedded in the narratives. We could also study regulations, in the shape of company policies, which formally set out enforceable measures such as incentive schemes to promote individual endeavour or rules to deal with dishonesty among

Box 3.4   Institutional constraints in action: politics, budgets and the UK National Health Service

The most widely recognized achievement of the post-war British Welfare State, the NHS is highly regarded by the population at large. Since 1945, there has been a shared understanding, accepted by all political parties, that the NHS provides the fairest and best quality health care system in the world and must be fully supported. Evidence which casts doubt on the credibility and sustainability of these commitments has emerged over the past two decades, and includes, amongst other things, the neglect and ill treatment of patients in some of the UK's major NHS hospitals, and the projected costs of providing health care for a rapidly ageing population. In response, successive Conservative and Labour governments have ordered 'reorganizations' of the structure of the NHS, but none have been able to control its rising costs, and, crucially, none have been able to make any public pledge to cut the funds provided to the NHS from the public purse. While the NHS remains a centrally controlled organization, there is no doubt that governments will continue to attempt to lower the costs of treatment, not least through the incremental hiving off of certain parts of its operations to private sector companies. But, over the last sixty years, a powerful combination of institutional constraints, in the shape of narratives, practices and rules, have closed down opportunities for effective political intervention:

Narratives have been constructed in relation to the NHS being 'the best system', a 'national treasure', 'free at the point of delivery' and 'fully

→

employees. Our purpose would be to trace the interaction between narratives, practices and rules which could make it very difficult for new employee not to conform to the institutions which, in combination, shape the company's ideal agent.

However, we may find that the 'fit' between rules, practices and narratives is not complete. Perhaps some of the older managers, who claim to know, may privately tell stories to newcomers which cast doubt on the founder as a hard-working entrepreneur, and may present him in a less heroic light, for example, as a beneficiary of good luck, or even inheritance. In their practices some experienced agents may employ well rehearsed routines which allow them to exploit the rules of the incentive scheme to achieve most additional income for least effort, and allow them to slack without being detected by management.

To take another example, which we touched on above, Box 3.4 focuses on how institutional constraints work together against politicians who would try to contain the rising costs of the UK National Health Service. As we shall see in Chapter 5, classical explanations of funded', following a logic which connects excellence to costs and thereby maintains high expectations of both. The concept of the NHS as a distinctively national health service leads to a demand that the same quality and quantity of treatment should be provided in every geographical location within the UK. Whenever attempts are made at local level to reduce or 'ration' any particular service, the accusation of 'postcode lottery' is used by patient groups, the media and opposition politicians to put pressure on central government to reinstate the services at their premium level.

Practices are important because, while the NHS operates top-down in a political and managerial sense, day-to-day diagnosis, treatment and referral by General Practitioners (GPs) actually drives the system from the bottom up. Although their services were incorporated into the NHS in 1945, GPs themselves retain the status of individual practitioners running their own businesses. As independent operators, GPs follow a 'logic of appropriateness' in which they prescribe the treatment they believe to be in the best interest of the individual patient, with attendant upward pressures on cost and volume.

Rules have been under the spotlight in the context of successive NHS scandals, with the aim of driving up quality and drive out abusive practices. An NHS Constitution was established in 2009 and 'patient charters' have been enforced through legislation, seeking to empower patients as service consumers. These formal written documents provide details of patients' rights including access to services which are free of charge, non-discriminatory, never refused on unreasonable grounds, obtainable from any UK NHS provider, and assessed locally on the basis of need.

institutional constraint tend to focus on path dependence, conceptualized as the reluctance of actors to deviate from a particular policy course because they calculate that the costs of doing so will outweigh the benefits. Here we provide a similar but more nuanced explanation for why the NHS budget has continued to increase in the past, and why it will probably do so in the future. Our account relies on the patterns of interaction between narratives, practices, and rules. On their own, each mode of constraint closes down alternative policy choices; in combination, they leave the would-be reformer with very few places to go.

Box 3.4 shows how narratives, which have been associated with the NHS since its inception, produce high public expectations of quality which are connected in turn to high levels of funding. We also explain the constraint which demands that the NHS is a *national* health service and therefore the same quality and quantity of treatment must be provided in every geographical location within the UK. When we look at practices, it is apparent that the demand for treatment is controlled on a day-to-day basis by General Practitioners (GPs) who refer patients for services from the community, and will prescribe the treatment which they believe best serves the interests of that individual. Considering the rules governing the NHS, central government itself has increased demand from the individual patient by positioning them as a consumer of services under a formal 'NHS Constitution', which specifies in writing a wide range of rights which can be exercised in terms of access to treatment.

In this way, the politician who tries to support an attempt to reduce or 'ration' any particular service is faced with the accusation that they are attacking the NHS and promoting a 'postcode lottery'. GPs' logics of appropriateness work against any local or central attempts to control costs, and government itself has given individuals the formal institutions through which to demand higher levels of service in terms of quality and quantity. These different institutional effects do not simply 'thicken' the same layer of constraint; rather, they act in combination to close down different avenues for policy reform which might otherwise have been available, in terms of questioning the sustainability of the NHS in its current form, the tailoring of local services to meet local needs, the engagement of GPs in cost control, and the possibility of persuading individual patients to accept different, and cheaper, treatment options.

It is perhaps not surprising, therefore, that in recent times UK governments have resorted to successively restructuring the NHS in what could be interpreted as attempts to sweep away some of the practices at the heart of the organization, and replace some of the actors who maintain these and the narratives which reinforce them. From an institutional perspective, however a 'new broom' can never 'sweep clean'. If we look at the history of the NHS from the 1940s, we can see that those pioneering institutional designers did not start with a blank sheet either. Indeed, they were required to work with the powerful institutions of private practice favoured by the GPs and consultants who sought to veto the project before it got off the ground. When the Labour health minister, Nye Bevan, admitted that he had 'stuffed' the consultants' 'mouths with gold', he was admitting that he had engaged in a political compromise which would allow the institutions of private practice to continue alongside the new, egalitarian institutions he was fighting to introduce. For the UK's coalition government, elected in 2010, these earlier narratives (subordinated for 60 years) provide an important resource as they seek to open up the health service to 'any willing provider'. The forms of change that become possible within a path dependent context depend upon the 'narratives and myths that were present at the founding of an institution' (Froese, 2009: 1).

Box 3.5 Breaking the rules: 'institutional racism' in London's Metropolitan Police

Within London's Metropolitan Police Force, profoundly damaging incidents of racist conduct towards citizens and fellow police officers have come to light at regular intervals over several decades. Looking at the interaction of different modes of institutional constraint, and accompanying gaps and tensions, helps explain why some officers have persistently disregarded the Met's formal institutional framework on anti-racism.

When black people first started immigrating to the UK in large numbers in the 1960s, racism was already institutionalized in the country. Private landlords were able to specify their own rules of occupancy in terms of 'No Blacks, no Dogs, no Irish'. Local authorities felt able to ask for changes to immigration rules so as to exclude black people from their boundaries. But from the 1970s onwards, new legislation and the equal opportunities movement put pressure on public bodies, including police forces, to deinstitutionalize racism from their organizations. Regulations, such as uniform requirements, which unintentionally discriminated against black people (e.g. Sikhs) were amended. Anti-racist practices and narratives were introduced through intensive training initiatives and sustained campaigns aimed at recruiting people from black communities to work in the Met.

The diagnosis of 'institutional racism' gained ground in the late 1990s when Lord McPherson examined the conduct of the police investigation into the murder of a young black man, Stephen Lawrence. The combination of institutional constraints in place within the Met should have led to the murder being treated in as serious a fashion as any other, but an alternative set of practices and narratives were also found to be in play, legacies of the pre 1970s era. At a narrative level, investigating officers assumed Lawrence, as young black man, to be a gang member and the victim of a gang killing. And the sloppy practices that typified the investigation were guided by an assumption that it was not important to find the killers of a black gang member.

The McPherson Report led to a second round of promoting anti-racist regulations, practices and narratives within the Met. In 2009, Trevor Phillips, head of the UK's Equality and Human Rights Commission, announced that the organization was no longer 'institutionally racist'. Against this the Metropolitan Black Police Association promoted a boycott of black recruitment to the Met from 2008, which only ended in January 2010 after the Deputy Commissioner admitted that racial discrimination is still practised by some of the force's officers.

No institution is ever 'complete' – it is a work in progress, the product of human agency and the outcome of political struggles. Institutional change emerges out of the interstices between rules, practices and narratives; just as stability arises from their alignment. Indeed, in all institutions (at some time and in some places) rules are broken, practices are ignored, and counter-narratives gain voice. Persistent or widespread 'non-compliance' may be a prelude to significant institutional change (Klijn, 2001), but it may also be tolerated at the margins or accommodated through rule adjustment. Processes of disobedience and change are related, but they are not the same thing. Rule-breaking is poorly understood within the literature, and our framework of distinct but interrelated modes of institutional constraint can help.

Box 3.5 provides a practical example of disobedience and resistance through a case study of 'institutional racism' in the Metropolitan Police Force (the 'Met'), which is responsible for policing London. The case highlights the importance of the Met's own history, which in turn is embedded in a long history of racism in the UK more widely. The timeframe used here is the period of 50 years from the 1960s when racist rules, practices and narratives were already rife in the British public and private sector. The racist institutions which persisted in the Met throughout this period were developed alongside those prevalent in society, creating a reinforcing effect. Against this backdrop, two extensive programmes of institutional change were implemented over this period in an attempt to deinstitutionalize racism in the Met. The first took place through the 1970s and 80s as the Met finally abolished the formal rules and regulations which had permitted racism in the force; at the same time, practices and narratives were shifting within wider British society. The second programme was developed specifically as a response to the death of Stephen Lawrence and the findings of the McPherson Report. The term 'institutional racism' was used to describe a situation in which informal practices and narratives allowed racism to continue *despite* the abolition of discriminatory rules. Officers' behaviour continued to be shaped by 'binding expectations' and 'constitutive schema' (Scott, 2008: 51) favourable to racism, even though rules had changed. Racism was no longer legally sanctioned but it was still morally and culturally acceptable in some groups of officers with the Met.

Consequently, the next stage of the reform strategy focused upon what Schmidt (2009) refers to as 'coordinative and communicative discourse'. New narratives were coined and promulgated which emphasized a moral case (the duty of the Met to serve all Londoners not just white communities) and a business case (policing would only be effective if it commanded the confidence of black communities as well as white). Mutually reinforcing practices were promoted and embedded including: neighbourhood policing initiatives; the recruitment of more black police officers and civilian staff; firmer disciplinary action against officers who exhibited racist conduct; the monitoring of arrest and prosecution statistics by racial origin; and support for the Metropolitan Black Police Association which acted as a professional association and support network for black police staff.

We can conclude that, cumulatively, these initiatives were at least partially successful, given the verdict of the head of the Equality and Human Rights Commission in 2009 that the Met was no longer 'institutionally racist'. This view remained bitterly contested, however, by the Metropolitan Black Police Association which promoted a boycott of black recruitment to the Met from 2008, on the basis of long-term concerns regarding the lack of career progression and disproportionate disciplinary action against people of colour in the Met. The more optimistic view is also undermined by the fact that the boycott was only ended in January 2010 after the Deputy Commissioner admitted that discrimination still exists among the Met's officers.

Our case example leads to three conclusions about the limitations of institutional constraint. First, most attempts at institutional reform are made in response to an existing set of rules, practices and narratives which are deemed undesirable. In the case of racism in the Met, these constraints were closely linked to institutions within wider British society. Even when the Met abandoned its discriminatory rules, less formal practices and narratives continued to shape behaviour. Attempts at deinstitutionalization which do not go beyond changing one set of formal regulations for another are unlikely to succeed. Second, reformers did not start with a 'blank sheet', and new rules, practices and narratives were promoted alongside the institutions they were supposed to supersede. Forced cohabitation in the institutional matrix of 'old' and 'new' institutions is always likely to produce opportunities for resistance to institutional constraint. Third, as Anthony Giddens (1999: 127) reminds us, institutions are 'instantiated' in the action of individuals – they do not have an objective existence beyond their effects upon actors' behaviour. Trite as it may sound, reformers need to take people with them and harness their efforts in the fashioning of new rules, practices and narratives. It is a very thin form of compliance that is secured by the imposition of new institutional arrangements.

Conclusion

In this chapter we have considered the central question of how institutions do their work, proposing that institutions constrain actors in three different ways: through rules, practices and narratives. We have argued that the character of constraint, and the way in which different modes of constraint are combined (or not), is an empirical rather than an ontological matter. Separating out the different modes is important not just analytically but methodologically, providing a guide as to what to look for in research on political institutions. But understanding how they related to each other is also vital to understand institutional dynamics. Through case studies, we have looked at how constraint is strengthened through the articulation of rules, practices and narratives, and at those circumstances in which rules are broken, dominant practices resisted and authoritative narratives disrupted. Next we consider how institutions empower (as well as constrain) and consider what an institutionalist conception of agency looks like.

Chapter 4

Power and Agency

We argued in our first chapter that institutions are 'Janus faced' – they both constrain action while also being the product of human agency. Institutions are created and adapted over time through agency. At the same time, in providing 'prescriptions' about behaviour, they empower some actors, and courses of action, while constraining others. But, while third phase institutionalism agrees that individuals and institutions are mutually constitutive, the role of agency and power remains under-theorized. The purpose of this chapter is to explain how institutions distribute power, and how actors exercise agency in an institutional context. We show how power tends to be concentrated with rule makers, who attempt to impose their will upon 'rule takers'. Such agency, however, goes beyond single acts of institutional foundation. Agency is also implicated in the diverse processes by which institutions develop over time, including rule shaping and rule breaking among less powerful actors. Borrowing from diverse power models, third phase institutionalism recognizes that power is exercised through regulation, practice and storytelling – and 'smart' mixes of these elements. We develop our own distinctively institutionalist view of agency, which highlights '5Cs' – that agency is collective, combative, cumulative, combinative, and constrained.

Actors, institutions and contexts

In the previous chapter we considered in some detail how the rules of the game limit the repertoire of action available to actors, but we also noted that scholars agree that institutions empower, as well as constrain. In this context, it is helpful to recall and link together points made in previous chapters. In Chapter 1 we argued that the study of politics is inextricably linked to the study of power. In Chapter 2 we noted the 'engaged' stance of institutionalists (from all three main schools) in the sense of recognizing that institutions are in essence mechanisms that sustain power differentials between the advantaged

Box 4.1   Rule takers and rule makers in Egypt's 'Arab Spring'

The first visible sign of the 2011 Egyptian revolution came in the form of a popular uprising which began on 25 January of that year. The uprising consisted of a campaign of non-violent civil resistance, typified by demonstrations, marches, acts of civil disobedience, and labour strikes in Cairo, Alexandria, Suez and Ismailia. Millions of protesters from a variety of socio-economic and religious backgrounds demanded the overthrow of the regime of President Hosni Mubarak. Tunisia had provided the template; President Zine al-Abidine Ben Ali had fled his country following a popular revolt earlier in that month.

Egyptian protesters articulated grievances in relation to Egypt's legal and political institutions, including pervasive police brutality, the use of state of emergency laws, the lack of free elections and freedom of speech, and punishing economic conditions including high unemployment, food price inflation, and low minimum wages. The primary demands from protest organizers were the end of both the Hosni Mubarak regime and of emergency law; freedom, justice, a responsive non-military government, and a say in the management of Egypt's resources.

Despite the protests themselves being predominantly peaceful in nature, violent clashes between security forces and protesters were frequent, with at least 846 people killed and 6,000 injured. Nevertheless, when the government attempted to impose a curfew, protesters defied the order and the police did not enforce it, and the presence of the Central Security Forces police, loyal to Mubarak, was gradually replaced by military troops who were less inclined to violent attacks on the protestors.

Mubarak dissolved his government and appointed military figure and former head of the Egyptian General Intelligence Directorate Omar
→

and disadvantaged. From this standpoint, our conceptualization of political institutions is as much concerned with what 'ordinary people' can and cannot do, as it is with the capacities of government and the behaviour of politicians and public servants who directly inhabit the political arena. In Chapter 3 we examined how the three modes of institutional constraint – rules, practices and narratives – each constrain actors, and how, when these are interconnected, their effects are amplified.

This recap brings us to the rather obvious, but crucial, point that our conception of power implies action by an actor, collective or individual, against another, that is to say, the *exercise* of power of one in relation to the other. In this way, our actors must possess two different, but closely related, types of capacity. First, they must possess the capacity to act in their own right, aided or hindered by the institutional config-

Suleiman as Vice-President in an attempt to quell dissent. Mubarak asked aviation minister and former chief of Egypt's Air Force, Ahmed Shafik, to form a new government. Meanwhile Mohamed ElBaradei emerged as a major figure of the opposition, with all major opposition groups supporting his role as a negotiator for some form of transitional unity government. In response to mounting pressure, Mubarak announced he did not intend to seek re-election in September 2012.

On 11 February 2011, eighteen days after 25 January uprising, Vice-President Omar Suleiman announced that Mubarak would be stepping down as President and turning power over to the Supreme Council of the Armed Forces (SCAF). This military junta, headed by de facto head of state Mohamed Hussein Tantawi, announced on 13 February 2011 that the constitution would be suspended, both houses of parliament dissolved, and that the military would rule for six months until elections could be held. The former cabinet, including Prime Minister Ahmed Shafik, continued to serve as a caretaker government until a new one was formed. Shafik resigned on 3 March, a day before major protests to get him to step down were planned; he was replaced by Essam Sharaf, the former transport minister.

Protests and pressure on SCAF continued through 2011 and in the last three months of that year elections were held for a People's Assembly where The Muslim Brotherhood's Freedom and Justice Party won 235 (or 47%) seats, the ultra-conservative Salafist Nour Party 121 and the moderate al-Wasat Party 10. At the end of 2012, public protests recommenced as dissatisfaction mounted with centralizing constitutional changes proposed by the new President, Mohammed Morsi. The Nobel Peace Prize laureate Mohamed ElBaradei summed up the demand for dialogue rather than imposition of new institutional rules: 'Cancel the constitutional declarations, postpone the referendum, stop the bloodshed, and enter a direct dialogue with the national forces.'

urations which impinge upon them. Second, they must be able, in some way, to impose their will on their environment and on other actors. In terms of the former, a good starting point in Hay's (2002: 94) succinct definition of agency as 'the ability or capacity of an actor to act consciously and, in so doing to attempt to realise his or her intentions', which captures both the strategic intent behind an actor's conduct, but also the possibility that this will not be realized. In terms of the latter, we again follow Hay in defining power as context shaping, that is 'the ability of actors (whether individual or collective) to "have an effect" upon the context which defines the range of possibilities of others' (Hay, 1997: 50).

Streek and Thelen (2005: 13–16) draw attention to the fact that actors and institutions are embedded in a societal context comprising other actors and institutions, while also emphasizing that the enactment of a social rule is never perfect and that there is always a gap between 'the ideal pattern of a rule' and how that pattern is played out in situ. Here we illustrate Streek and Thelen's four key points about institutions with regard to the negotiation between rule makers and rule takers about the institutions of government during the 'Arab Spring' of 2011 (see Box 4.1). The highly contested context in which the negotiation takes place serves to expose the importance of agency in the shaping, bending and challenging of institutions, and the flexibility and ambiguity which this dialectic relationship builds into the rules themselves.

- First, 'the meaning of a rule is never self-evident and always subject to and in need of interpretation'. Echoing our argument regarding 'ordinary people' as significant actors in institutional theory, Streek and Thelen suggest that 'applying a general rule to a specific situation is a creative act that must take into account, not just the rule itself, but also the unique circumstances in which it is to be applied'. Hence rule takers, as well as rule makers, are afforded some degree of discretion in the initial interpretation, the fitting of cases to rules, and the fluctuating logics used to justify institutional constraints over time.

- Second, there is inevitably a certain amount of ambiguity in the way in which rule makers frame rules in the first place. Following a feedback loop, the creative interpretations of rule takers set in motion 'another sequence' of exploration of conflicting interpretations, observations of impacts, and revision in the light of this information.

- Third, rule takers may resist institutional constraint and, in many instances, will actively seek to revise institutions by exploiting their imperfect fit.

- Finally, rule makers and enforcers themselves accept that there are limits to the extent to which they 'can prevent or correct unintentional or subversive deviation' from institutional constraint.

Our case study of the ways in which rule makers responded to demands for institutional change in Egypt's 'Arab Spring' shows how the deeply embedded institutions in force throughout Hosni Mubarak's 20-year period in power rapidly became the subject of re-interpretation and negotiation in the face of popular protest. And so, as the 'rules of the game' were changing in neighbouring Arab countries (Tunisia, for example), the Egyptian people themselves discovered the time-honoured practice of reclaiming the streets to challenge the legitimacy of central government. Curfews were broken and military authority defied, with the result that Mubarak stood down and power was turned over to a military junta. The rule takers continued to protest in the face of alternative leadership from within the same political elite. The rule makers were eventually forced to hold elections in a significant, though still contested, move towards multi-party democracy.

So, while power tends to be concentrated with rule makers, its exercise is often flawed in its outcomes. As Bevir and Rhodes (2008: 732) argue, 'the centre has rubber levers; pulling the central policy lever does not necessarily mean something happens at the bottom'. It also builds in both a temporal and constructivist aspect to our consideration of agency and institutions. Streek and Thelen (2005: 16) argue that 'an institution is defined by a continuous interaction between rule makers and rule takers', during which each new interpretation of rules contributes to the manner in which institutions are 'discovered, invented, suggested, rejected, or for the time being, adopted'. Agency in relation to institutions is thus both collective and contributory. For Streek and Thelen, institutions are 'continuously created and recreated by a great number of actors with divergent interests, varying normative commitments, different powers, and limited cognition'.

However, Streek and Thelen's pragmatic approach to power and agency also leaves undisturbed key theoretical dilemmas. They leave unanswered some basic questions about the origins and extent of the 'powers' possessed by actors, and the qualities of agency which is at once heavily constrained and, at the same time, capable of continuously reinterpreting institutions in an interventionist and dynamic fashion. To cut into these debates we need to go back a step and consider the contribution of different approaches to understanding power within political science.

How different perspectives on power have influenced institutionalism

To help us formulate a distinctively institutionalist conceptualization on agency we must first understand how institutionalists conceive of power. Here we show how pluralism, elitism, Marxism and post-structuralism, respectively, have contributed to institutionalist thought. Table 4.1 provides a comparative summary.

82

Table 4.1 *Power and institutions: contrasting perspectives*

	Pluralism	Elitism	Marxism	Post-structuralism
Key theme	Power is dispersed fairly evenly across groups in society and this is a desirable state of affairs.	Power is concentrated in national government, large business corporations, and the military.	Power as economic power and the gulf between those who own the means of production, and those who sell their labour.	Power is dispersed and pervades political time and space as a constant. Power has a brutal quality and cannot be controlled, only exposed to criticism.
Core ideas	The centrality of groups to the political process; power is always disaggregated, rather than concentrated; consensus, not continuing conflict, is the main driver in politics.	Three unconnected layers: the politically fragmented 'society of the masses'; in the middle, interest groups competing with one another; at the top the three elite groups as above.	Structural constraints of class, gender and race shape access to the three key resources actors use in trying to shape political outcomes: money; knowledge; and political power.	Power and knowledge are mutually constitutive of and feed off one another. The political environment is a complex set of overlapping, mutually constraining discourses, which have no fixed anchorage or point of origin.
Connections with the three strands of institutionalism	Enjoys best fit with 'old' institutionalism. Focus on the formal policy and its context as stable and agreed. Lindblom's neo-pluralism crosses over with elitism in Urban Regime Theory.	Historical: the state as the key actor. Sociological: particular groups dominate governance in both formal and informal settings. Rational choice: elite groups are intent on pursuing self-interest.	Historical: through the 'varieties of capitalism' school. Sociological: the power of the ideas which sustain capitalism. Rational choice: capitalists exploit their workers in pursuing self-interest.	Historical: through 'discursive' institutionalism (Schmidt, 2006). Sociological: the causal and constitutive role of ideas in politics, and the re-use of templates for policy, the creation of identities and 'the other'.

Perspective on institutions	Pluralists privilege a form of agency which is largely unconstrained by institutions. The way we do things is agreed and therefore only a backdrop to highly visible decision making.	Elite actors are constrained by clusters of rules, practices and narratives, but these also empower them to compete for dominance with one another.	In the 'varieties of capitalism' school states develop their own distinctive institutional configurations. More traditional Marxists are concerned with how institutions sustain structured inequalities.	Institutions are another form of idea and may be a constituent of a discourse – which is the basic unit of analysis. Some institutionalists have adopted the concept of discourse to explain why institutions change.
Added value for institutionalism	Politics is about mobilizing groups of actors; how such groups form and acquire power is important at both the grass roots and higher levels; any form of institutionalism that neglects formal rules and arenas is radically incomplete.	Politics is about decision making and agenda setting; informal practices are as important as the formal rule based processes. Power can be invisible, i.e. visible only to the agenda setters. Elite actors are not necessarily unified to a common cause – they may compete amongst themselves.	Politics is about decision making, agenda setting and preference setting. The exercise of power has significant material impacts which sustain disadvantage. Capitalism exhibits a variety of different institutional configurations and impacts.	Politics is about agenda setting, shaping preferences and reforming perceptions and identities. We should be suspicious of the notion that the ideas put forward by politicians are 'new' and progressive. A respect for context and the fine grain of politics.

Pluralist thought has developed around three core principles: the centrality of groups to the political process; the assumption that power is always disaggregated, rather than concentrated; and the belief that consensus, rather than continuing conflict, is the main driver of the political process (Smith, 2006: 26). This third principle is particularly important from an institutionalist perspective. The implication is that, where conflict does occur, it is not about the rules of politics (because these are taken for granted and agreed by all parties), but concerns who gets what slice of the cake. Pluralists assume that consensus is a sign of agreement; if groups are not engaged in active lobbying or mobilization, 'they are assumed not to have a grievance of sufficient strength to warrant concern' (Smith, 2006: 26).

Critics argue that pluralism promulgates three fundamental errors (see Smith, 2006; McAnnulla, 2006; Marsh, 2008), even in its 'neo-pluralist' guises, which acknowledge the consistent dominance of certain groups within the political system. First, plurality is mistaken for pluralism: because there are many groups in society, it is assumed that power is dispersed roughly equally, and government, if it features at all, is neutral and open. Second, an empiricist perspective leads to the assumption that, if groups are present in formal policy-making processes, they necessarily have a significant influence on key political decisions. Finally, a voluntaristic view of agency leads to the belief that associations and networks are inherently open, thus ignoring institutional barriers to inclusion, such as racial and gender discrimination.

How does the pluralist tradition inform institutionalist thought? It fits best with the 'old' institutionalism, which Stinchcombe (1997) and Rhodes (2006) have stoutly defended, and which we have argued in Chapter 2 remains the essential core of institutionalism. Hence there is a common focus on the formal arenas in which policy is developed and an assumption that this context is relatively stable and predictable. As we move into second and third phase institutionalism, however, the relationship has become more strained. Neo-pluralists remain generally empiricist in orientation, while institutionalists have become more theoretically orientated (if not wholly deductive). While institutionalists have developed more complex understandings of rules, practices and narratives, neo-pluralists have shown limited interest in the nuanced nature of institutional constraints on the behaviour of groups and the outcomes of their interactions. But there is still scope for productive synergies. For instance, in our own work, we have sought to show how both the formal structure and the informal practices of government influence the creation and mobilization of social capital.

Putnam neglects the way in which the relationship between social capital and democratic performance is institutionally framed. Governments play a crucial role in determining the degree of influence that organized interests have upon public policy: are they asked to participate, are they listened to when they do, and are they kept informed of the impact of their interventions? Research shows that such factors, along with the resource and regulatory framework for civil society bodies, are critical (Lowndes and Wilson, 2001; Lowndes and Pratchett, 2008).

How we conceptualize power is closely interlinked with how we view the agency of actors; in general, pluralists privilege a form of agency which is largely unconstrained by institutions. This optimistic outlook presents great problems for 'engaged' institutionalists, with their sensitivity to the way in which the rules of the political game are structured to distribute power and advantage. However, pluralist perspectives remind second and third phase institutionalists to keep their 'eye on the ball' in respect of the importance of formal decision-making arenas (despite the significance of less formal practices), and the centrality of organized interests (at the grass roots and in the higher echelons) in the political process.

Elitist perspectives of the twentieth and twenty-first centuries can be traced back to C. Wright Mills' work on *The Power Elite* (1956). This proposed a gradation of the distribution of power within the nation state: the bottom level contains the politically fragmented 'society of the masses'; the middle level is occupied by the semi-organized interest groups competing amongst themselves for resources; and the top level is the preserve of three sets of actors – the executive branch of national government, the large business corporations, and the military establishment. In this way, Mills sought to distance his approach from both the contemporary pluralist and Marxist models. He argued that the pluralists only saw the middle tier of society, which they mistook for the power structure of the whole nation. Marxists were equally blinkered, focusing on just one part of the 'power elite' – those who exercise economic power.

Elitist thought has had a continuing influence on the development of second and third phase institutionalism, with the move to 'bring the state back in' (for example, Katzenstein, 1978; Skocpol, 1979; Krasner, 1980; Skowronek, 1982). In this context, Evans (2006: 47) suggests that 'By the mid-1980s, virtually every significant current of theoretical work in political science was united in a renewed interest in the state itself as the fundamental unit of analysis.' These scholars were not only institutionalists, they were also elitists. Theda Skocpol was one of the first to argue that, rather than being theorized simply as an arena for political cooperation or conflict, the state should be treated as an autonomous set of actors and institutions in its own right. In a crucial distinction from Marxist models, she saw the organizations which make up the state as being independent of control by the dominant economic class, often pursuing their own interests in defiance of class interests. At the city level, urban regime theory had its roots in Charles Lindblom's neo-pluralism and, in particular, his observation that business and political actors within city elites need to cooperate to achieve their respective goals (see Elkin, 1986; and Stone, 1989). Mossberger and Stoker (2001: 812) explain how urban regimes work, taking a specifically institutionalist approach: 'Regimes overcome problems of collective action and secure participation in the governing coalition through the distribution of selective incentives such as contracts and jobs. Collaboration is achieved not only through formal institutions, but also through informal networks.'

Focusing on the state as actor, elitism has informed the development of historical institutionalism; at the same time, sociological institutionalists (like Clarence Stone) have documented the capacity of particular groups to dominate governance in both formal and informal settings. The central premise that groups are intent on pursuing self-interest also resonates with the principles of rational choice institutionalism. In all three cases, institutions are the means by which group actors inherit, accumulate and consolidate power. But elitism is not without its particular weaknesses and dedicated critics. First, its conception of power tends to be static. Some dynamism may be allowed through competition between groups within the power elite (whether at the level of the state or urban regime), but groups are seen as having defined and permanent boundaries. Allied to this is a top-down view of the exercise of power which denies those outside these boundaries any significant influence. In terms of agency, those actors within the elite are empowered through dominant institutions, while those outside in civil society are permanently and comprehensively isolated from power. For many institutionalists, while the over-optimism of pluralism is located at one extreme of a continuum, elitism's counsel of despair is to be found at the other.

In classical **Marxism**, power is defined exclusively in relation to economic power and the opposing interests of those who own the means of production and those who sell their labour. Marxists have looked to institutionalism to address the question of why capitalism has not collapsed in the face of its internal contradictions, notably the concentration of capital, polarization of social forces and acceleration of political conflict. The 'varieties of capitalism' school takes a spatial approach, considering the capacity of individual national states to develop and adapt their own distinctive institutional configurations (Hall and Thelen, 2008; Thelen, 2009; Schmidt. 2009). The regulation school takes a historical perspective looking at the way in which a particular 'regime of accumulation' (like Fordism) becomes coupled with a 'mode of regulation', that in effect provides an 'institutional fix' capable of (temporarily) ameliorating the crisis tendencies of capitalism (Aglietta, 1979; Boyer and Saillard, 2002; James, 2009). The mode of regulation comprises an interlocking ensemble of institutional forms and practices in the political, economic and social domains, as in the combination of welfare state, corporatism and mass consumption during Fordism. Seeking to apply the perspective to empirical research, Stoker and Mossberger (1995) detected the emergence of a 'post-fordist local state' in the UK from the mid-1980s, with privatization, partnerships and non-electoral participation as the key institutional features.

Although broadly within the Regulationist tradition, Jessop (1990: 267) proposes higher levels of contingency and indeterminacy in institutional formation, arguing that the state has 'multiple boundaries, no institutional fixity and no pre-given formal or substantive unity'. For Hay, the state is loosened further from its material bearings, with institutions defined as 'codified systems of ideas and the practices they sustain' (Hay, 2006a: 58). But it is not the case that 'anything goes'. The institutions of the state are 'strategically selective', presenting 'an uneven playing field whose complex contours favour certain strategies (and certain actors) over others' (Hay, 2006b: 75). From a different direction, Marsh (2002: 167–71) also moves towards a more contingent understanding of how political institutions empower the interests of capital *vis-à-vis* those of labour, acknowledging three-fold 'structural constraints' of class, gender and race.

Marxist scholarship has influenced the development of historical institutionalism, and particularly the study of 'varieties of capitalism'; it continues to reinvigorate sociological institutionalism through exploring the power of the ideas which sustain capitalism; and its fundamental concern with the state as an instrument of class interest resonates with the premises of rational choice institutionalism. In general terms, Marxist thinking reminds us that power is exercised through agenda and preference setting, as well as formal decision-making; that the exercise of power has significant material impacts which sustain disadvantage across generations; and that capitalism is coupled with, and stabilized by, a variety of institutional configurations, which differ over both time and space.

Post-structuralism would seem, on the face of it, an unlikely bedfellow for institutionalism. Power is taken to have a disembodied, dispersed and pervasive quality, and also a brutal character that cannot be controlled, only exposed to criticism. Power and knowledge, which feed off one another, exist within a political environment made up of overlapping, mutually constraining discourses, which have no fixed anchorage or point of origin. Institutionalists have come relatively late to post-structuralism, due to its implied rejection of 'structure' but also to its fatalistic take on prospects for institutional reform, which belie an 'engaged' approach. But third phase institutionalists are paying increasing attention to the way in which discourses – rather than 'hard' structures – set preferences and shape perceptions and identities (Moon, 2012). In his 'analytics of government', Mitchell Dean (2010: 30) argues that established ways of acting and framing (the traditional meat of institutionalism) are reinforced by distinctive ways of seeing and thinking. Sørensen and Torfing (2008: 40) coin the phrase 'poststructuralist institutionalism' to draw attention to the role of institutions in constructing particular subjectivities, and in creating 'an operational closure by including and excluding various issues, particular forms of knowledge and certain actors'.

A loose cohort of historical institutionalists (Schmidt, 2006, 2008, 2010; Hay, 2001, 2006a, 2010; Blyth, 2007) has developed variations of constructivist or discursive institutionalism which privilege ideas as constitutive *of* institutions. On the sociological wing, Barnes *et al.* (2007: 54) import insights from post-structuralism into their institutionalist analysis of public participation, thus revealing how new practices are not only 'empowering' citizens, but also drawing them into 'new fields of power'. In a similar vein, John Clarke (2005) has argued that new discourses (or 'technologies') of citizenship make individuals more 'responsible' and hence more 'governable' (Clarke, 2005). 'Crossovers' into post-structuralism retain the quality of 'work in progress', and there is always the danger that the materiality of 'institutions' is lost in a fascination with the power of language and ideas. But the value of the post-structuralist perspective is its reminder that politics is not only concerned with decision-making in public and agenda setting behind closed doors, but also with a more fundamental manipulation of preferences, perceptions and identities via pervasive, continuous and 'social' processes (Finlayson and Martin, 2006: 159).

It draws our attention to groups who are discursively marginalized as 'not one of us', and reinforces institutionalists' suspicion of the 'new', particularly when the adjective is used by politicians to describe and legitimize their latest policy initiative. It also appeals to institutionalism's respect for context and the fine grain of politics.

Our discussion so far has revealed considerable overlaps in theorization between the main approaches to understanding power in political science. Pluralism has crossed the boundary into elitism with urban regime theory; elitism and Marxism are linked within work on 'varieties of capitalism'; post-structuralism, while often openly critical of Marxist theory, shares its concerns about the coercive power of the state. Each approach has left its imprint upon the development of institutionalism. But institutional power is clearly not the whole of the story. If dominant actors are empowered to act by institutions, and institutions alone, then we have simply returned to the determinist view of agency contained in Marx's early work, or indeed in structural-functionalist traditions within social science. If this is the case, then just as those who are subjugated by institutions have 'no choice', so those who inherit power are unable to do other than wield that power to reinforce the institutions which advantage their sectional interests. Against such determinism, we have argued that actors should be conceived as possessing the capacity (if not always the opportunity) to act in their own right, aided or hindered by the institutional configurations which impinge upon them; and are potentially able to impose their will on their environment and on other actors.

As positions on power and agency converge within third phase institutionalism, we can make two key observations. First, under certain circumstances, actors will not do what is demanded of them. Second, the context within which agency takes place is crucial: as environments change, different possibilities emerge in terms of actors' capacities to resist constraint and seize opportunities for empowerment. In different temporal and spatial contexts, different sets of actors are able to act strategically and exercise power in different ways. Over the long term, structural inequalities persist because privileged actors benefit from 'an uneven playing field' tilted to their advantage, although this elite may be structured in relation to dimensions beyond Mills' triad of economy/government/military – the role of patriarchy, ethnic cleavages and religious hierarchies (for instance) deserve attention. But, in the medium term, non-elite actors are also able to shape the direction of politics and policy in ways which remain hidden from those who only observe the formal arenas of rule making.

Indeed, 'subaltern' institutions, such as trades unions and social movements, can empower even the most marginalized actors to resist the imposition of institutions from above. Understanding the significance and dynamics of political institutions requires that we look beyond the structures and sensibilities of elites; we need also to consider how 'ordinary people' can develop capacities and seize opportunities to change the rules of the game, albeit with the constant threat of the re-imposition of dominant institutional constraints. The robustness and/or fragility of elite institutions affects this context. As we showed in Chapter 3, disconnects and slippages between different modes of constraint – rules, practices and narratives – open up spaces for rule breaking or shaping.

We look next at the specific relationship between the different modes of constraint and questions of power and agency.

Power through regulation

As a mode of institutional constraint, formal rules clearly distribute power. From an immediate and specific perspective, laws, regulations and policies state which actors have the licence to act in a certain way and who has the authority to police and punish those who do not comply with a rule. From a medium-term perspective, we can see how rules take on a normative dimension over time, indicating not just what is possible, but also what is desirable. Rules come to tell us which groups of actors *should* have power in particular situations and provide justifications as to why it is right and fair that they do so. Taking the long view, the writing and rewriting of rules (and their enforcement) tends to confer power on particular elites (including, but not only, dominant economic classes) by creating and sustaining an uneven playing field which in turn makes it more likely that they will exercise power in the future.

We showed in the last chapter that rational choice scholars were motivated to bring institutions into their work to reduce the volatility implied by their theorization of individual actors able to pursue self maximizing behaviour at will. For these scholars, the existence and distribution of agency and power are largely taken for granted, and the key question relates to how such capacities can be reined in, and channelled for the collective good. The principal–agent model deals with these concerns in the simplest way possible by assuming the presence of a powerful, hierarchically superior actor, who has the capacity to design rules which coerce the rule taker into compliance. As Peters (2005: 55–6) suggests, the authority of the principal to wield such power within a specific context is usually unquestioned because that actor is clearly at the top of the organizational or state hierarchy (e.g. Congress or the Minister of State). Peters points to the ubiquity of the principal–agent model in analysing regulatory policy in the US; in the UK the model has underpinned the institutional design and reform process itself, whether in education, health or the (attempted) regulation of banks and financial services.

But more complex conceptions have also developed within rational choice institutionalism. As Crouch (2005:7) argues: 'Fundamental to the concept of the market is the idea that no one actor is big enough or strong enough to affect price by its own actions; and individual actors are not permitted to combine to act strategically.' In the ideal market, therefore, the groups of actors who have been able to break through the barriers to entry are assumed to be more or less equal in power, and the aim of regulation is to sustain this natural balance by discouraging cartel or monopoly formation. In a similar vein, Mayntz and Scharpf (1995) have developed an 'actor-centred institutionalism' which 'gives equal weight to strategic actions and interactions of purposeful and resourceful individual and corporate actors and to the enabling, constraining, and shaping effects of given (but variable) institutional structures and institutionalized forms' (Scharpf, 1997: 34). The model has been applied within political arenas characterized by 'highly structured and frequently recurring interactions among a limited number of actors with a high capacity for strategic action' (Scharpf, 1997: 105), as in encounters between countries in international relations, opposing political parties in legislatures, or multinational companies in global markets. There may be a 'principal' lurking in the background, but its relationship with multiple agents is more ambiguous, and the main focus in on competition between the agents themselves.

Putting to good use Scharpf's actor-centred and game-theoretic approach, Eric Schickler (2001) develops a notion of 'disjointed pluralism' in his study of the US Congress, where he finds coalitions of actors built around a wide variety of different 'collective interests'. The analysis does not explicitly identify the empowerment of 'ordinary people', but it does suggest that Members of Congress are far more open to influence from actors based outside the House and Senate than the elite model would normally allow. In relation to the latter, policy-making by this plurality is disjointed in the sense that over time it comprises an accumulation of different innovations from groups with different, often conflicting, interests. The resulting legislation builds in conflicts and compromises and is often unsatisfactory, in some regard, to all parties. Schickler's approach to power and agency has formed something of a blueprint for third phase institutionalists, with its emphasis upon the collective, combative and cumulative character of power and agency, and the tendency for actors to build on existing institutions rather than start from scratch.

Sociological institutionalists have long been interested in the close relationship between rules and roles. In the 1960s, Berger and Luckman (1967: 73) drew attention to the requirement for institutions to become embedded in the identity of the actor by regular rehearsal of role. At the beginning of second phase institutionalism, March and Olsen (1989: 23) argued that 'rules define relationships among roles in terms of what an incumbent of one role owes to the incumbents of other roles'. However, the rules embedded in certain roles also tell us how those actors are empowered, as well as constrained. In this vein, Clarke and Newman (1997) examined how, in the neo-liberal reforms of the 1980s and 1990s in the UK, the roles of elite actors, such as 'professionals and bureaucrats', were recast by a managerialist narrative. As Newman (2005: 717–18) observes, power was 'apparently devolved to "local" managers with high degrees of autonomy to develop the best ways of delivering policy outcomes in line with a government's political goals and aspirations'. The use of the term 'apparently' reveals a paradoxical coupling of empowerment and constraint within the reforms. Just as local government professionals, police, clinicians and administrators were the beneficiaries of formal rules, which increased their capacity for context shaping, so these delegated powers existed alongside a suite of rules about audit, inspection and the removal of powers from 'failing organizations'.

A decade later, Leach and Lowndes (2007) show how the next stages of this 'modernization' agenda impinged upon the roles of political leaders and chief executives (and a wider cast of local stakeholders) within UK local authorities. Not only were empowering rules balanced by constraining legislation, but each of the newly introduced rules had the potential to empower one set of actors, while draining power away from another. In this way, for example, the 'executive' rule, contained in the Local Government Act 2000, gives the leader of the council the opportunity to take on a prime ministerial type role as leader of a cabinet, or even wield presidential type power as a directly elected mayor.

Where leaders are able to establish themselves in a more dominant role, the expected effect is a reduction in the power of the chief executive of the council and 'back bench' elected members. Potentially empowering rules are actually layered on top of existing practices, which offer deviant actors opportunities for 'effectively incorporating (even emasculating) new formal expectations' (Leach and Lowndes, 2007: 23–4).

From the 1970s onwards, historical institutionalists argued that the state should be treated as an autonomous set of actors and institutions in its own right. In a crucial distinction from Marxist models, the organizations which make up the state were understood as independent of control by the dominant class, often pursuing their own interests in defiance. In developing the 'varieties of capitalism' approach, Hall and Thelen (2008: 9) stress that understanding the firm is as important as understanding the state, and that there exist high levels of agency on the part of actors, and complex webs of constraint and opportunity originating from the prevailing institutional matrix:

> First, as a firm-centric and broadly rationalist approach, it conceptualizes the political economy as a terrain peopled with entrepreneurial actors seeking to advance their interests as they construe them, constrained by the existing rules and institutions but also looking for ways to make institutions work for them. Although some institutions rely on sanctions for their operation, the 'varieties of capitalism' approach moves away from a view of institutions purely as factors that constrain action towards one that sees them also as resources, providing opportunities for particular types of action, and especially for collective action (see Hall, 1998). Second, the varieties of capitalism framework emphasizes that the political economy is replete with a multiplicity of institutions, many of which are nested inside others. Some can serve as functional substitutes for other institutions, at least for some purposes. Thus, any strategy adopted by a firm or other actor is likely to be conditioned, not by one, but by a number of institutions.

Power through practice

As we saw in Chapter 3, behaviour is also shaped by informal practices that are conveyed through demonstration rather than written rules. Actors new to a particular political arena learn about institutional practices through observing what others do, rehearsing these practices, and responding to associated incentives and sanctions. If we take a snapshot of a particular arena, we are unlikely to recognize immediately the shaping effect of informal practices; these are likely to remain obscure, overshadowed by the formality of rules. But with a longer-term focus, we can see how the practices developed by certain groups are legitimized over time, generally strengthened through their links to narratives which provide normative justifications for particular ways of acting, and work to embed practices as 'common sense'. Indeed, practices may eventually be elevated to the status of rules. For those rational choice institutionalists who continue to privilege parsimony above all else, the exclusion of complicating factors such as invisible practices remains a key concern of their methodology. However, as shown in Chapter 3, many rational choice institutionalists have accepted for some time that institutions are transmitted not only through rules, but also through informal processes of demonstration and narration. In methodological terms, this has tended to mean expanding both the spatial and temporal dimensions of study to examine how individuals and groups interact with one another over time. In game-based experiments, where cooperation is necessary, this has had the effect of surfacing practices which engender trust and reciprocity. Walker and Ostrom (2007) observe that the literature on social dilemma games now 'overwhelmingly supports the conclusion that social norms such as reciprocity play a key role in understanding the cooperation within groups'.

Indeed, Elinor Ostrom's body of work provides an example of the trajectory of third phase institutionalism in this respect. Not only does it consider informal practices as an element of 'rules-in-use' (building on John Commons' original 'institutional economics' of the 1930s), but it also examines how actors lower down the hierarchy develop practices which can achieve the status of rules over time. Ostrom emphasizes that institutions specify not only what actions are forbidden, but also those which are permitted on the part of certain actors. She shows how rule takers are able to exercise a degree of agency in putting rules into practice, and conceptualize practices in terms of the enactment of rules in a specific context by specific actors. In terms of agency and empowerment, rule takers can only make what they can of the rules handed down to them by the rule makers.

In later work, however, we see a change in emphasis towards a concern with how local actors develop their own 'rules-in-use' from the bottom up. This orientation emerges from continuing work on 'common pool resources', within which she includes forests, fisheries,

oil fields, grazing lands, irrigation systems, and knowledge. Here
Ostrom develops her critique of the assumptions behind Hardin's
(1968) 'tragedy of the commons' into an extensive research
programme which demonstrates how practices can be developed by
small groups in indigenous communities, which are more effective in
sustaining the 'commons' than the imposition of institutional frameworks from outside or above by local and central government. In char-
acterizing 'policies as experiments', she strikes a distinctly pluralist
note in explaining 'why a series of nested but relatively autonomous,
self-organized, resource governance systems may do a better job in
policy experimentation than a single central authority' (Ostrom, 2007:
18).

From a sociological perspective, Clarke and Newman (1997)
remind us that many of the activities which we take for granted as
being 'professional' and which are now embedded in national legislation, were once unincorporated and originated in what were, at the
time, rather obscure practices, developed by organizations independent of state control, such as the church. Scott (2001: 55) calls our
attention to the bottom-up progression of practices to rules when,
referencing Hughes (1958) on professions, he suggests that 'much of
the power and mystique associated with these types of roles comes
from the license they are given to engage in "forbidden" or fateful
activities : conducting intimate examinations or sentencing individuals
to prison or death'.

Although much of the sociological literature deals with agency on a
collective basis, its emphasis on roles also focuses attention to those
political institutions in which agency and power is concentrated in one
person's hands. The President of the United States is often referred to as
'The Most Powerful Man in the World' and yet, as we saw in the example of President Obama's health care reforms (Box 1.4), high degrees of
agency are accompanied by high degrees of constraint. In another
setting, Foley (1999) and Heffernan (2003) have suggested that Tony
Blair 'presidentialized' the role of British Prime Minister by drawing
power into himself during his tenure in office. The cabinet as a collective decision-making body was downgraded and Blair relied increasingly on bilateral discussions with individual ministers, and the
guidance of special advisers and media experts. However, the adoption
of 'sofa government' did not rely on Blair removing the existing rules
and structures of cabinet government. Cabinet still met but, as in the
elitist power model, the important decisions were made out of purview
of the collective. New informal practices, which initially existed along-

Box 4.2　The power of practice: Ecuador's 'ghost coalitions'

An enduring combination of political institutions appears to militate against the prospects of radical policy change in Ecuador. Since the transition to democracy in 1979 no Ecuadorian President has held a majority in Congress because of strong regional and ethnic cleavages, which are reflected in the number of political parties in the parliament. Additionally, term limits combined with mid-term elections have undermined attempts at long-term policy development, and numerous veto opportunities are built into the legislative process itself.

Outside Congress, narratives developed by the media and the Ecuadorian public also severely constrain the incumbents' capacity to form coalitions for substantial reform. Voters have felt betrayed by parties who had attempted market-based reforms of the economy despite campaign promises not to do so, to the extent that the term 'gobiernista', or government supporter, has become an insult, implying the politician is being bribed by the government, or 'in their pocket'. The media have pursued this narrative theme by portraying bargaining between political parties as synonymous with corrupt and illegal practices.

And yet during the 1980s and 90s, Ecuador liberalized its economic institutions to a greater degree than comparable countries like Mexico and Venezuela, and avoided the economic crises which engulfed many other Latin American countries during that period. In particular successive presidents passed legislation to improve tax collection and limit public spending, and opened up the financial, trade and banking sectors, despite having little or no formal party support in Congress.

How was this possible? The answer lies not so much in the agency of individuals but in the existence of a set of established practices, or informal institutions, which ran alongside the constraining forces outlined above, and allowed for the formation of 'ghost coalitions'. These in turn

$\rightarrow$

side and in the shadow of the formal institutions, became increasingly significant in structuring behaviour, in effect 'displacing' (Streek and Thelen, 2005) or neutering traditional rules. Nevertheless, McAnulla (2006: 132) challenges the presidential thesis, arguing that, despite his accumulation of personal power, Blair remained constrained by the formal rules which made him dependent on the support of the parliamentary party to stay in office. Rawnsley's (2010) account also identifies the limitations on Blair's presidential practices originating from the simultaneous evolution of the role and practices of Chancellor of the Exchequer, Gordon Brown (who eventually become Blair's successor as Prime Minister).

Both rational choice and sociological institutionalists tend to assume the primacy of rules over practices. Hence, in the top-down were dependent on the maintenance of 'clientelist' institutions in the Ecuadorian political system which allowed presidents the discretion to distribute rewards to potential and actual coalition partners, such as appointment to government posts, granting of licences and contracts, and the allocation of government resources to the constituency represented by the politician in question.

The significant characteristics of the ghost coalitions concern both secrecy and their ability to facilitate long-term policy making. Hence, because of the risk of public and media approbation, the agreements on which they are based have to remain secret, and high-profile cabinet posts, for example, are not on offer, but appointments to head powerful state-owned enterprises are. Additionally, no public record of legislative votes is kept in the Congress. Hence elected representatives are free to attack a policy on the floor of the house, while voting for it secretly in the lobby.

In terms of enforcing coalition agreements, partners have subverted available formal sanctions to discipline possible defectors from a ghost coalition, and are able to employ a range of threats of punishment. Presidents, for example, have the power to remove defectors from the lucrative and influential posts to which they have been appointed; those co-opted into the coalition enjoy the discretion to request impeachment proceedings against cabinet members, thereby disciplining the government. But the most important sanction available to both sides has been the threat of 'going public' and bringing the media down on the coalition. And yet far from being opportunistic and transient arrangements, ghost coalitions seem to have provided the stability for successive Ecuadorian governments to accumulate radical policy reform and 'muddle through' in the face of severe external financial shock.

Source: Acosta (2006: 69–84).

accounts, practices as rules-in-use are essentially defined by the rules which precede them, while, in the bottom-up versions, practices which become rules have been 'elevated' to that status. Although this tendency amply illustrates the importance of the interconnections between rules and practices (and narratives) which we drew out in Chapter 3, there is no reason why this relationship should be conceptualized as hierarchical with rules at the top. With its longitudinal perspective and emphasis on the importance of ideas in shaping policy, historical institutionalism has come to theorize practices in terms of the sustained enactment of a set of ideas, which conceptually, at least, are elevated above rules, rather than hierarchically subservient. Hence, Crouch and Keune (2005) refer to 'changing dominant practice' as a frame through which to analyse the particular characteristics of different countries' versions of Keynesianism. While Crouch and Keune focus upon the ways in which actors are able to change practices gradually, Mark Blyth (2002a) considers moments at which the formal rules governing economic policy are discredited and collapse. At this point, freed from the constraints of formal institutions and empowered by new sets of ideas, actors are able to construct a new set of rules for the future.

The way in which formal rules and informal practices confer power differs not only over time but also between national political systems and cultural contexts. The case study from Ecuador in Box 4.2 shows how political actors, who are heavily constrained by formal rules, can access covert practices – 'ghost coalitions' – to achieve their policy goals, while still appearing to conform to the dominant institutional configuration. Using Helmke and Levitsky's typology (discussed in Chapter 3) Acosta (2006: 84) argues that this relationship between rules and practices is complementary, in the sense of 'helping to improve the (poor) policymaking capacity of a fragmented legislature'. Practices do not displace the existing rules, nor do they bring in 'more of the same', but they harness a different sort of institutional effect which operates beneath the surface and compensates for failures in the formal configuration. Acosta himself, however, acknowledges the 'double edged' nature of this effect, in that it clearly runs against other efforts at institutional change designed to 'clean up' Ecuadorian politics. From an engaged perspective, we must weigh the claims of Ecuadorian presidents that they have 'saved' the country from financial disaster against the knowledge that large swathes of the Ecuadorian public were opposed to the neo-liberal economic policies which were effectively imposed by stealth. This appears to be an example of a ruling elite using embedded practices to subvert the checks and balances that have been imposed upon them by a suspicious electorate.

Power through storytelling

We showed in Chapter 3 how third phase institutionalism has increasingly embraced the significance of collective understandings in shaping political behaviour. Summarizing Linde's (2001) vivid study of induction into the institutions of MidWest Insurance, we illustrated how ideas and beliefs about an organization are not simply embedded within that setting, but are continuously transmitted between actors by narration (Box 3.4). These understandings are fashioned into stories, and these, in turn, are built into narratives which 'distil and reflect a particular understanding of social and political relations' and lead to a normative conclusion (Feldman *et al.* 2004). Whether in a corporate environment like MidWest, or in a political arena like a parliament or a civil service department, narratives tell new entrants how they are expected to conduct themselves and relate to others, and are backed up by both incentives and sanctions (although these may be informal as well as formal).

As an account of the narrator's 'grand conception', narratives rely for their potency on iteration and elaboration over time, and transmission across an expanding collective of actors. As with practices, therefore, their empowering effects may not be apparent in forms of rational choice institutionalism that focus on the 'here and now'. However, as third phase institutionalism gained ground, rational choice scholars began to widen their spatial and temporal horizons and admit to their analysis the role of ideas and beliefs. In developing game theory in corporations, Aoki (2010: 71, his emphasis) argues that, although shared beliefs among players may be seen as constraining by individuals, 'they are actually *enabling* at the same time', because they reassure players that the possibilities for action on the part of other players are not unlimited, and give them some indication of how other players might respond under certain conditions. Shared understandings of an informal and intangible nature empower actors through reducing the disabling effects of uncertainty.

Also from a rationalist perspective, Sabatier has developed Heclo's (1974) approach to the interaction of political elites within a policy community, as they attempt to respond to changing socio-economic and political conditions. Sabatier's body of work differs from conventional rational choice institutionalism in several significant ways. First, pre-empting Schickler (2001) above, it focuses on coalitions of actors, rather than individuals, and significantly expands the number of actors (i.e. coalitions) 'in play'. Second, it expands the timescale for study to ten years and beyond. Third, it uses the concept of shared beliefs, as opposed to interests, as the glue which holds together coalitions of actors. Fourth, in accordance with this rejection of pure selfishness as a motive force behind agency, it holds that the strategic intent of coalitions is concentrated on translating the value base behind their shared beliefs into legislation, rather than simply producing policy which reflects their group's interests. Fifth, this context shaping is achieved as much by trial and error and reflective learning, as by the exercise of raw power. In terms of agency and power, therefore, Sabatier sees the shared belief system as not only promoting the stability of the elite coalition, but also providing the motive force for its strategic intent.

As sociological institutionalists, Schneiberg and Lounsbury employ a more pluralistic model in their discussion of social movements and institutional analysis. Giving an account of how 'eco-activists' have promoted recycling initiatives in the US, they promote the 'movements' themselves as the actors in their analysis, and emphasize 'their role as agents of theorization, classification and diffusion of codified arguments, frames and theoretical resources'. They describe how initially, the eco-activists narrated 'recycling as a way to rebuild community, create local closed-loop production and consumption, and reduce community dependence on conglomerates and capitalist commodity systems'. But in the face of isolation and industry and state indifference, the movements changed their approach, forging ties with commercial waste handlers, and 're-theorizing' recycling as an activity which could generate profits for the private sector:

> Coupled with grass-roots mobilization against new incinerators, and negotiations with state agencies to buy recycled materials, theorizing recyclables as commodities transformed cultural beliefs and discourse about waste in the industry, creating institutional conditions for diffusing recycling practices. (Schneiberg and Lounsbury, 2008: 655)

In this example, therefore, 'ordinary people' appear to enjoy high degrees of agency. From a 'Man as Scientist' perspective (e.g. Bannister and Fransella, 1971), they are empowered principally by their 'theorizing' capacities, that is to say, their ability to form ideas into stories about the world, and radically rework these when their strategic intent is not being realized.

Also from a sociological perspective, Newman (2005) considers the role of the 'transformational leader' in network governance in the UK. Here she uses concepts from discourse theory but, following Rose (1999), her approach is modified from the traditional Foucauldian perspective 'to allow for the possibility of creativity and experimentation on the part of human actors'. Implicitly employing a combination of both Marxist and elite perspectives, she examines 'the technologies of power through which public service "leaders" are constituted as the proactive agents of state modernization'. In summary, she argues that the state, in the form of the New Labour government in the UK, has attempted to both re-ignite, and closely direct, the agency of elite actors in the public service. It has done this by proselytizing a narrative of the manager as a leader who can transform his or her area of the public service by the sheer force of his or her personality, and particularly through the 'embodiment of characteristics such as integrity, vision and charisma'; but, at the same time, channelling this new found zeal through 'key "success criteria" against which managerial actors are judged' (Newman, 2005: 720). Critical of the 'thin' conceptions of agency in rational choice (e.g. Dunleavy, 1991) and other network studies (e.g. Rhodes, 1997), Newman concludes from her study that, while some elite actors have used the narrative of transformational leadership to enhance their 'managerial power', others have found an enlarged space in which they could 'self author' and subvert some of the state's strategic intentions to more closely meet the demands of 'ordinary people' (Newman, 2005: 730).

As we saw above, historical institutionalists have embraced the significance of ideas since Peter Hall's (1986, 1989) early work on Keynesianism and monetarism. But the conception of narrative here is more constraining than empowering, in the sense of limiting the field of feasible policy alternatives. Schmidt (2009: 532) offers an alternative with her 'discursive institutionalism' which prioritizes the role of creative agents – political leaders, government spokespeople, party activists, spin doctors – whom she sees as 'political actors engaged in a mass process of public persuasion'. In this way, even more so than Newman, Schmidt departs from discourse theory assumptions to allow high degrees of agency in the creation, and strategic mobilization, of narratives as institutional resources. As Schmidt (2009: 533) explains:

> actors can gain power from their ideas as they give power to those ideas. Discursive power comes from the ability of agents with good ideas to use discourse effectively, whether to build a discursive coalition for reform against entrenched interests in the coordinative policy sphere or to inform and orientate the public in the communicative political sphere. Conveying good policy ideas through a persuasive discourse helps political actors win elections and gives policy actors a mandate to implement their ideas.

In recognizing the power of narrative within political institutions, we should not assume that this is accompanied by any expansion of the scope for deliberation or democratic inclusion. Box 4.3 shows the role played by discursive power in communist China through a case study of stock market reform (Bell and Feng, 2009). Against a backdrop of

Box 4.3 Power through storytelling: stock market reform in China

In the last thirty years, China has established institutions intended to liberalize its economy, within an authoritarian state ruled by the communist party. This 'developmental' strategy is intended to ensure the survival of the communist regime through strong economic growth and improving citizens' living standards. In this context, the communist party elite perpetuates, and is shaped by, an institutional storyline of 'management by exception'. Senior party members generally take a 'hands off', strategic role, but are required to intervene directly in disputes and crises which cannot be managed at the subordinate and intermediate levels of the Chinese state bureaucracy. By invoking 'management by exception', senior figures (including the Premier) are empowered, in certain circumstances, to exercise power in arenas outside their normal scope, and directly impose solutions on actors lower down the hierarchy.

With the economy dogged by a weak banking sector and cautious overseas investors, the Chinese stock market was set up by the communist leadership to draw in funds from the Chinese public to support failing state-owned enterprises (SOEs). The institutional design of the stock market was specifically engineered to achieve this aim. The government drove citizens to invest in the stock market by imposing penalties on alternative forms of savings, retaining state ownership of most listed companies, and, within the market itself, imposing a split between tradable and non-tradable shares, with the majority being non-tradable. From the beginning, this institutional design offered both central and local government actors a range of opportunities to 'loot' public funds to prop up their own pet SOEs. A weak regulator was unable to make other than cosmetic reforms and the SOEs themselves had a strong vested interest in resisting

→

corruption scandals and impending political crisis, Premier Wen Jiaboa sought to dissociate himself from the original design of the stock market by promoting the storyline of the state's 'helping' rather than 'grabbing hand'. Invoking a linked narrative of 'management by exception', he was able to break down the firewall between the political and bureaucratic institutional apparatuses (at least temporarily) to enable his Vice Premier, Huang Ju, to 'persuade' key bureaucratic interests of the wisdom of cooperating with stock market reform. Like our case study from Ecuador (Box 4.2), Bell and Feng's (2009) research highlights the utility of an institutionalist approach to understanding power and agency in contexts beyond the US and Europe. Indeed, in the Chinese context, elite actors are able to respond to a political crisis by reaching out beyond their immediate context to effect change across institutional reform to their 'cash cow'. Furthermore, actors within the state bureaucracy were implicated in the corrupt operation of the market, and Premier Zhu Rongji himself had strongly backed the strategy in 1999.

By 2003, the stock market was on the point of collapse in the wake of a prolonged downturn and widespread public resentment at the corruption within the market. The crisis threatened the legitimacy of the regime itself. At this point Zhu Rongji was replaced by Wen Jiaboa who had not been directly involved in setting up the stock market. Wen appreciated the need to reform the market radically and realized that the series of piecemeal institutional changes promoted under Zhu were insufficient to rebuild public confidence. He prepared the way for radical institutional reform by narrating 'the need to protect the interests of small and medium investors' and the state's role as 'a helping rather than a grabbing hand'. In 2004 he issued a Nine-Point Guide to cabinet which laid out a new set of rules for the stock market, including removing the tradable/non-tradable shares split at the heart of the market's failure.

His strategic intent was initially neutralized by the vested interests outlined above, and a stalemate between the two major bureaucratic entities that regulated stock market activity. Little progress was made for the next two years until Wen invoked the narrative of 'management by exception' and, in an unusual move in Chinese politics, brought the heads of all the relevant bureaucracies together into one group under the leadership of himself and the vice premier, Huang Ju. Wen's storyline left the bureaucrats in no doubt that disagreements and rivalries would receive speedy arbitration, while Huang was sent to explain the urgency of the reforms in a closed-door session with brokers and fund managers. Two months later radical reforms were underway and a collapse of the Chinese stock market was averted.

Source: Bell and Feng (2009).

configurations which normally rest outside their sphere of influence. And, while the case study focuses on the role of narrative, this is invariably backed up by formal rules (e.g. the Nine Point Guide) and embedded practice (e.g. political patronage of state owned enterprises).

The recognition of third phase institutionalism that power is exercised through regulation, practice and storytelling – and judicious mixes of the three – provides important intellectual traction for both analysing and challenging entrenched institutional power. As we know from foreign policy analysis, 'hard' power (using inducements and threats via military and economic means) may be combined with 'soft' power (shaping preferences via social, cultural and ideological means) for maximum effect (Nye, 2008). As Andrew Heywood (2011: 215–16) notes, George W. Bush's approach to the 'war on terror', particularly the 2003 invasion of Iraq, has been criticized as counter-productive given the anti-Americanism it provoked on the 'Arab Street'. The Obama administration has put more emphasis on 'winning hearts and minds' through influence and persuasion at the political level, alongside institutional capacity-building and development programmes. Because such strategies are actually backed up by the possible use of massive military force, the concept of 'smart power' has been coined to refer to combinations of soft and hard mechanisms.

So the conceptual distinction between rules, practices and narratives has real significance for the institutional bases of political strategy on the ground. This is relevant not just for dominant global actors (like China or the USA) but also for new forms of political resistance, which increasingly deploy subtle and differentiated mixes of hard and soft power – examples include storytelling (through the use of social media, music and culture), and forms of protest based upon embedding new practices (what you eat, what you wear, what you buy). These are not *replacing* traditional mechanisms like demonstrations and strikes, or indeed armed insurrections or terror campaigns, but are more frequently visible within 'smart' strategies – whether in relatively developed countries (animal rights, environmentalism, anti-capitalism) or in other regions of the world (the 'colour revolutions' in parts of the former USSR or the uprisings of the 'Arab Spring', for example).

What is an institutionalist conceptualization of agency?

So what, in theoretical terms, have we learnt from our institutionalist analysis of power and agency? Third phase institutionalists insist, quite correctly, that institutions and individuals are mutually constitutive. But the first half of this equation has (unsurprisingly) dominated institutionalist thinking. 'Animating' our understanding of institutions requires that we spell out a distinctively institutionalist conception of agency. If an 'institutionalist conception of agency' sounds like a contradiction in terms, that is because institutions are themselves paradoxical. Individuals are not simply constrained by institutions, they are also responsible for the crafting of these same constraints (this is the subject of Chapter 7 on institutional design). Beyond such foundational moments, actors are also creatively engaged in the enactment of institutions. 'Rule takers' are not passive implementers, but creative agents who interpret rules, assign cases to rules, and adapt or even resist rules. To understand institutions, we need to understand power and agency as well as constraint and compliance (as discussed in Chapter 3).

At the beginning of this chapter we argued that, if we are to dig down to the roots of how institutions empower, we must understand actors as possessing two different, but closely related, types of capacity: for agency, in the sense of seeking to realize intentions, and for power, in the sense of having an effect on the context 'which defines the range of possibilities of others' (Hay, 1997: 50). Examining Streek and Thelen's schema of rules, rule makers and rules takers, we saw how power tends to be concentrated with rule makers, who attempt to impose their will from the top down, but, equally, that this exercise of power is often flawed in its outcomes. Added to this, subordinate actors are not just 'rule takers', they are also rule benders and rule breakers. Over time, the ways in which these actors interpret and modify rules, practices and narratives, becomes a potent force for change. Both power and resistance play their part as institutions are 'discovered, invented, suggested, rejected, or for the time being, adopted' (Streek and Thelen, 2005).

Reviewing dominant conceptions of power in political science, we have argued that the main strands of institutionalism have borrowed widely across these, as they have come to appreciate that in different temporal and spatial contexts different sets of actors are able to act strategically and exercise power in different ways. Our exploration of rules, practices and narratives within this frame of reference helped us understand the various processes by which institutions empower actors, and how shifting power settlements characterize trajectories of institutional change. In concluding the chapter, we outline our distinctively institutionalist '5Cs' conception of agency (see Table 4.2 for a summary of the key elements).

Third phase institutionalists tend to theorize agency more in *collective* than individualistic terms. Rational choice institutionalists, who were most concerned with actors as individuals, have been influenced by scholars including Sabatier, Schickler, Ostrom and Pierson towards the adoption of a medium- and longer-term view of politics as the mobilization and maintenance of coalitions of actors for collective action. Sociological institutionalists have observed how, over time, large groups of actors embed their activities into the professional, political and public roles that constitute their collective power base. When particular roles such as prime minister or president appear to confer

Table 4.2 An institutionalist conception of agency: the 5Cs

	Collective	Combative	Cumulative	Combinative	Constrained
Key characteristics	The mobilization of actors to work together, rather than as individuals, under the same institutional configuration.	Direct action by actors with the intent of opposing and defeating other groups and their institutional defences.	The impacts of agency on institutions are only apparent over time and rely on the contributions of many actors who may not know each other.	Actors use the institutional materials to hand, often exploiting lack of fit between different types.	There is no pure free will or absolute power. Actors are always constrained to some extent by their institutional context.
A practical example	The formation of workers' cooperatives (Ostrom, 2007).	The conduct of political parties (Schickler, 2001).	The impacts of labour regulation (Thelen, 2004).	The emergence of the Californian high tec economy (Crouch, 2005).	The development of health care systems (Pierson, 2004).
Connections to the other Cs	Coalitions of actors are often formed for combative purposes (e.g. to oppose or generate institutional change).	Political combat is not a single event: it is sustained and attritional and relies on cumulative effects from a number of different actors.	Cumulative effects overlap with collective action, but are distinguished by the fact that they are often unintentional in the outcomes they produce.	Actors have a limited range of institutional material to work with. They are constrained in their scope of materials to combine.	Actors are particularly constrained in coalitions where they must respect the institutions of the other group(s) as well as their own.

| *Exceptions and conditioning contexts* | Some actors attempt to deploy presidential power, others work across institutional boundaries as individual 'reticulists'. | Collaboration and partnership working offers an alternative in some contexts (e.g. coalition governments). | Agency may come to the fore during crises and powerful actors may have the opportunity to make an 'immediate' impact. | Actors may rely on reinforcing a single set of existing institutions (e.g. UK/US penal policy and the 'prison works' approach). | Degrees of constraint vary according to context: in authoritarian regimes the agency of elite actors may be enhanced (see Box 4.2). |

large degrees of agency and power on individual actors, institutionalists show how actors' scope for context shaping is constrained by the need to hold supportive coalitions together, and the oppositional agency of other actors, individual and collective. In this way rational choice and sociological scholars have converged with historical institutionalists, who have always tended to see agency and power in wider spatial terms and in a longer temporal context.

If the collective aspects of agency stress the need for actors to cooperate in order to exercise power, then we must also observe that such coalitions are usually formed with *combative* intent. Our understanding of context shaping needs to include direct attempts at conduct shaping by one set of actors in relation to another (Hay, 2002: 186). In this way the principal–agent model, which underpins new public management, assumes that sustained action from the centre can change the conduct of large groups of citizens. From a pluralist perspective, sociological institutionalists consider the bottom-up agency of social movements who form to challenge the policies pursued by the centre. Historical institutionalists, and those with longer-term rational choice perspectives, borrow from the social movements school the idea that in politics the 'losers from the first round' do not disappear, but actually 'hang around' looking for opportunities to exact their revenge.

Third phase institutionalists have been influenced by Paul Pierson's (2004) plea to view politics in the longer term, as the movie rather than the snapshot. Hence there is now a *cumulative* element to institutionalists' conceptions of agency and power which goes beyond the collective and the combative. The impacts of agency and the exercise of power by a wide variety of different actors accumulate over time to produce effects which cannot be foreseen by any of the actors involved. In this way, those intended and unintended effects produced by actors, who may be opposed to one another, interact together and reinforce the structured inequalities recorded by Marxist scholars, while also producing opportunities for deviance and resistance on the part of less institutionally powerful actors (as institutionalists of a pluralist and elitist hue have observed).

Despite the obsessions of both politicians and political scientists with establishing what is 'new', third phase institutionalists have developed a conception of agency and power that focuses upon reforming the materials to hand (March and Olsen, 1989). Hence third phase institutionalists are interested in the *combinative* activities of actors who bring together existing institutions and ideas in attempts to form or reinforce coalitions and combat their political opponents. Actors find opportunities for the recombination of institutional elements to pursue their strategic advantage (Crouch, 2005), often exploiting the lack of fit between different modes of institutional constraint (as described in Chapter 3), and the tendency of narratives, in particular, to incorporate elements which weaken as well as strengthen the overall impact of the institutional configuration. In the process of recombination, as we saw in the US health care example in Chapter 1 (Box 1.2), actors attempt to align their own mixed motivations and those of others implicated in coalition building. Goodin (1996: 28) reminds us that 'Typically, there is no single design or designer', arguing that students of institutional reform should pay attention to 'the multiplicity of designers and to the inevitably cross-cutting nature of their intentional interventions in the design process'.

But, whatever the empowering effects of institutions, and in some particular contexts (and for some actors) these can be considerable, third phase institutionalists continue to demonstrate that agency and power are always *constrained*. In this way, from an institutionalist perspective, there is no such thing as pure free will, or absolute power. Actors with strategic intent to exercise power are constrained by a number of ubiquitous factors which limit both their capacity to act, and their ability to make their desired impact. First and foremost amongst these are existing institutions and the modes by which different forms of institutional constraint act together and separately. And, as we have shown, actors cannot achieve their strategic intent alone and must act collectively. In their attempts at institutional design and reform, they do not have access to a 'blank slate' – they encounter both the resources, and the constraints, characteristic of a world replete with institutions. Institutional effects also accumulate over time (creating path dependencies), constraining actors in ways which they and their opponents could not have foreseen at an earlier moment. We finish by reiterating Hay's point about power as conduct shaping. Not only do political actors seek to empower themselves and their allies; they seek also to constrain their opponents in a direct and combative manner.

Thus we conclude that the same mechanisms which empower also constrain and that for institutionalists the two processes need to be considered as cohabiting forces. While third phase institutionalism retains a strong link to pluralism, this tendency is significantly conditioned by a recognition of struggles against state and elite power, within which 'ordinary people' are mobilized through their own institutions. Political institutions are not the prerogative of the state or of elite actors. The world of protest and campaigning is itself a rich institutional landscape. Social movements, trades unions, community groups, and revolutionary struggles are subject to their own formal rules, informal practices and narratives. But, as elite perspectives remind us, powerful actors will seek to circumscribe the space within which such institutions can thrive. And, from a Marxist viewpoint, institutionalists observe that those who are historically empowered tend to retain those capacities, and pre-structured inequalities continue to put limits on the effectiveness of any attempt to empower those lower down the hierarchy.

These broad conclusions begin to throw light on why institutional change can be a messy, conflicted and even dangerous process. It is to this issue – central to the development of third phase institutionalism – that we now turn.

Chapter 5

Institutional Change

In the next three chapters of this book we address three of the most difficult questions for institutionalist theory. How do institutions change, why do institutions vary so much, and can institutions be 'designed' in any meaningful sense?

Throughout its second phase of development, institutionalism was routinely criticized for its tendency to be 'rather better at explaining stability than change' (Hay, 2002: 15). Behind this observation lay two distinct sets of criticisms which related more to the *quality* of the explanations offered, rather than the quantity of theories available. The first set observed that explanations of institutional change were typically 'thin', in the sense of being sketchily drawn and consequently unconvincing (Peters, 1999: 147–8; John, 1998: 65; Rothstein, 1996: 153). The second, more specific, set of criticisms identified a tendency to call on external, or 'exogenous', forces to produce the motive forces for change, rather than looking to the role played by actors and institutions within the local political space ('endogenous' forces) (e.g. Gorges, 2001). In this chapter we look at how institutionalists have made the transition from thinner to thicker theories of institutional change, and from conceptualizations which privilege one dimension of political time and space to schemata which are multi-dimensional.

In the first section of the chapter, we show how, in the case of early attempts at explaining institutional change, scholars aligning themselves with rational choice and historical institutionalism were influenced by the legacies of institutionalist economics, and more recent developments in neo-Darwinian evolutionary theory. We argue that the two key concepts developed at this time, path dependence and punctuated equilibrium came to dominate second phase institutionalism. By contrast, sociology as a discipline was already embedded in a long tradition of social, as opposed to biological, evolutionism; hence sociological institutionalism adopted an evolutionary approach which privileged slower, incremental processes of change. The chapter provides a mapping of different perspectives in relation to two variables – the tempo of change (from punctuated to incremental) and the

111

balance between structure and agency in explaining drivers of change. The mapping shows how, in third phase institutionalism, any clear distinction is breaking down between the explanations of institutional change offered by rational, historical and sociological approaches. Institutionalists of all colours are exploring novel themes, recognizing that gradual change can have transformative effects, that change can be stimulated by endogenous as well as exogenous factors, and that agency has relevance beyond periods of crisis. The chapter finishes by presenting a perspective on institutions and institutional change which we term 'Politics – the Movie' because we believe it produces an analysis of the roles of institutions, actors and their environments in a way which captures the rich temporal and spatial characteristics of political drama and is informed by a specifically institutionalist approach to agency.

Change: an institutionalist dilemma

As we saw in Chapter 2, when institutions were 'rediscovered' in the 1980s, the challenges facing the 'new' institutionalism were rather more basic than finding explanations for institutional change. Looking outwards, institutionalists made a priority of presenting the case against the individualism of behaviouralism and first generation rational choice perspectives. Looking inwards, institutionalists sought to develop the theory to respond to the well-rehearsed criticisms of the 'old' institutionalism. They did so influenced by, and borrowing from, not only the old institutionalism in politics, but also the versions which had been developed in economics and organizational theory. In early attempts at explaining institutional change, scholars aligning themselves with rational choice and historical institutionalism were influenced by the legacies of institutionalist economics and more recent developments in neo-Darwinian evolutionary theory. The two key concepts developed from the 1980s onwards – path dependence and punctuated equilibrium – continued to shape the debate around how institutions change through second and into third phase institutionalism.

As the primary beneficiary of institutional economics, rational choice institutionalism saw institutions as necessary to stabilize markets by controlling the volatility of individual choice. In these early second phase accounts of institutional change, actors were free to decide that the rules were not working as intended, and, as Peters and

Pierre (1998: 570) explain, produce 'another round of explicit choices about structures and rules' on a planned basis. But, as we have seen in previous chapters, from the earliest stages of second phase institutionalism, some boundary spanning rational choice institutionalists were intent on introducing broader spatial and temporal horizons to this minimalist conception. In this way, as soon as longer time spans were used, and gaming and principal agent relationships were exposed to more than one iteration in empirical research, more complex ideas on change emerged. While Williamson (1985) and North (1990) saw economic institutions as developing to ease problems of exchange, political institutions were increasingly seen by rational choice scholars as *obstacles* to effective exchange, subject as they were to processes of 'path dependence'.

Path dependence assumes the presence of calculating actors but argues that they are subject to forces of positive feedback. Once policy makers have started down a particular path, the probability of remaining on that path increases over time. As Pierson (2004: 21) argues, 'the costs of switching to some previously plausible alternative rise'. As we saw in Chapter 2, there is no reason to assume that the path which gets 'locked in' is superior to those that were foregone. The QWERTY keyboard, for instance, persists in tablet computers and smart phones purely because the costs of changing the industry standard are too high.

Political actors are constrained by the cumulative effects of institutional reinforcement and, as Rothstein (1996: 152) explains, the expected costs of institutional change are complex, and include the costs of learning how to operate within a new structure, of dealing with new sources of uncertainty, and of engaging in change itself. In the political domain, rational choice accounts may see path-dependent processes as driven by the personal utilities of powerful politicians or civil servants (budgets, prestige, patron–client links) (Niskanen, 1971; Dunleavy, 1991). For historical institutionalists like Paul Pierson, path dependence may be driven by more altruistic actors who calculate that public policy goals are best served by working within existing state structures and paradigms (however rusty) rather than diverting resources towards institutional change. Other historical institutionalists focus less on the prospective agency of actors in maintaining path dependence, but on the retrospective constraints on agency provided by the structured nature of existing institutions (Lowndes 2005: 295). They work with a 'softer' version of path dependence, relying on 'the basic, and deceptively simple, idea ... that the policy choices made when an institution is being formed, or when a policy is initiated, will have a continuing and largely determinate influence over the policy far into the future' (Peters, 2005: 71).

Unsurprisingly, path dependence has also stimulated theorizations of what happens 'in between' these periods of relative institutional inertia. Political scientists have adapted the theory of punctuated equilibrium, which was developed in biology in the 1970s in opposition to the prevailing theory of 'phyletic gradualism', which argued for an uninterrupted process of evolution. Instead, it was proposed that most sexually reproducing species experience little evolutionary change over geological time; when evolution does occur, it is a rare event in which one distinct species splits into two, rather than one species gradually transforming into another. These rare events are the punctuations which occur in an equilibrium, which is otherwise maintained by the large numbers of organisms which comprise the species, and by the continuous process of gene flow (Mayr, 1963). While rational choice scholars first applied the principles of punctuated equilibrium to political analysis (Krasner, 1984; True, Jones and Baumgartner, 1999), it has also been adapted for use by neo-Marxists like Jessop (1990) and Thelen and Steinmo (1992). Hay (2002: 161) provides an overview definition of the concept: 'a discontinuous conception of political time in which periods of comparatively modest institutional change are interrupted by more rapid and intense moments of transformation'.

Although the definition does not eliminate the possibly of modest change during 'normal' as well as 'exceptional' times (to use Hall's, 1993, terms), second phase institutionalists came to focus upon the punctuations, variously understood as 'crises' (Skowronek, 1982), 'critical junctures' (Collier and Collier, 1991) and 'critical institutional events' (Baumgartner and Jones, 1993). Rational choice scholars saw punctuations as moments in which strategic agents are able to act beyond the confines of existing institutional constraints. As John and Margetts (2003: 412) explain: 'there are critical junctures when the agenda of the political system shifts, such as when parties have an influence on policy outcomes ... or when the indivisibility of a new programme demands a large scale policy change, an example being space exploration'.

Historical institutionalists also adopted the concept of punctuated equilibrium, tending to focus on 'formative periods' in institutional development – the critical junctures at which new institutions are born and path dependence set in train. Rather than the motive force for change coming from the calculations of rational actors inside the political space, the emphasis was on changes in the external environment, such as wars, or, for example, the rise to prominence of new policy ideas. Change was therefore theorized as 'disruptive', in the sense that there 'is a sharp break with the past and the setting forth of a new path of policy and institutional development' generated primarily by exogenous forces (Peters and Pierre, 1998: 578).

But second phase institutionalism was influenced also by the long tradition of social (as opposed to biological) evolutionism, associated with the work of Comte and Spencer. Sociological institutionalists were little affected by theories of path dependence and punctuated equilibrium as they took hold in second phase institutionalism during the 1980s. They remained committed to an incremental, rather than a punctuated, version of institutional change, with a particular interest in the ongoing relationship between organizations and their environment and whether this was a reactive or proactive process (Peters, 2005: 118–19). In reactive theorizations, sociological institutionalists adapted Spencer's principle of 'Survival of the Fittest'. In a hostile and competitive world, the types of organization which could not adapt their institutional forms to fit with the demands of the external environment gradually disappeared. Equally, where there was a 'good fit', both the organizations and their associated institutions were likely to survive and prosper. In proactive theorizations, sociological institutionalists proposed that organizations attempted to shape their environment through strategic responses to institutional processes.

Although not using the language of path dependence, sociological institutionalists recognize pressures for institutional reproduction. The 'garbage can model' of policy making, for example, shows how organizations tend to fit problems into pre-existing solutions which they have used in the past, rather than analysing every situation from first principles and designing a bespoke solution. Hence adjustments made by actors in response to environment change are remarkably uniform in character over time, because of their tendency to use the same set of templates. In developing the concept of 'isomorphism', DiMaggio and Powell (1991b) adapt Spencer's original concept of 'social fitness' or 'the acquisition of a form regarded as legitimate in a given institutional environment' (Scott, 2001: 153). They theorized coercive, normative and mimetic mechanisms which 'make organizations more similar without necessarily making them more efficient' (DiMaggio and Powell, 1991b: 64). The result is that similarities in institutional form within a 'population' of organizations are reinforced over time (as further discussed in Chapter 7).

Within second phase institutionalism, a long-standing commitment to social evolutionism (among sociological institutionalists) combined with an emerging interest in punctuated equilibrium (in historical institutionalism) to produce a privileging of 'exogenous forces' as drivers for institutional change, whether conceived in broad terms as 'the environment' or more specifically in relation to events such as wars or ideological shifts. At the same time, rational choice institutionalists' insistence of a role for strategic agents provided raw material for the converging approaches in third phase institutionalism that we examine below.

Charting third phase theories of institutional change

Third phase institutionalism is marked by a yet more vigorous engagement with questions of institutional change. Indeed, attempts to theorize change beyond the classic 'stop-go' models are a defining feature of this third phase. We see a progressive blurring of distinctions between rational choice, historical and sociological perspectives as scholars grapple with similar dilemmas and increasingly borrow tools and insights from one another. Common lines of enquiry include:

- How do external and internal factors combine to stimulate institutional change?
- Can gradual change have transformative effects?
- Over what time period can we make sense of institutional change?
- What role do ideas and discourses play in precipitating and shaping change?
- How does 'real' change relate to planned processes of institutional design?
- What is the role of collective *vis à vis* individual actors?
- How is institutional change resisted as well as facilitated?
- Does it make sense to separate institutional from agential processes?

To explore some of these questions, we map third phase perspectives on institutional change in relation to two analytical continua: the tempo of change (the horizontal axis in Figure 5.1, below) and the balance between structure and agency (the vertical axis). The purpose

Figure 5.1   *Charting theories of institutional change*

Tempo of change

Most incremental   Most punctuated

A	B	Highest structure
structured, incremental change *'big, slow moving and invisible'*	**structured, punctuated change** *'any more bright ideas?'*	

Structure agency balance

D	C	Highest agency
agential, incremental change *'bringing the actor back in'*	**agential, punctuated change** *'bringing the state back in yet again'*	

(boxes: A2, A1 in quadrant A; B2, B1 in quadrant B; D1, D2, D3 in quadrant D; C1, C2 in quadrant C)

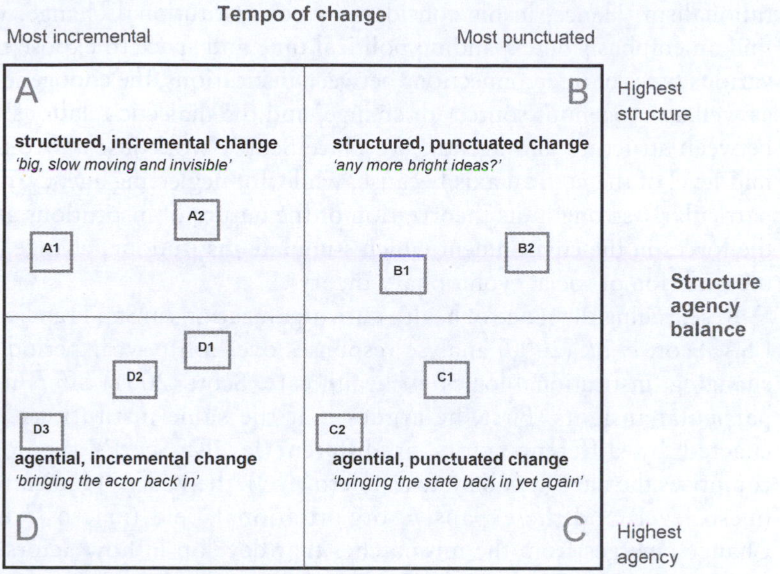

of mapping approaches in this way is to detach them from assumptions about 'schools of institutionalism'. Rather than asking whether an approach belongs in the historical, sociological or rational choice camp (or the new discursive grouping), we look at how its conception of institutional change is positioned in relation to the core variables represented by the axes. This allows us to get closer to understanding what third phase institutionalism has to offer in response to the lines of enquiry we have identified, and further away from the prevalent sectarianism of the academy.

Quadrant A: Structured, incremental change – 'big, slow-moving and invisible'

Quadrant A captures approaches to institutional change which, on balance, give rather more emphasis to structure than agency, and privilege incremental, over punctuated, change. In this quadrant, the work of Scott (2001) at A1 and Pierson (2004) at A2 illustrates the convergence between sociological and rational choice perspectives (respectively) that we have argued characterizes third phase institutionalism.

Scott's theoretical and empirical work typifies much of the boundary spanning scholarship which we see developing in third phase institutionalism. Hence, in his consideration of institutional change, we find an emphasis on expanding political time and space to expose the various types of interconnections between institutions, the endogenous as well as exogenous sources of change, and the dialectic relationship between structure and agency. We place Scott's work just above the mid-level of the vertical axis because, while not neglecting agency, it is particularly strong in its theorization of the nature of institutions and the forces in the environment which stimulate institutional change (in the tradition of social evolutionary theory).

Researching the range of health-care organizations in San Francisco, USA, Scott *et al.* (2000) analyse responses over a fifty-year period to changing 'institutional logics' of health care. Scott (2001) offers two particular insights. First, he argues that the same institutions are enacted by different actors at different levels. Scott's typology comprises the narrow sub-system (micro level), the wider organization (meso level) and the expansive organizational field (macro level). Change emerges from the mismatches that develop in how actors at various 'vertical' levels transmit and interpret institutions. Second, health-care institutions are connected 'horizontally' to institutions in other domains within the external environment. As these external institutions change, so the mismatches between levels are forced wider.

Scott's is largely a structural explanation, which theorizes change in terms of the gradual opening up of gaps in institutional configurations. But he acknowledges endogenous, as well as exogenous sources of change, recognizing that institutions are themselves internally structured and that actors will exploit opportunities afforded by gaps in institutional fit. Scott (2001: 195) draws our attention to the 'interweaving of top-down and bottom-up processes' and the importance of the agency of actors lower down the hierarchy as well as at the top. Nevertheless, deploying Giddens' concept of structuration, Scott emphasizes that agency is always constrained by its dialectic relationship with institutions.

We place Scott's work at A1, close to the incremental pole of the horizontal axis because of his fifty-year time horizon, and the marked absence of the concepts of punctuation or crisis within his theorization. Consistent with the much smoother theorization of change in social evolutionism, Scott's methodological approach emphasizes the importance of charting changes over time in the numbers and types of actors in the organizational field, in the nature of institutional logics, and in the characteristics of governance systems which impinge on the organization from outside and inside. By cross referencing data from these three streams, he argues that evidence can be produced to show how institutions have changed in respect of their regulative (in our terms, rules), normative (practices), and cultural-cognitive (narrative) dimensions (Scott, 2001: 202).

From a rather different direction, Paul Pierson (2004) converges on very similar territory to Scott. As a critical friend of rational choice institutionalism, Pierson's chief goal is to rework the concept of path dependence to include the social and historical contexts in which actors pursue their interests. Pierson's work (2004: 103–32) is particularly strong in exploring the temporal effects which place restrictions on the effectiveness of intentional projects of 'institutional design'. We place Pierson's work at A2, some way above the mid-level of the vertical axis, because, while paying due attention to agency, it lays heavy emphasis on 'the ways in which institutional outcomes channel and constrain later efforts at institutional innovation' (Pierson, 2004: 133). Pierson's calculating individual actors are capable of high levels of agency, but their attempts at change are met by even higher levels of institutional resilience, and equally animated opposition from actors who see change as threatening their interests. Pierson cites Hacker (2004: 246) to summarize the argument:

> Consider for a moment a highly simplified model of the options open to political actors who wish to change an existing policy. In the starkest calculation, they must decide whether to 'work within' this extant policy framework to achieve their ends or 'work outside' it by revising or eliminating it. Seen this way, it immediately becomes clear that two questions loom large. First, how easily can these actors achieve their aims through the existing framework? And, second, how costly would it be to replace it with a policy more closely tailored to the ends they desire? If the answer to the first question is 'very easily', then the actors may pass up challenging even a policy that would be relatively costless to change. If the answer to the second question is 'very costly', then they may try to work within even a policy framework that is heavily biased against the ends they seek.

Borrowing from Schickler (2001) and Thelen (2004), Pierson (2004: 156) argues that, where replacement costs are high, potential reformers will either abandon efforts at change, or opt for partial solutions, such as placing a new institution on top of an existing one ('layering'), or adapting an existing institution to achieve the policy objective in mind ('conversion'). We locate Pierson's work towards the incremental pole of the horizontal axis because of his characterization of the processes of institutional development as 'big, slow-moving and invisible' (2003: 177–207). Nevertheless, we do not place him as far to the left as Scott because implicit in Pierson's theorization is the concept of a formative period of institutional creation, in which path dependence is set in train.

Quadrant B: Structured, punctuated change – 'any more bright ideas?'

Quadrant B is home to approaches which, on balance, give rather more emphasis to structure than agency, and privilege punctuated, over incremental, change. In illustration, we discuss the coalition-based perspective of Paul Sabatier (2007) at B1 and the ideas-based approach of Mark Blyth (2002a) at B2.

In a project which spans two decades and running, Sabatier and colleagues have developed the Advocacy Coalition Framework (ACF) for analysing the interaction of political elites within a policy community, as they respond to changing socio-economic and political conditions. An elitist perspective on policy making, the ACF takes these groups of 'legislators, agency officials, interest group leaders, judges, researchers and intellectuals from multiple levels of government' (Sabatier and Weible, 2007: 196) to be the most important actors in politics. Adopting March and Olsen's notion of a 'logic of appropriateness', Sabatier argues that shared beliefs rather than interests are the glue that holds coalitions of actors together. Such 'belief systems' relate not only to goals but to understandings about how best to achieve these ends.

Following Kiser and Ostrom (1982), the objective for actors in devising strategies for institutional change is to 'structure action situations – chiefly via institutional rules regarding the range and authority of participants – so as to produce the desired operational decisions' (Sabatier, 1988: 160, note 2). Conflicting strategies from various coalitions are normally mediated by a third group of actors, or 'policy brokers', whose task is to find some reasonable compromise which will reduce intense conflict between coalitions. Nevertheless, locked into 'group thinking' and distrust of other coalitions, 'it is exceeding unlikely that members of a coalition will change policy core beliefs voluntarily' (Sabatier and Weible, 2007: 198). Sabatier argues that major change in the belief systems in coalitions and therefore, major change in policy, can only come about from an external source. Marginal change may be affected by 'policy-oriented learning' but major change is stimulated by exogenous shocks, including changing socio-economic conditions, regime change, outputs from other sub-systems, or a disaster.

Some may regard Sabatier as a 'borderline' institutionalist, because he is somewhat cagey about explaining how far institutions themselves are central to policy change. Nevertheless, it is clear that his actors are heavily constrained by their logics of appropriateness and the relatively fixed nature of their belief systems (or practices and narratives in our conception of institutional constraint). We place the ACF at B1, relatively high to the structure end of the structure–agency axis, because of its emphasis on stability and constraint, and also relatively high on the punctuated end of the second axis because of its reliance on external shock to explain major change.

Mark Blyth's (2002a) work, at B2, focuses on case studies of 'great transformations' in economic policy in the USA and Sweden. In his theoretical approach, Blyth employs a 'constructivist institutionalism' which suggests that it is ideas rather than institutions themselves which are important at times of significant institutional change. In so doing, he adapts the concept of punctuated equilibrium, developing a conceptualization borrowed from rational choice, which theorizes crises as exceptional times, in which existing institutions are delegitimized and actors lose sight of their 'real interests' (Knight, 1921). As new ideas arrive, some actors are able to use these to stabilize the situation, diagnosing the problems which have precipitated the crisis and offering solutions in the form of a new policy paradigm and associated institutions. For Blyth, 'in the struggle over existing institutions, ideas are weapons'. But, 'following the delegitimisation of existing institutions, new ideas act as institutions'. And, 'following institutional construction, ideas make institutional stability possible' (Blyth, 2002a: 34–45).

Blyth's work is positioned on the far right of the 'tempo' axis, concerned as it is with the causal effects of ideas during punctuations in institutional stability. New ideas are seen as bursting forth, employed by combatants in short, concentrated explosions of political warfare. But, as Hay (2006a: 70) suggests, the question of constraint and structure–agency balance poses some problems for Blyth. Are all institutions delegitimized during a crisis or only those relevant to the cause of the crisis? If most institutional interconnections remain intact, just as in times of equilibrium, how are some actors able to escape constraint and take the lead in building replacement institutions? In short, Blyth's conceptualization seems to swing from long periods where all actors are constrained, to brief episodes where some actors are granted great freedoms, but without explanation of who they are and why they are able to do this. We place Blyth's work just above the half way point on the structure–agency axis because for most of the time (in equilibria) his actors are constrained. However, we should note that when it really matters, that is to say in times of crisis, it is neither institutions nor even actors who are centre stage but ideas themselves. In this way institutions are simply the object of change rather than being implicated in the process.

Quadrant C: Agential, punctuated change – 'bringing the state back in – yet again'

Quadrant C captures approaches which, on balance, give rather more emphasis to agency than structure, and tend to be more concerned with the formative periods during which institutions are created or reformed rather than the periods in between revision. We look here at Eric Schickler's classic study of 'disjointed pluralism' in the US Congress (C1) and at Vivien Schmidt's 'discursive institutionalism' (C2).

Taking four historical periods, Schickler analyses different aspects of institutional change in Congress: changes in rules, procedures and practices, changes in scope and powers in the committee system, and changes in the types and roles of members who become leaders in Congress. Each change he discovers is treated as a discrete event, but he also seeks to place it within the context of the ten-year period in question. As a rational choice institutionalist, central to his concept of context are the 'distinct and partially contradictory kinds of collective interests' which 'motivate the design of legislative institutions' (Schickler, 2001: 5). Echoing our discussion of actors' mixed motivational demands in Chapter 1, Schickler argues that collective interests simultaneously seek to: ensure re-election, maintain a power base, enhance the party's reputation, achieve policy based outcomes, and improve the prestige of Congress itself.

Schickler's findings can be summarized thus:

- Multiple collective interests typically shape each important change in congressional institutions.

- Entrepreneurial members build support for reform by framing proposals that appeal to groups motivated by different interests.
- Congressional institutions usually develop through an accumulation of innovations that are inspired by competing motives.
- The adoption of a series of changes intended to promote one type of interest typically provokes contradictory changes that promote competing interests.

The outcome tends to a tense layering of new arrangements on top of pre-existing structures. Anticipating substantial opposition to change, coalitions choose to add an additional layer to existing institutions rather than attempt to replace them. While each layer is itself a product of conscious design, the overall configuration of institutions as they develop over time will appear haphazard. While path dependence is important, insofar as layering builds on existing institutions, 'its emphasis on continuity underestimates the incidence of major changes in congressional institutions' (Schickler, 2001: 16). Schickler (2001: 17) argues that 'members who are disadvantaged by current organizational arrangements will have strong incentives to reform them' and the multiple interests themselves which motivate members are ultimately irreconcilable. As Schickler (2001: 18) explains: 'The interplay of coalitions promoting contradictory objectives produces institutions that are tense battlegrounds rather than stable, coherent solutions.'

Although Schickler recognizes structural constraints through an element of path dependence and a built-in requirement to (seek) compromise, the approach has a voluntaristic flavour whereby actors appear to select strategies in a relatively unconstrained manner. Hence, like Thelen in Quadrant D, we place Schickler's work halfway between the mid-line and the agency pole. On the horizontal axis, disjointed incrementalism is harder to place. There is a recognition of the ongoing nature of demands from the external environment to which multiple collective interests must respond. But, at the same time, his focus is chiefly upon the formation of institutions, and based upon decade-long time capsules. Hence we place his work in the middle of the Quadrant on this axis too.

As we saw in Chapter 4, Vivien Schmidt (2009) offers discursive institutionalism as an alternative to a historical institutionalism increasingly dominated by rational choice principles. Her focus is upon explaining the dynamics of institutional change through a focus on 'the discursive political coordination, communication, and deliberation' (Schmidt, 2009: 517) of public action. She argues that the significance of the state as an actor in its own right has been lost by scholars like Kathleen Thelen (see Quadrant D, below), who had previously championed 'bringing the state back in'. For Schmidt, discursive institutionalist approaches offer greater purchase to the comparative study of national economies than a form of historical institutionalism increasingly dominated by rational choice assumptions. In place of a standard bifurcation between liberal and coordinated forms, she sets out to analyse the role of 'real politics, the politics of leadership and opposition' in fashioning economic institutions and policy (Schmidt, 2009: 540). Hence 'varieties of capitalism persist not just because of path-dependent structures and market or managed logics of coordination but because of differing ideas and discourse about state action and business and labor interaction' (Schmidt, 2009: 541).

In a similar fashion to Mark Blyth (Quadrant B, above), Schmidt (2009: 530) argues that ideas are used by actors 'to (re)conceptualize interests and values as well as (re)shape institutions'. And they come in a variety of forms: specific policy ideas (for example, neo-Keynesianism); more general programmatic ideas, (for example, a shift from neo-Keynesianism to neo-liberalism); underlying public philosophies (for example, the French government's approach to supporting infrastructure investment); foundational economic ideas (as per Blyth's (2002a) 'great transformations', above); or collective memories that are generated at critical moments (for example, the state-framed agreements for wage bargaining in Sweden, which persist from the 1930s).

But actors are far more central for Schmidt than Blyth in explaining institutional change. In Blyth's account ideas seem prior to actors, functioning as some kind of exogenously generated independent variable. But Schmidt (2009: 532) explains 'processes of change through the ideas and discourse of the agents who reproduce those rules – and change them – in everyday practice'. Institutional change is 'the product of sentient agents engaged in thinking up new ideas about what to do and how to do it and then engaging in discussions in efforts to persuade others that this is indeed what one needs to do and ought to do' (Schmidt, 2009: 533). At the same time, the battle of ideas is structured differently in different countries according to the existing political institutional context, leading to different outcomes (or 'varieties of capitalism'). The state remains the key reference point for Schmidt, albeit a differentiated composite of reflexive actors. For this reason we position Schmidt's work at C2, towards the agency pole of the structure–agency axis. In terms of tempo, Schmidt sets out to explain punctuations in a different way from 'mainstream' historical institutionalism, but she recognizes the continuous and iterative nature of the discursive processes involved.

Quadrant D: 'Agential, incremental change' – 'bringing the actor back in'

Quadrant D is home to approaches which, on balance, give rather more emphasis to agency than structure, and, like those in Quadrant A, privilege incremental, over punctuated, change. At D1, we look at Schneiberg and Lounsbury's (2008) work on the role of social movements in institutional change; at D2, we draw on our own research on 'institutional emergence' (Lowndes, 2005); and at D3 we consider Kathleen Thelen's typology of forms of 'gradual institutional change' (Mahoney and Thelen, 2010; Thelen, 2009; Streek and Thelen, 2005).

Schneiberg and Lounsbury (2008: 648–9) are concerned with 'how groups coalesce to make claims for or against certain practices or actors in order to create or resist new institutional arrangements or transform existing ones'. Like Pierson in Quadrant A, Schneiberg and Lounsbury theorize energetic actors who meet intimidating institutional and agential resistance. But, the social movements they study are organized collectives, who are value driven, digging in for the long haul, and thus, in the main, not engaged in cost-benefit calculations. We place their work just below the mid-line of the vertical axis, because their theorization of the structure–agency balance is marginally tilted towards agency, not least by the sheer persistence of their actors in attempting to produce institutional change. They emphasize 'deliberate or strategic action, and self-conscious mobilization around alternatives' but in a context in which we cannot assume sufficient capacity or reflexivity on the part of social movements to ensure that agency is translated into institutional change (Schneiberg and Lounsbury, 2008: 649).

For Schneiberg and Lounsbury, 'change flows from combinations of movements and institutional processes'. What movements can achieve is conditioned not just by dominant political institutions but by the achievements of previous waves of struggle, which come to structure the institutional environment of politics. New social movements seeking to change conventional politics are able to build on alternative, oppositional institutions established by their predecessors. Schneiberg and Lounsbury (2008: 652) argue that interest group politics have become a key feature of US politics 'through successive waves of mobilization and transposition by three outsider/challenger groups', namely unions, then farmers, and then women's groups. A new institutional repertoire has been established, including not just strikes, boycotts and protests but also cooperatives, mutuals, apolitical clubs, and single issue associations. Such oppositional institutions can also be experienced as constraining by new movements, who seek precisely to disrupt the expectations of elites (as in the women's peace movements of the 1980s, 'queer' politics in the 1990s, or the current wave of anti-capitalist street 'occupations'). The success of such strategies depends, however, upon movements' access to resources, the receptivity of those with specific institutional power, and the resonance of new models within a broader institutional environment.

At the heart of this work is an oscillatory rhythm of political protest and institutional change that provides an alternative to the two main evolutionary perspectives, relying, as they do, on a particular tempo of change. We are confronted by two competing populations rather than a process of adaptation within a single population in response to environmental forces. As a distinctively political, rather than biological or social, process, the struggle between the parties is rarely decisive and often contingent in its conduct and outcomes. In particular, if a social movement fails in one attempt at institutional change, it is at liberty to bide its time to make another. Furthermore, when significant institutional change is successfully forced through by one group, those on the losing end lie in wait for opportunities to reverse the defeat. Hence, it is the strategic and opportunistic nature of the parties' struggle for advantage which is prominent. The agency of one group is conditioned by the direct and continuous opposition of another, in addition to the structural constraints which impinge upon it. The movement/institution dialectic means that we position the approach at D1, near the central point of the structure–agency axis. The oscillatory pattern of institutional change (with successive waves of mobilization) places the work close to the midpoint of the tempo axis too.

At D2, we position our own research on institutional change in English local government, which looks at why some institutions appear to have been transformed, while others are 'unmoved'. Following North (1990), institutions themselves are conceptualized as part of a densely interconnected 'matrix' in which 'different rule-sets change at different rates and in different directions, reflecting power relation-

ships and the "embeddedness" of local governance in specific historical and spatial contexts' (Lowndes, 2005: 292). Echoing Pierson
above, Lowndes emphasizes the coexistence, and interaction, of forces
for continuity and change within organizations. The former originate
from path dependence, but on forces for change, Lowndes tilts the
balance towards agency rather than structure, by allowing her actors
considerable combinative capacity. Here the cracks in the institutional
fabric, which result from processes of uneven development, open up
'creative spaces' in which local managers and politicians as 'institutional entrepreneurs seek to adapt the "rules of the game" in order to
respond to changing environments and protect (or extend) their influence' (Lowndes, 2005: 299). Adapting Crouch and Farrell (2004), she
suggests such entrepreneurs expand and recombine their institutional
repertoires through strategies of 'remembering', 'borrowing' and 'sharing' (see Chapter 7). The resulting process of institutional emergence is
messy in so far as it is characterized by contingent and context-dependent effects.

We place this work fairly close to the mid-point of the vertical structure–agency axis in Figure 5.1 because actors are constrained within a
dense institutional matrix, by path dependence, and more specifically
by a 'garbage can model' (Cohen, March and Olsen, 1972) which
limits actors' access to institutional materials to what is already to
hand. D2 is plotted substantially to the left of the horizontal axis
because it is clearly the incremental aspect of change that is of most
concern:

> Exploring institutional change in 'normal times' is important
> because it draws our attention to the many small steps that, over
> time, contribute to the making and breaking of path dependency.
> Conceptually, it helps to 'bring the actor back in'. It shows how
> paths tend to become broader over time as they gradually encom-
> pass other smaller tracks, their overall direction and character
> changing subtly in the process. (Lowndes, 2005: 299)

While Lowndes' work is conducted at the micro level, Thelen (at D3)
moves up a level to consider system-wide institutional change. A key
contributor to the 'varieties of capitalism' debate, Thelen (2009: 475)
observes the remarkable resilience of political and economic institutions in the face of major external shocks (for Germany she points to
defeat in two world wars, foreign occupation and regime changes). Her
specific studies lead her to a general conclusion:

[B]ig breaks do not necessarily mean big openings for radical insti-tutional reconfiguration. But conversely, it is also not at all clear that all significant change has to have its source in a major exogenous shock that upends old arrangements and somehow clears the way for new ones... [S]ignificant change often takes place gradually and through a cumulation of seemingly small adjustments... in the absence of some obvious historic rupture.

Theoretically, Thelen is engaged in a sustained critique of the punctu-ated equilibrium model of institutional breakdown and replacement. Her counter proposition is that significant change in the form and function of institutions arises from shifts in the political coalitions on which such institutions rest. The seemingly paradoxical phenomenon of 'gradual transformation' can take four distinct forms (see Streek and Thelen, 2005: 31; and Thelen, 2010: 15–16):

- **Displacement** – This is the rising salience of subordinate relative to dominant institutions, which Thelen also calls 'defection'. Previously suppressed, or latent, institutional resources may be reactivated, or there may be an 'invasion' or assimilation of new rules from outside the institutional setting.
- **Layering** – This is where new rules are introduced on top of or alongside existing rules. New elements attached to existing institu-tions gradually change the original institution. Through a process of 'differential growth', the 'new fringe eats into the old core'. We see 'a compromise between old and new slowly turning into defeat of the old'.
- **Drift** – Here a neglect of institutional maintenance ('deliberate neglect'), in the face of a changing external environment, leads to a 'slippage in institutional practice on the ground'. Rather than the introduction of new rules, existing rules have a different impact because of changes in the environment.
- **Conversion** – Here new purposes become attached to old institu-tions, which are effectively 'redirected' or 'reinterpreted'. This may arise from 'subversion' as 'rules are reinterpreted from below' or it may be the outcome of intended or unintended 'ambiguity' in insti-tutional design. Again, rather than introducing new rules, there is a 'changed enactment of existing rules' for strategic reasons.

Central to Thelen's theorization of institutional change is the idea that institutions 'are never "simply" applied, they are always interpreted, enforced and enacted, and, of course, by actors who have divergent and conflicting interests' (2009: 490). Gaps between the design of institutions and their 'on-the-ground implementation' are vital in explaining endogenously derived processes of change. First, gaps emerge because institution-building at inception is often a matter of political compromise. Hence designers intentionally build in ambiguities in an attempt to please all parties, but these fault lines widen over time and under pressure. Second, institutions are not neutral. Because they instantiate power, they continue to be contested. The 'losers' from the first round of contestation do not go away, and actors who are not part of the 'design coalition' may find ways to occupy and redeploy institutions not of their own making. Finally, over time, space opens up further to enable 'reinterpretations that are very far from the intent of the designers, who may be long gone' (Thelen, 2009: 491–2).

Over decades, a multitude of actors, many of whom are not aware of each others' existence, contribute to the formation of institutions over which they, at best, have only fleeting control. Within these parameters, however, Thelen's actors are less constrained than those we have already considered in this section, because their rational intent produces a form of collective voluntarism in which group actors appear to be able to implement strategies and take opportunities without hindrance. Where Schneiberg and Lounsbury emphasize iteration, Thelen stresses aggregation. Gradual institutional change arises out of the accumulation over time of moves towards satisfying group interests, although such moves are varied and complex, able to subvert as well as reproduce dominant paths, and occur over the long *duree* rather than only at moments of externally generated crisis. In Figure 5.1, we place Thelen's work at D3, close to both the agency end of the vertical axis and the incremental end of the horizontal axis.

Understanding change: institutions, actors and environments

Our review reveals considerable movement beyond second phase institutionalism's preoccupation with stop–go models of change driven by periodic external shocks. While positions vary according to the continua represented by the axes of Figure 5.1, for us there are three key conclusions:

- change can be stimulated by endogenous as well as exogenous forces;
- gradual change can have transformative effects; and
- both institutional stability and institutional change are the product of human agency.

Such conclusions ensure that, for third phase institutionalists, change is no longer a problematic adjunct to the main business of explaining how institutions shape political behaviour and structure political outcomes. Change and stability must be understood simultaneously, not separately. Both change and stability are actively constructed out of the ongoing interaction of actors, existing institutional constraints, and contextual challenges. We are reminded of March and Olsen's (1989: 16) seminal description of institutions as 'creating and sustaining islands of imperfect and temporary organization in potentially inchoate political worlds'. Stability has to be constantly worked at, as individual and collective agents *act out* rules, practices and narratives. Sustaining stability requires constant adjustment on the part of actors, who assign cases to rules and also bend rules to fit cases. Change may emerge slowly over time out of the aggregation of such adjustments. Or it may come suddenly when cases are novel enough to offer a funda-mental challenge to existing rules, practices and narratives (that is, they cannot be accommodated within existing institutional arrangements), or where actors mobilize purposefully to change or resist existing insti-tutional constraints, talking advantage of gaps and contradictions in the institutional fabric. The acting-out of institutions may be inter-rupted by decisive action on the part of rule takers, rule makers or rule enforcers. Institutions both constrain the efforts of change agents and are the target of them. Whether the trigger to change is classified as internal or external depends on how the boundary between 'institu-tion' and 'environment' is understood. As we saw above, actors may expand their institutional repertoire through 'borrowing' and 'sharing' across political space (different 'action arenas' in Ostrom's terms), or through 'remembering' across political time (reactivating 'paths not taken').

From here we argue that any credible analysis of institutional change must examine three factors – institutions, actors and environ-ments – and, of course, their interaction. We call this theoretical and methodological orientation 'Politics – the Movie', because we believe it produces an analysis of the three factors in a way which captures the rich temporal and spatial characteristics of political drama and is informed by a particularly institutionalist approach to agency. We can explore the implications of such an analysis through two related case studies that focus on President Obama's first term of office.

As we saw in Chapter 1, the Obama presidency succeeded in pushing through health-care reforms in the face of ferocious opposition from the Republican Party and interest groups outside Congress. While we must acknowledge that this change was hard won and remains fragile, we also need to bear in mind that the succession of these reforms to law contradicts the predications of many (including some institutionalists) who have convincingly argued that the USA's dependence on institutions shaped by private health-care provision would not allow for state intervention of this sort, and, if anything, would pull welfare policy in the opposite direction (e.g. Hacker, 2004). The case gives us some insight, therefore, into the circumstances under which actors can cut against established path dependence, but reminds us that the personal and political costs of doing so are likely to be high, and the losers from that round of contestation lie in wait for an opportunity to stage a policy reversal. Above all, we show how what Obama can achieve at this particular time is facilitated and constrained by the institutional configurations at his disposal, and by the positive and negative influences of institutions and actors in the wider political environment.

The second example of institutional change is in the reshaping of the institutional configuration of the American right, through the emergence of the Tea Party as a faction which is heavily critical of US politicians en bloc, and succeeds in pulling the Republican Party, in particular, towards its low-tax, low-spend orientation (see Box 5.1). Here our 'Politics – the Movie' approach shows us that the potency of the Tea Party narrative lies not so much in it being perceived as 'new', but more in its appeal to deeply embedded values and folk memories which can be traced to the American War of Independence – and in fact to 'old virtue'. In tracing the Tea Party's impacts on US politics forward from 2008, we also illustrate in true dramatic style how the faction's interventions not only severely constrain the Democrats' capacity to progress economic policy, but also weaken the credibility of the Republican Party and its capacity to find an outstanding candidate to take on Obama in the 2012 general election. Because, while the Tea Party were not strong enough to force their preferred choice on the GOP (Grand Old Party), they were powerful enough to make sure that the more socially liberal candidates, such as John Huntsman and Newt Gingrich were eliminated in the early stages of the primaries. Furthermore, the candidate who eventually won the nomination, Mitt

Box 5.1   Agency and institutional change: Obama and the Tea Party

In the US elections of November 2008 the Democratic Party led by Barack Obama won a clear victory over their Republican opponents in voting for both houses of Congress. The party captured six Senate seats from their rivals, increasing their majority in the 100-seat chamber, and made further gains in the House of Representatives, easily exceeding the 218 seats needed for a majority. The victory was attributed by political analysts to the Democrats' capacity to massively outspend their opponents in their campaign activities, a huge registration drive to bring out the latent Democratic vote, Obama's personal appeal as an anti-Bush candidate, and his ability to build support from white and black voters, as well as Hispanic and Jewish voters who had previously voted Republican.

However, the first two years of Obama's presidency were marked by resignations from his administration, a sluggish economy, and a sharp decline in the President's approval ratings amongst American voters. Despite majorities in both houses, the administration found it difficult to enact its programme, but in early 2010 Obama finally pushed through his health-care reforms against ferocious opposition from the Republican Party. He justified state intervention and the spending of tax dollars on health care on the grounds that the rules and practices of the private health-care companies were unjust in their exclusion of many thousands of poorer members of US society (see Chapter 1, Box 1.2).

Following their defeat in 2008, the attempts of the Republican Party to regroup were both helped and hindered by an emerging faction known as the Tea Party. Recalling the resistance of the early American colonists who threw taxed British tea into Boston harbour, the Tea Party was founded on a groundswell of populist anger over government bail-outs of failing banks, insurers and auto companies following the economic meltdown of 2008. Campaigning under the early settlers' slogan of 'no taxation without representation', the Tea Party helped the Republican effort by presenting Obama's health-care reforms as an invasion of the state into the lives of ordinary Americans, and the Democrat administration as profligate, wasting extra tax dollars at a time when ordinary people were already

→

Romney, was forced to 'woo' the Tea Party with speeches in which he accused Obama of presiding over a kind of economic civil war that pits rich against poor, thereby reinforcing the Tea Party's narrative of the President as 'a dangerous Marxist'.

Institutions and institutional change

It seems to us axiomatic that institutions themselves should be at the centre of any explanation of institutional dynamics, and, indeed, this is suffering economic hardship. The Tea Party hindered the Republicans insofar as they expressed 'a vociferous anger' against all members of Congress and the Senate, directly opposing some Republican candidates in the run-up to the mid-term elections, and repelling some voters with their deeply conservative views.

In the mid-term elections of 2010, the Republican Party regained their majority in the House of Representatives, winning over fifty seats from the Democrats. However, the Democrats narrowly retained control of the Senate, despite losing six seats, including some to candidates backed by the Tea Party. The Democrat loses were attributed to stay-at-home voters who were disillusioned with the economic and jobs situation in the US, and to the Tea Party's capacity to mobilize 'angry' voters against 'Obama's Big Government'.

The second half of Obama's presidency was characterized by stalemate in key areas of economic policy. Threats and inducements by the Democrat administration failed to move a Republican grouping which had made pledges over reducing big government and protecting tax cuts for the better off, and was 'locked into' the Tea Party narrative in this respect. In late 2011, the US's credit rating was downgraded for the first time ever; a Democrat/Republican 'super-committee' failed to find a way to reduce the government's $15bn debt, concluding with accusations of bad faith from both sides. One of the sticking points in the negotiations focused on Republican attempts to reverse Obama's health-care reforms. Although Obama and the Democrat Party continued to be seen as weak during this period by voters, the credibility and effectiveness of the Republican Party were also affected by its incorporation of the Tea Party. Battles within the Grand Old Party between the socially liberal and socially conservative factions led to the elimination early on in the presidential primaries of preferred candidates of both persuasions. The Republican Party finally nominated Mitt Romney, a businessman and Mormon by faith, to run against Obama in 2012, after what was seen by many in the party as the most brutal and abrasive campaign for several decades. Romney sought to appeal to Tea Party voters by criticizing Obama's plan to raise taxes on the super-rich as a kind of economic war intended to pit poor Americans against their more successful compatriots.

the case in most of theorizations we reviewed in the section above. For example, in Quadrant A, Scott (2001) focuses on changes in institutional logics and Pierson (2004) argues that institutional change can only be understood in terms of institutional stability. In Quadrant C, Schickler (2001) focuses on change to institutions as rules, practices and roles. In Quadrant D, Thelen (2009) stresses the dynamic qualities in the interpretation, enforcement and enactment of institutions. Nevertheless, it is less clear that the fledging discursive or constructivist institutionalism accepts our proposition. For Schmidt (2009),

Hay (2006a) and Blyth (2002a), the focus is on ideational change with institutions relegated to mere context. Ideas are treated as external to, and prior to, institutions and as the key driver for change. Despite the couplet 'discursive institutionalism', institutions appear to be empty vessels into which ideas can be poured, rather than exercising any constraining effect upon the adoption of ideas or the subsequent shaping of behaviour.

Our tripartite conceptualization of institutional constraint (Chapter 3) – as operating through rules, practices and narratives – not only provides a helpful schema for understanding the nature of institutions themselves, but also our 'Politics – the Movie' approach to explaining how they change. Institutions are, essentially, configurations of rules, practices and narratives, which are interconnected in a variety of ways. These different modes of constraint may combine to produce institutional stability over time; but it is also possible for gaps and contradictions to open up, creating instability – and possibilities for change. Rules, practices and narratives may reinforce one another (the 'over-determination' of relatively stable institutions) or abrade and undermine each other. If we think about the banking crisis in the UK (see Box 1.1, p. 7), customers still abide by the formal rules of financial institutions (managing their bank accounts, loans and savings plans) but the narratives that used to reinforce institutional constraint (about the reliability and trustworthiness of the banking system) have weakened to the point that they no longer reinforce these rules and, indeed, start to make space for the evolution of alternative practices (buying gold or property or accessing the stock market independently). Creative spaces open up (for better or worse) when the 'fit' between different elements of an institutional configuration weakens. Indeed, change strategies may focus upon just this – how to undermine existing narratives, or model new practices, as a precursor to changing formal rules. Further complexity arises from the fact that institutional configurations outside the political domain also act to shape the behaviour of political actors – the sexual division of labour continues to affect assumptions about men's and women's roles, for instance, despite the outlawing of discrimination via formal rules.

With regard to our case studies, the different forms of institutional constraint and empowerment constitute powerful forces in shaping the unfolding political drama. The opposing sides draw upon institutionalized accounts of how the relationship between the US state and the individual citizen has developed over centuries, relationships that are enacted in practices which demonstrate how public and private bodies do, and should, treat the individual citizen. In relation to rules, the central arguments are about how far the state should legislate to provide for its citizens, what these rules should be, and whether the use of state funds can be justified to implement them.

In pushing through his health-care legislation, Obama evokes the US government's historic and current responsibilities to treat all its citizens equally, and then creates a tension between this normative institution and the practices of the private health-care companies and the rules which allow them to exclude the poor. At the same time, however, he exposes interconnections between his argument about the state's responsibility to intervene and a much more powerful institutional configuration which is rooted in the origins of country itself. For the narratives, practices, and rules associated with the Founding Fathers are clustered together specifically to protect the citizen from state intervention, and are much more securely interconnected in the minds of much of the American polity than Obama's conflicting configuration.

Hence, the ideas brought into the arena by the Tea Party after 2008 are not in any way 'new', or separate from existing institutions. In fact, they are, in every way, institutional, in that they derive their power from the fact that Americans are keenly aware that these ideas are deeply embedded in their constitution, and their shared understandings of 'the American Way', as freedom from constraint in any form. When Obama and the Democrats win their victory in Congress over health care in early 2010, the lack of fit between their approach and the American Way is highly visible, and offers a potent line of attack for their opponents in the run up to the mid-term elections.

In the second half of the presidency, Obama and the Democrat Party generally continue to be constrained by a powerful configuration of rules, practices and narratives which the Republicans are able to exploit to demand concessions from the President. The most notable of these is found in the restoration of the Republican majority in the House of Representatives which gives the party the opportunity to introduce legislation to attempt to overturn Obama's health-care reforms. In terms of practices, it is clear that the logic of appropriateness in such circumstances demands not only 'behind the scenes' attempts to broker compromise in the national interest, but also the setting up of an ad hoc structure, the 'super-committee', to fortify these efforts. However, both sides are so securely bound into their narrative positions that the conflictual approach sponsored by the Tea Party faction in the Republication Party prevails and as a consequence the stalemate over economic policy continues.

Actors and institutional change

Although they exert a powerful influence on actors and are central to any theorization, institutions remain dependent on actors for their maintenance, defence, revision and rediscovery (Streek, 2001: 31). As we have repeatedly noted, institutions are revealed through the action of individuals, shaping relatively stable patterns of behaviour. They are effective only insofar as they are acted out by individuals, and enforced by 'third parties'. An 'institutionalist conception of agency' may sound like an oxymoron, but it is at the heart of the project of third phase institutionalism, and of particular significance in seeking to understand change (and resistance). It is not helpful for institutionalists simply to 'add agency and stir'. To state that agency must be taken into account alongside institutions is simply to re-describe the contested terrain of social science. Our 'Politics – the Movie' perspective must include a distinctive perspective on agency. To this end, in Chapter 4 we developed our 5Cs conception of agency – as collective, combative, cumulative, combinative, and, ultimately, constrained. We are now in a position to say more about the 5Cs, and about the tension between actors and institutions in relation to institutional change.

Considering Figure 5.1, agency is viewed as collective and combative by all the third phase theorists we discuss. There is a clear tendency to see coalition building as a prerequisite for actors seeking to promote institutional change. The oscillatory rhythm which typifies the consequent struggle for ascendency between opposing parties is most vivid in Schneiberg and Schickler's work, but is also present to varying degrees in Thelen, Pierson and Scott. The notion of combat denotes protagonists who, while constrained by the rules of the game, also seek to use them strategically to protect (or extend) their influence, in opposition to the other strategic actors. In Quadrant D, particularly, there is a strong affective dimension in the motivation for institutional change; combat is often between those who see themselves as the 'losers from the first round' and those who gained the advantage. In this context, both sides are constrained not only by the institutional environment in which they operate, but also by the direct action of opponents who often feel aggrieved about the impacts of a previous round of change. But not all agency is collective. Lowndes, Schickler and Blyth each find room for individual actors who work across the boundaries of political space and, in doing so, shift from being outsiders to become insiders, and back again. But such individual actors are essentially mobilizers and 'reticulists', who seek to bring actors together to launch sorties for institutional change.

As we explained in Chapter 3, the concept of cumulative agency differs from that of collective agency in that the former does not necessarily imply any conscious attempt to cooperate on the part of the various actors who contribute to the process of institutional change. In Quadrant C, Schickler draws our attention to the fact that the institutional configurations which are currently apparent in political assemblies are the haphazard creations of many different legislators, separated not only by party allegiance, but also by significant periods of time. Even more vividly, in Quadrant D, Thelen (2009: 477) explains how 'institutions created for one set of purposes and resting on the shoulders of one set of actors could be carried forward on the shoulders of another coalition altogether'. Such actors may not have any knowledge of, or contact with, one another; and, if they did, might not be inclined to cooperation.

The work plotted in Figure 5.1 produces several different insights into combinative agency in institutional change. Thelen, as above, suggests this might involve hijacking the opposition's institutions to use for one's own purpose, but also argues that combination involves knowingly building in ambiguities in the design and enactment of institutions so as to disguise potential conflicts within coalitions (see also Mahoney and Thelen, 2010). Also in Quadrant D, Schneiberg argues institutional change involves actors recombining new elements with prevailing models, myths or concerns. And, for Schickler in Quadrant C, the creation of the 'common carrier' is the process by which coalitions come together around multiple competing interests. Lowndes reminds us that processes of combinative agency may involve actors from adjacent 'action arenas', thus questioning the ease with which we can meaningfully describe particular actors as being located inside or outside a particular political space (see also Crouch, 2005: 24).

Unsurprisingly, work located in Quadrant A ponders specifically the notion of constraint upon agency in securing institutional change. The weight of institutional processes as they are theorized in Pierson (2004), for example, might leave us wondering how recognizable institutional change is ever achieved. However, within Figure 5.1, the overall tendency was to seek to balance structure and agency, by theorizing high levels of agency for change which are met both by institutional 'stickiness' and high levels of agency expressed as opposition. Indeed, from an engaged perspective, the maintenance of such a balance is not just a theoretical question. On the one hand, a higher agency-to-structure balance reveals more opportunities for less powerful actors to shape the context in which they pursue their strategic intent. On the other hand, if this tendency is taken too far, then we fall into over-optimistic pluralist assumptions of a level playing field in which the victims of structured inequalities are to blame for their failure to impose themselves upon their environment. The trick for third phase institutionalism is to hold together in the same analytical space 'the strategic actions and interactions of purposeful and resourceful individual and corporate actors' and 'the enabling, constraining, and shaping effects of given (but variable) institutional structures and institutionalized forms' (Scharpf, 1997). Agency is constrained by, but constitutive of, institutions. We need to understand agency 'in and against' institutions. Institutional change occurs when the balance between constraint and creativity shifts in favour of the latter.

We can put the 5Cs to good use in our case studies. The emergence of the Tea Party provides a good example of how collective action involves coalition building. In this case, a core of white, largely male voters, who tend to be in their late forties and above, has been able to network and organize its activities across the United States, while drawing in citizens from other demographic profiles, who feel disenfranchised by 'Big Government' and 'taxation without representation'. Their agency is fiercely combative in the sense of transmitting both an anti-elitist and anti-statist message, which views both political parties as corrupt and 'part of the system'. Their anger and sense of grievance are focused on Obama who they disparage as a 'socialist', because of policies like his health-care reforms, but their preferred option is to 'throw out' *all* members of Congress and replace them with 'ordinary Americans'.

As we have seen, their combinative agency is distinctively institutional in that they have been able to pull to the surface ('remember') institutions from the eighteenth century which are deeply embedded in both the formal precepts and the shared narratives of the American Constitution and the day-to-day practices of American life. Rehabilitating the name, 'Tea Party', is particularly evocative in this context, and they have been able to combine these institutional legacies with modern-day normative accounts of the need for fiscal responsibility, limited government and free markets. As Pierson and Thelen, amongst others, point out, the cumulative nature of agency usually takes some time to produce outcomes, but we can already glimpse some contingent effects of agency pushing to the surface. In particular, the Tea Party's attacks on Republicans, as well as Democrats, may have cost the Republicans a larger majority in the House of Representatives and a chance to regain the Senate as well, producing an unintended cumulative effect in terms of resisting the resurgence of that party in tandem with the efforts of the Democrats.

Finally, the apparent lack of constraints on the agency of Tea Party activists in the first half of the Obama presidency gives us some insights into how movements such as these become empowered. For the Tea Party's initial success seems to be based on its ability to locate the movement, at least temporarily, outside normal political time and space. In terms of time, as we have seen, the Tea Party has reactivated an institutional configuration which appears to express 'timeless' truths, deemed to be self-evident and therefore uncontestable. In terms of political space, by attacking both main parties, the Tea Party has placed itself outside the formal arena of the Congress and thus able to present Democrats and Republicans alike as self-interested and corrupt. The Tea Party's own recourse to highly normative accounts of how things *should be* provides a striking contrast, inviting audiences to draw the conclusion that this a politics based purely on values.

However, from the mid-term elections onwards, the Tea Party has accepted that it cannot work indefinitely outside the mainstream of politics and needs the Republication Party and its institutional configuration as a larger vehicle within which to progress its more conservative policies. Hence the Tea Party candidates for the 2012 presidency were launched under the Republican Party banner but because of their extreme views were rejected by mainstream Republican voters early on in the primaries. However, during the same period, the Tea Party's narrative was strong enough to force out of the running socially liberal candidates such as Gingrich and Huntsman, and force the eventual winner of the nomination, Romney, to make considerable concessions to their normative stance.

Environments and institutional change

Returning to Figure 5.1, the approaches on the right hand side (Quadrants B and C) rely most strongly on established concepts of path dependence and punctuated equilibrium. Blyth produces a coalitional model of change which is principally driven by externally generated ideas. In a similar vein, Sabatier argues that, for all the infighting between coalitions, only external shock can change core beliefs. In their different ways, therefore, these theorizations are based on the evolutionary metaphor where rapid and intense moments of transformation are characteristic of institutional change. On the left hand side of Figure 5.1, Pierson follows the Spencerian, rather than the neo-Darwinian, path, and conceptualizes change as dependent on the capacity of actors to exploit the slow emergence of cracks in a dense institutional fabric. A third approach is evident in the work of Schneiberg and Schickler, and to a large extent in Thelen and Scott. Here, the emphasis is not so much on how institutions and actors respond to changes around them, but more on how the struggle for ascendency between groups of actors leads to intended and unintended changes in institutional processes and effects.

Of course it is possible to construct more complex evolutionary models in which some change is incremental, some rapid, and some created through internal conflict between competing 'populations' of institutions and actors. But this prospect leads us to question whether the evolutionary metaphor itself has run its course as a heuristic for politics, based as it is on the desire to explain the emergence of organisms over hundreds of thousands of years. This is not to say that what happens in the environment surrounding institutions is unimportant. Nor is it to deny that some change happens slowly, almost imperceptibly, and some is sharp and disruptive. Rather it is to suggest that each of these propositions requires some scrutiny in the light of our review of the latest work on institutional change.

For it seems to us that rather than invent new or more complicated metaphors for institutional change, it may be more productive to start from a constructivist perspective which sees politics, as we have defined it from Hay (2002), as an uniquely human activity. Such an approach places institutions and actors at the centre of both institutional stability and change, and explains fast, slow and conflict-based dynamics as products of the tensions between actors and institutions. From this perspective, how can we better conceptualize 'the environment' so that it more than a portmanteau term for anything outside the immediate political space?

From an institutionalist perspective, the environment is best conceptualized as a dense matrix of other institutions which are shaped by, and shape the conduct of, other groups of actors. In this way if we wish to locate the source of particular changes in slow shifts in 'the environment' then we need to trace these back to institutions and actors who are interconnected with the institutions which are at the centre of the change. Similarly if we wish to argue that an 'external' crisis or a shock is the cause of change, we need to show how such a disruption was constructed by interconnected actors and institutions and how this was transferred to the institutions and actors in question. In this way a crisis cannot be viewed as an 'event' independent of actors and institutions and contained in a brief time capsule. Rather it is the product of the interconnections between actors and institutions which may go back some time in history. Equally as Thelen (2004) demonstrates, changes, which are only now apparent in institutions, have their origins in an accumulation of effects which have matured over several decades. In both a temporal and a spatial sense, the boundary between an institution and its environment is a constructed one.

What is 'inside' and what is 'outside' is also likely to be contested. Women Parliamentarians, for instance, have contested established understandings of 'work–life balance'; government contracts with business have brought with them frequent disputes about how close or distant the parties and their practices should be; and federal systems typically involve ongoing renegotiation of the respective powers and responsibilities of constituent units. The timelines that 'matter' are also subject to contest, as 'foundational moments' and key decision points are argued over. The environment does not 'do things' to institutions. The transmission of effects between institutions across political space and time can only take place through chains of human action and interaction. As Colin Crouch (2005: 24) explains, by focusing on 'networks of structured relationships' between actors in overlapping institutional domains, we start to 'break down the rigid dichotomy between endogeneity and exogeneity as sources of actors' responses'. These are issues we return to in Chapter 6.

When we apply this sort of approach to our case study, the benefits are apparent. For if we deploy a theorization, which relies on the concepts of punctuation or shock, then the arrival of the Tea Party on the scene in 1998 can be viewed as a critical juncture in US politics in which a new set of ideas disrupts the Obama presidency and foreshadows significant institutional change. From this perspective, the causes for this coalition's ascendency can be located in immediate factors such as the impact of poor economic growth on the American middle class, and the timing of Obama's legislation on health care. This analysis is useful as far as it goes, but, as Pierson (2004) suggests, offers us the snapshot rather than 'Politics – the Movie'.

As we have argued above, to understand any significant institutional change we need a wider lens in terms of political space, and a longer view in terms of political time. In respect of the long view, while many of the actors involved in the coalition may be 'new' in the sense that they are new to politics, the rules, practices and narratives with which they are connected go back at least as far as the American War of Independence, and can be traced through the fears of many after the

American Civil War that the North would impose totalitarian rule on the South. From here a 'principled anti-government radicalism' (Dionne, 2010) became the motive force behind a number of similar political movements in the twentieth century. Drum (2010) goes so far as to argue:

> It is what happens whenever a Democrat takes over the White House. When FDR was in office in the 1930s, conservative zealotry coalesced in the Liberty League. When JFK won the presidency in the '60s, the John Birch Society flourished. When Bill Clinton ended the Reagan Revolution in the '90s, talk radio erupted with the conspiracy theories of the Arkansas Project.

In the longer view, therefore, the Tea Party and its institutions are explained as part of a continuing struggle between groups in the US who have always opposed government from the centre, and those who favour 'a centralized government revolving around a forceful, moralistic presidency' (Morris, 2010).

This approach helps explain why anger is a central feature of the Tea Party narrative and why members feel a more deep-seated sense of dispossession than might be justified by Obama's relatively moderate health-care reforms and modest stimulation package for the economy. Most of all, it suggests that the Tea Party carries forward a set of institutions which are deeply embedded in US politics, have a highly affective and normative texture, and will not go away. In terms of political space, it focuses our attention on the interconnections between the Tea Party and the Republican Party, and how their respective institutional configurations fit together, or abrade against one another. Hence from its emergence there were clear indications that the Tea Party both helps and hinders its host, with the negative aspects of this relationship becoming more apparent as the Obama presidency reached the end of its first term, and Republicans struggled to find a candidate who satisfies both institutional configurations.

Conclusion

This chapter has challenged the idea that institutionalism is neither interested in, nor adept at, theorizing change. It has challenged too the idea that theoretical leverage is to be gained from a sectarian contest between 'schools of institutionalism'. Our analysis demonstrates that each of the main schools is grappling with similar insights, and enduring puzzles. We have identified the key variables in research on institutional change, specifically relating to the tempo of change and the balance between structure and agency. Research has moved way beyond the preoccupation of second phase institutionalism with stop–go models driven by periodic external shocks. We conclude that institutional change can be stimulated by endogenous as well as exogenous forces, gradual change can have transformative effects, and both institutional stability and institutional change are products of human agency.

Moreover, understanding change requires that we focus upon the interaction between institutions, actors and environments. With our cinematic metaphor, we have sought to capture the rich temporal and spatial characteristics of political drama by putting institutions first – metaphorically 'setting the stage'. Only then can we bring on the actors who are empowered and constrained in very specific ways by their institutional setting. Finally, we pan across that landscape for the institutions and actors outside the immediate focus of the camera which are producing intended and unintended impacts on the possibilities for action and the eventual conclusion to the movie. And, when the sequel follows, the storyline of 'Politics – the Movie 2' is unmistakably shaped by the institutional legacies of what came before.

Chapter 6

Institutional Diversity

Why do we see such a variety of political institutions, even within democratic systems? Might we not expect that institutions would converge on forms that fitted particular purposes? Indeed, the functionalist tendencies of first phase institutionalism produced an expectation that similar forms could flourish in quite different contexts – for instance, the assumption that newly independent colonies could replicate elements of the 'Westminster model' or French republicanism. Such expectations are reproduced today in many transnational policy programmes on 'good governance', 'democratization' and 'state building'. Second phase institutionalism was also dominated by reproductive theories: in their sociological form, they saw institutions as converging in form in response to dominant templates within the environment; in rational choice interpretations, convergence was seen to arise out of rational design processes aimed at solving problems of complex exchange.

Whether through mimicry or intent, the assumption was that institutions would become more similar to one another over time. In contrast, third phase institutionalism is characterized not by reproductive but by *generative* theories, which see political institutions as context-specific, and deeply contingent, phenomena. Enduring institutional diversity is to be expected. Institutionalists have been criticized for retreating into an 'anything is possible' position that over-emphasizes contingency (Jordan, 1990). But, in this chapter, we seek to show that such a criticism is unfair because third phase institutionalism is able to identify the specific factors that are implicated in this diversity: time, space, agency and power. As we saw in the last chapter, third phase research shows how actors adapt rules, practices and narratives over time as they seek to match endlessly varied cases to existing institutional frameworks, leading institutions to develop and combine in novel ways. At the same time, political institutions are embedded within environments made up of other institutions and this too is a source of variety. Actors moving between spaces borrow and share institutional prescriptions. The variety of forms taken in different places by superficially similar political institutions is quite striking, as they co-evolve with institutions in other social and economic domains. The diverse form taken by institutions is also the outcome of political contestation, given that any set of rules and practices distributes power and advantage in particular ways and is likely to be challenged by oppositional actors. Third phase institutionalists do not just 'bring the actor' back in, they bring back actors with real human heads and hearts, who engage critically and strategically with institutions rather than simply playing pre-assigned roles. As we will see in Chapter 7, research on institutional design increasingly sees the impetus to institutional variation (and ambiguity) as a resource rather than an obstacle for programmes for reform.

Using a series of illustrative vignettes, the chapter starts by reviewing the shifting emphasis from similarity to diversity within different schools of institutionalism. We go on to show how the boundary-spanning scholars of third phase institutionalism are focusing on the mix between similarity and diversity, rather than one or the other, and how this is illuminating the debate on stability and change. In considering spatial and temporal dynamics, we argue for the need to move beyond binary oppositions. We show that the boundaries between old and new institutions and between institutional 'insides' and 'outsides' are inevitably blurred, and that this blurring may be exploited strategically by political actors seeking to form and hold together coalitions for either maintaining or challenging the status quo.

What makes institutions similar?

As we showed in the early chapters of the book, new institutionalists of all hues define institutions in relation to the regularized patterns of behaviour that they shape. Indeed, such a definition marks a break with old institutionalist definitions that refer simply to formal structures or organizations. As with the linked concept of stability, there is a presumption towards similarity within institutionalism, although the understanding of what drives this has differed between sociological and rational choice schools. Building on earlier work (Lowndes, 1996), we present a series of vignettes based upon theorizations of institutional similarity. The dictionary defines a vignette as an 'illustration not in definite border', a 'character sketch' or a 'short description'. The term captures our aim here: each short account exposes a particular aspect of institutional life; it is not a definitive statement; and the borders of one vignette blur with those of another. These images allow us to compare the different perspectives present in the literature, and to identify the direction of travel within institutionalism.

The mythic institution

Sociological institutionalists, rooting their work in organization theory, highlight processes of 'institutionalization' whereby 'mythic' or 'symbolic' elements of an organization's environment are incorporated into its structures, cultures and outputs (Scott, 2001: 181). Such elements form 'templates' for organizing and derive from professions, educational and training programmes, legal and public policy frameworks, public opinion and prevalent ideologies. Compliance with taken-for-granted beliefs about how best to organize, and towards what ends, become more important than the actual efficacy of dominant structures and practices (DiMaggio and Powell, 1991a: 28; Meyer and Rowan, 1977). Institutions are dominated by a sense of 'this is how things are done'; in institutional life, 'the moral becomes the factual' (Zucker, 1991: 83). Organizations' shape and style reflect the 'myths' of the institutional environment (e.g. around human relationships, and financial or marketing practices), instead of the demands of specific work activities. The power of 'institutional environments' lies in their capacity to confer legitimacy, which is linked to organizations' survival prospects. By adapting to cultural expectations, organizations are better able to recruit staff, gain funding from governments or credit from banks, build alliances with other organizations, and market their products to consumers. The power of 'institutional myths' is such that increasing homogenization (or 'isomorphism' – see Chapter 5) is evident among populations of organizations. The demand for similarity of structure and functioning, rather than for increased efficiency, drives organizational change (DiMaggio and Powell, 1991b: 63–6). Zucker (1991: 105) calls this the 'contagion of legitimacy'.

The efficient institution

Institutional form has also been explained with reference to a universal economic logic. Institutions are 'efficient' frameworks, which arise to solve problems of complex economic exchange. Such a formulation produces convergence on a limited range of institutional options, as illustrated by Williamson's classic work (1985) on 'markets and hier-archies'. Williamson asks under what conditions economic functions are performed within the boundaries of a firm, rather than through market processes which cross firm boundaries. He proposes that transactions which are uncertain in outcome, recur frequently and require 'transaction-specific investments' (i.e. time, money or energy which cannot easily be transferred to other types of interaction) are more likely to take place within firms. The institution of the firm allows association between transacting agents to be secured through hierarchical authority rather than market exchange. Such arrange-ments are more efficient for transactions which are characterized by bounded rationality (difficulty in anticipating and specifying all contingencies) and by opportunism (the possibility for one party to pursue its interests by guile or deceit). By internalizing this type of transaction, there is no need to anticipate and weight all contingen-cies, and the possibility of opportunism is reduced through authority relations and closer identification between (internal) transacting partners. At the same time, exchange in the open market remains the most efficient institutional arrangement for transactions which are straightforward, non-repetitive and require no transaction-specific investments (such as a one-off purchase of standard equipment). Put most simply, the approach sees the main purpose and effect of insti-tutions as economizing on transaction costs (Williamson, 1985: 1). As Coase (1937: 404) put it much earlier: 'The question always is, will it pay to bring an extra exchange transaction under the organiz-ing authority?'

The predictable institution

North's (1990) analysis of institutional similarity contains elements of both an 'efficiency' and a 'mythic' approach. Using rational choice assumptions like Williamson, North sees institutions as incentive struc-tures which impact on individuals' utility-maximizing behaviour. However, he stresses predictability rather than efficiency as the rationale for institutional similarity. Like the organization theorists reviewed earlier, North attributes the stability of institutions to their basis in culture and tradition. North sees institutions as arising to cope with problems of bounded rationality, thus reducing uncertainties in human interaction. While institutions are one determinant of transaction costs, their existence need not reduce costs. In contrast to his early work (North and Thomas, 1973), North is at pains to stress that institutions reduce uncertainty by providing a predictable, *but not necessarily efficient,* framework for human interaction. Technically inefficient institutions persist because they contribute to predictability and harmony in interaction and because they are deeply embedded in culture and tradition. North argues that the most powerful institutional constraints are informal (codes of conduct and norms of behaviour), which allow actors to express their values and ideologies at little or no cost. Because they have become part of expected behaviour, these subjective variables do not jeopardize exchange relationships – despite their departure from 'rational' premises. The mix of formal and informal institutional rules determines the 'opportunity set' that actors face in making choices. It is the tenacity of informal constraints that produces institutional predictability.

The manipulated institution

Williamson and North see economic institutions as developing to ease problems of exchange, through maximizing efficiency and/or predictability. In contrast, political institutions may be viewed by rational choice scholars as *obstacles* to effective exchange. Pursuing assumptions of utility maximization, they predict a generic process of 'institutional entropy' in the political arena. Manipulated by utility-maximizing politicians and bureaucrats, institutions degenerate over time; they come to serve the individual, private interests of officials and any conception of the public interest is lost (Dunleavy and O'Leary, 1987: 112–13). The most well-known claim about the maximizing behaviour of public officials is that they seek to augment their status and material well-being through increases to budgets under their control, producing a convergence towards bureaucratic expansion and 'mission creep'. At the same time, utility-seeking politicians attempt to maximize votes by promising benefits and service enhancements. Together these manipulations result in waste and 'over-supply' of government goods and services (Niskanen, 1971, 1973). An alternative to the budget-maximizing thesis is provided by bureau-shaping theory which accepts that bureaucrats are self-serving, but proposes that bigger budgets do not always serve their utilities. Rather, Dunleavy argues that senior bureaucrats have strong preferences about the kind of work they do and the kind of organization they work in. Institutional manipulation leads to a different sort of convergence – towards the splitting off of routine operational functions from strategic cores where work is less routine and less visible, and subject to greater discretion and status. Dunleavy (1991: 247–8) claims empirical justification for his theory on the basis that British senior civil servants have not only cooperated with, but promoted, reforms which reduced their management of large budgets through the separation of 'executive agencies' from wider departments.

The globalized institution

While rational choice-inspired accounts see institutional convergence arising out of the fundamentally similar motivations of individual actors, there is another type of theory which sees institutional similarity as arising in response to macro-level structural forces. Theories of globalization point not only to the transfer of policy making responsibilities from national governments to international organizations (like the World Trade Organization or the European Union), but also to the increased similarity of domestic institutions as their scope for autonomy is reduced. In contrast to the 'mythic institution', it is an economic rather than a cultural contagion that drives convergence, and the forces at work are international rather than organization or society-specific. Countries in the Eurozone, for instance, are supposed to pursue the same type of fiscal and monetary policy, regulated and supervised by European-wide institutions like the European Central Bank. The post-2010 Eurozone crisis is linked to the breaking (or at least bending) of rules by countries like Greece, Spain and Italy, and further integration of economic and political institutions is the favoured way forward. 'Hyper-globalists' argue that it is world markets rather any international political institution that actually dictates the shape and direction of nation states (Ohmae, 1995). The success of globalization, it is argued, is predicated upon nation states adopting a domestic institutional formula characterized by reduced welfare spending, lighter business regulation, weaker trade unions, open borders and flexible economies (Heywood, 2011: 11). Opponents of such 'neo-liberalization' concur that such homogenization is occurring, but point instead to its social and environmental costs (Held and Kaya, 2006). While often having a humanitarian and social democratic inflection, global campaigns for 'good governance' can serve to reinforce such institutional convergence, especially when linked to economic liberalization (as in the World Bank's 'structural adjustment' programmes for developing countries) or backed-up by the threat of force (as in agendas for 'regime change' in counties deemed hostile by leading powers).

What makes institutions different?

Accounts of reproduction and convergence have come in for a lot of criticism from third phase institutionalists. Borrowing across different schools of institutionalism, their starting point is an empirical observation of the continuing extent of institutional diversity, despite the top-down pressures of globalization or the bottom-up demands of utility-maximizing actors. Providing examples not just from politics but from shopping, work, sport and leisure, Elinor Ostrom (2005: 4–5) sets out the challenge in her book *Institutional Diversity*:

> A major problem in understanding institutions relates to the diversity of situations in contemporary life. As we go about our everyday life, we interact in a wide diversity of complex situations... Our implicit knowledge of the expected do's and don'ts in this variety of situations is extensive. Frequently, we are not even conscious of all of the rules, norms, and strategies we follow. Nor have the social sciences developed adequate theoretical tools to help us translate our implicit knowledge into a consistent explicit theory of complex human behaviour.

As we noted in Chapter 1, the 'new institutionalism' in political science has been challenged to develop new theoretical tools by the proliferation of *new institutions* – as in the growth of multi-level and multi-actor governance arrangements, for instance, or the emergence of social media as vehicles for political deliberation and mobilization. It has also been challenged by *new environments* as attention has turned to understanding political institutions across the globe, not just in Europe and the USA or the 'developed world'. These new contexts have proved highly dynamic, with novel institutional arrangements accompanying democratic transitions (for example, South Africa's 'Truth and Reconciliation' process or forms of Islamic democracy in the Middle East) or hybrid development pathways (from Chinese 'market Stalinism' to the Latin American 'pink tide'). And it is has often been *new actors* who have driven political change – social movements, religious leaders, bloggers, celebrities even.

Three further vignettes reflect critiques of institutional sameness, expressing instead the impulse to diversity:

The embedded institution

Critics of the 'mythic' institution ask how can we account for the empirically observed diversity of institutional forms if processes of isomorphism are so strong? And how can we account for change over time if environmental 'templates' are so influential? While society-wide institutional templates may affect what happens in individual organizations, it seems clear that pressures for convergence are mediated by local circumstances and power relations. The specificities of local practice and conceptions ('how things are done around here') may either reinforce or undermine institutional templates circulating in the wider environment.

At the same time, proponents of the 'efficient' institution have been criticized for an ahistorical and over-abstract take on reality, which drastically simplifies the motivational complexities involved in creating and maintaining different institutional arrangements. Granovetter (1992) criticizes Williamson's characterization of both market and hierarchy, arguing that each is 'embedded' in prevailing social relations. Markets are not necessarily anonymous and disordered; firms are not necessarily tightly controlled nor ordered. How each institution operates is dependent upon personal relations and networks of relations between and within firms. Granovetter (1992: 72) argues that, '*both* order *and* disorder, honesty *and* malfeasance have more to do with structures of such relations than they do with organizational form'. This type of argument has been developed in comparative studies of economic structure and performance. It is clear that different arrangements of hierarchy-market relations become institutionalized and relatively successful in particular contexts. 'Efficient' firms and markets may look quite different in, say, Japan and Britain, as they are embedded in different patterns of social relations, which in turn relate to the distinctiveness of the state, financial system, education and training, family life, and culture.

Similar processes are observable in politics. As we have seen above, the globalization thesis tends to support a claim that capitalism creates a homogeneous set of institutions across the Western world, which broadly produce the same effects on citizens living under those regimes and, to a great extent are 'inevitable' (Thelen, 2004:1–4). Against this perspective, the 'varieties of capitalism' literature (see Chapter 5) points to a fundamental distinction between advanced economies based on a neo-liberal agenda which allow the market to rule ('liberal' varieties), and more egalitarian economies where the power of employees in shaping the industries in which they work is much more pronounced ('coordinated' varieties) (Thelen, 2009). Schmidt (2009: 527) adds a third category to the established liberal and coordinated economies, which she terms 'state-influenced market economics', and which particularly applies to countries like France and Spain. The diverse institutional arrangements present within emerging economies (notably the so-called BRIC countries – Brazil, Russia, India and China) only expand further the varieties of capitalism.

At the other end of the spatial scale, our own research on local government has shown how embeddedness in wider institutional frameworks leads to the emergence of distinctive local political institutions. When central government required English local authorities to select from three new models for political leadership (elected mayor, council manager or cabinet), their choice – and interpretation – of approach was deeply influenced by political and non-political elements of the local institutional milieu – the organization of civil society, the structure of the local economy, traditions of political campaigning and party organization (Leach and Lowndes, 2004). John Stewart (2000: 43) has commented upon how such institutional resources provide both a force for continuity in particular places, but also for diversity across local government as a whole. Top-down and bottom-up institutional influences interact in important ways to shape arrangements for local political leadership. The extent of local distinctiveness relates to the degree of autonomy and diversity that higher levels of government will tolerate. At the same time, the impact of higher-level regulation or influence is mediated by the strength of local institutional commitments (which vary across time and space), as seen in our study of the diverse outcomes of New Labour's 'modernization' programme for British local government (Lowndes and Wilson, 2003). To paraphrase Karl Polanyi (1992), politics is an 'instituted process', embedded in institutions political and non-political.

The conflicted institution

In contrast to the mythic and efficient vignettes, culture is highlighted as a variable within our vignettes of the 'predictable' and 'manipulated' institution. North and Dunleavy add depth to the rational actor account through recognition that institutional form is crucially influenced by cultural and value imperatives. But they both treat culture and values as a 'given' – they are a kind of wild card, which we are asked to accept into our theoretical hand. Dunleavy may be correct to argue that bureaucrats maximize utilities through bureau-shaping, but the nature of the 'shape' they seek would be better considered as an open question deserving of research in its own right. It is not just the choice of utility-maximizing strategy that varies in different periods and contexts, it is also the values that underpin these strategies. We should expect these to vary over time and space (as in the 'embedded' institution) but also to be an object of contest and competition. In a similar vein, critics of sociological concepts of the 'mythic' institution, point to struggles within organizations to determine value systems; there is no uncritical adoption of dominant cultural templates. Anyone who has worked in a big organization (a university, for example) will know that influence over institutional myths and symbols is as important a power resource as control over material factors like budgets and buildings.

North's stress on stability makes it hard to grasp the dynamics of institutional change within his analysis. He argues that change in formal institutional rules occurs when it is in the interest of those with sufficient bargaining strength to make adjustments. It remains unclear, however, how all-important informal rules change. North (1990: 37) links informal constraints to 'our heritage', 'socially transmitted information', or 'culture transmitted between generations'. But culture remains an exogenous variable, something 'out there' which shapes institutional life. In contrast, organization theorists like Clegg (1990: 7) point to competition between groups of actors over cultural resources and to the existence of multiple and competing 'modes of rationality'. And, through their ongoing project on 'varieties of capitalism', historical institutionalists study the role of competing coalitions in fashioning, over time, distinctive welfare states in different country contexts.

Power is endemic to institutions and a significant source of institutional diversity. Shifting power relationships unsettle existing institutional settlements, which are – in effect – a means of distributing advantage between different groups of actors, and privileging certain sets of values over others. This is March and Olsen's (1989: 17) seminal insight: that seemingly neutral procedures and arrangements embody particular values, interests and identities. More recently, Mahoney and Thelen (2010: 7–8) have described institutions as '*distributional instruments* laden with power implications' (original emphasis). Even when institutions are relatively stable, this is the product of ongoing power play. Like a football match that ends with a nil-nil score, something (rather than nothing) has been happening. The result generally reflects an ebb and flow of advantage and disadvantage over time, not a stasis or a stand-off. Third phase institutionalists have started to address Peter John's (1998) challenge to look at the 'fine grain' of institutional power. Institutions do not just vary between themselves, they are also internally differentiated with a range of rules, practices and narratives (promoted and defended by different interests) coexisting in 'teeth-gritting harmony' (to borrow Louis Athusser's evocative phrase). This picture of an inevitably 'conflicted institution' represents a significant departure from first phase institutionalism's assumptions of integration and functional fit.

As we saw in Chapter 2, many third phase institutionalists take an 'engaged' perspective, pointing to the challenge to prevailing power relations that strategies for institutional resistance and reform present. Just as disadvantaged groups are marginalized by existing institutional configurations, so too can they use these or other institutions (in certain circumstances) to 'redefine the parameters of what is socially, politically and economically possible for others' (Hay, 1997: 50). Institutions are inevitably 'conflicted' – indeed, this is what sustains them as political phenomena.

The ambiguous institution

Sounding initially like an oxymoron, this vignette captures the thrust of much third phase theorizing, and is increasingly dominating the agenda for research on institutional diversity. As we have seen, institutions have been understood in relation to characteristics like stability, regularity and predictability. New concepts of ambiguity (Mahoney and Thelen, 2010), heterogeneity (Schneiberg and Clemens, 2006), redundancy (Crouch, 2005), polycentricity (Ostrom, 2005) and emergence (Lowndes, 2005) have come into play as third phase institutionalists have turned their attention to understanding sources of both institutional stability and change.

As with so much in the new institutionalism, the origins of these developments can be traced back to March and Olsen's pioneering work in the 1980s. The central claim of their work is that institutions are sustained by 'a confidence that appropriate behaviour can be expected most of the time' (March and Olsen, 1989: 38). But appropriateness is not seen as a given; rather as the outcome of an ongoing work of interpretation by reflective actors. Rules produce variation and deviation as well as conformity and standardization. Situations are assigned to rules through a comparison of cases, but there are always areas of ambiguity in the interpretation and application of rules. Such ambiguity provides a source of institutional change as does the changing external environment – novel cases and novel interpretations are 'encoded' into 'new routines' (March and Olsen, 1989: 34). Institutions are never closed or complete.

These insights have been picked up by third phase theorists seeking, in Ostrom's words, to 'animate institutions'. As agency has been brought to the fore, research has shown how strategic actors (or coalitions) exploit redundant institutional resources, or ambiguities in the interpretation of existing institutions, to shift rules and practices. The form that institutions take depends critically upon the creative work of reflexive actors. Adapting a concept from anthropologist Levi-Strauss, 'bricolage' (patching together of disparate materials at hand) may be the only route to institutional innovation in the face of path dependency, resource constraint, risk aversion and a generalized lack of trust (Lanzara, 1998: 27). Ambiguity can also become a power resource for competing groups of actors. Mahoney and Thelen argue that many institutional arrangements reflect 'ambiguous compromises' among actors 'who can coordinate institutional means even if they differ on substantive goals' (Mahoney and Thelen, 2010: 8). Because such compromises are inherently unstable, the 'ambiguous institution' contains within it opportunities for further change and diverse reconstructions, as interpretations of interest and the balance between competing actors shift over time.

Institutional diversity and ambiguity are not only inevitable but also provide institutional designers with an important resource. Rather than going for a technically 'efficient' institution, they may seek robustness over time and a capacity for learning and adaptation. This is where the 'ambiguous' institution comes into its own. In her work on 'common pool' resources, Elinor Ostrom (2005: 283) argues not for efficiency but for polycentricity, including multiple and overlapping governing authorities at different scales:

> Because polycentric systems have overlapping units, information about what has worked well in one setting can be transmitted to others who may try it out in their settings… can be encouraged to speed up the exchange of information about relevant local conditions and about policy experiments that have proved particularly successful. And, when small systems fail, there are larger systems to call upon – and vice versa.

The embedded, conflicted and ambiguous nature of institutions means that diversity is to be expected, although institutional similarity may pertain in specific temporal and spatial contexts. Tendencies to institutional reproduction and generation coexist. Consistent with a view of institutions as dynamic processes, rather than static forms, concepts of 'similarity' and 'diversity' should be understood to refer not to settled states but to shifting patterns of convergence and divergence.

Temporal and spatial dynamics

It is clear that time and space matter in shaping patterns of institutional similarity and diversity, and in contributing to the 'essential indeterminacy' (Hay, 2002: 141) of institutional outcomes. But how can we best understand these variables? We formulate the problem in terms of 'contingent effects'. We use this term for three reasons which reflect the overall perspective taken by the book. First, the adjective 'contingent' comes from the Latin *contingens*, which means 'touching together' and expresses the inevitably interconnected nature of institutional processes and effects. Second, the noun 'effects' brings with it the idea of continuing processes which contribute to, but do not cease at, the emergence of multiple outcomes. Finally, the expression of the indeterminacy of institutional change within the phrase 'contingent effects' itself has the effect of balancing an emphasis on institutions and their core characteristics with a recognition of the importance of agency in the long-term development of institutions. As Colin Crouch (2005: 19) reminds us, these effects are generated by, and impact upon, 'real human individuals'.

In this vein, Hay (2002: 114) theorizes agency itself as a primary source of contingent effects, but also emphasizes that the varying contexts in which political actors operate introduce elements of indeterminacy into political conduct. More specifically in relation to institutional change, Blyth (2002a) specifies the contestation, which occurs during the ideological struggle over institutional change, as the origin of contingent effects which shape the public policy paths which actors take during and immediately after conflict. Such an approach resonates with Premfors' (2004) work on the contingent effects to be seen in the different paths which the Scandinavian countries have taken to democracy. Thelen (2004),in contrast, emphasizes the institutional conservatism of actors at times of crisis and conceptualizes contingent processes as effects which unfold over time as actors over-layer institutions and gradually convert them, unwittingly for the most part, to uses different from those intended by their initiators. This approach is very much in tune with Hochschild and Burch's (2004: 34) research on the effects of contingency and agency in US immigration policy, and particularly in relation to their analysis of how two very different pieces of legislation have, in combination over time, produced very different effects from those intended by the law makers:

> Changes in the composition of the United States over the past few decades were contingent on the unexpected choices of millions of individuals around the world who used a law devised for other purposes; changes in how we understand and practice race in the United States might be equally contingent on the unknown choices of millions of Americans, old and new, over the next few decades. Contingency probably does not always rule politics, but sometimes it does.

Paul Pierson's *Politics in Time* (2004) is a landmark work in third phase institutionalism and suggests rich lines of enquiry related to contingent effects. He proposes that, under perceived pressures of time, political actors create institutions characterized by tension, contradiction and compromise. He also notes that actors may be aware of the likelihood of the contingent effects of longer term or wider political consequences, but take a 'calculated risk' that these effects will not materialize in their worst forms (Pierson, 2000: 478). Pierson (2004: 115) quotes Garret Hardin's maxim that 'we can never do merely one thing' to illustrate the complexity and interrelatedness of political activity, the failures of cognition on the part of actors and the contingent effects which flow from this.

We can begin to identify the key characteristics of contingent effects. First, they cannot be credibly attributed to 'events', 'globalization', 'luck', or the 'forces of nature', but, from a humanist and constructivist perspective, must be traced back, however tortuously, to agency, and the indeterminacy which the element of choice, inherent in the concept of agency, brings to political conduct. Second, although contingent effects are always traced back to human agency, this itself is characterized by failures of cognition and the inability of actors to contain the effects of their conduct in environments which themselves are highly complex and widely differentiated. Third, contingent effects have a spatial dimension, whereby the conduct of actors outside the immediate space impacts on the actors within that public policy arena in ways which these peripheral actors did not intend, and may not even be aware of. Fourth, contingent effects have a temporal dimension; some effects have an immediate influence on actors' conduct, but the impact of others may only become apparent over time. Finally, attempts at institutional change invite contestation from actors who oppose reform; the battle for ideas that ensues produces contingent effects, as do the compromise solutions that actors employ in an attempt to bring contestation to an end.

We now distinguish in more detail between temporal and spatial contingent effects.

Temporal contingent effects

Temporality is a term from general philosophy which indicates that our perceptions of time are constructed and experienced in different ways in different contexts (Wood, 2001). Temporal contingent effects manifest themselves as unintended impacts on an actor or actors in the present time period which have been generated by agency in the past. As an example in British public policy, Leach (1995: 49–67) analyses 'the strange case' of the Local Government Review. He argues that its origins lay in 'the political ambition of one individual', Michael Heseltine, who in the 1980s as Secretary of State for the Environment set in train in a long drawn-out restructuring of English local government in which the boundaries and functions of particular local authorities were reviewed in tranches. Over more than a decade, the purpose of reorganization became less and less clear, political support fell away, and the costs and disruption mushroomed (Leach argues that the negative impacts of the Review are 'difficult to over-emphasize'). The temporal contingent effects here, as Leach explains, relate to the inability of successive Conservative ministers to escape from a set of institutionalized policy commitments for which they themselves had no enthusiasm and could find no 'plausible rationale'.

Going beyond grand statements of 'path dependency', we can differentiate between the effects of sequencing (the order in which actors do things), timing (the point at which one particular action takes place within a sequence), and tempo (the pace of political time as constructed and perceived by key actors). Sequencing and timing effects can be intended as well as unintended, originating from actors' strategic and tactical decisions. Actors may attempt to sequence their own and others' actions to further their strategic intent, or to force a timing effect with the intention of 'stealing a march' on the opposing actors. We look at each in turn, with illustrative examples.

Sequencing effects originate in actions being completed in a particular order. As an example, Hacker (1998: 59) studies the comparative development of health-care systems in Britain, Canada and the USA and argues that 'the evolution of national health policies cannot be explained without an understanding of the sequence and timing of major government interventions in the medical sector'. Echoing the potential for strategic intervention by actors in these effects, which was outlined above, he traces in detail the actions taken by the British government from the 1911 National Insurance Act through to the post-war establishment of the NHS. Hacker demonstrates that it was the order in which these actions took place which led to universal health care being established in Britain, while in the USA such sequencing was absent, with contemporary institutional reformers 'left facing insuperable political barriers to the passage of national health insurance' (Hacker, 1998: 127–8), as illustrated in our discussion of Obama's health policies in Chapter 5. Taking a different cut, Gerry Stoker's (2002) work on New Labour's 'modernization' of public services in the UK reveals a 'lottery' in which a plethora of reform initiatives (and agents) were unleashed with a view to destabilizing existing institutional configurations and providing space for innovation. We might consider this a strategic 'de-sequencing' of actions.

Timing effects originate in a single action or event taking place at a particular point within a sequence of events. As one example, the sudden death of the British Labour Party leader, John Smith on 12 May 1994, was particularly significant for its timing in the sequence of events in the run-up to the 1997 general election. Indeed, as Marr (2007: 487–9) points out, Smith had already suffered one major heart attack and the populist *Sun* newspaper had greeted his succession to Neil Kinnock 'with an eerily accurate and predictive headline: 'He's fat, he's fifty-three, he's had a heart attack and he's taking on a stress laden job.' Furthermore, Smith 'did not believe Labour needed to be transformed, merely improved' and this frustrated the emerging New Labour faction in the party to the point where 'Blair was contemplating leaving politics, so despairing was he of Smith's leadership.' The timing of Smith's death in the sequence of events between Kinnock's loss in the 1992 election and the next election in 1997 turned out to be highly significant. It gave Tony Blair (the new leader) and Gordon Brown (the shadow Chancellor) a three-year 'window' within which to fashion and embed the 'New Labour' narrative and, with their influential 'spin doctors', to plot their strategy for winning the election after 18 years in opposition. Radical institutional change within the Labour Party was made possible (the abolition of 'Clause 4' and the introduction of 'one member, one vote' for example), as was the re-fashioning of many of the institutions of the core executive once Labour came to power.

As a second example, in the US Presidential Election of 2012, the arrival of Hurricane (or 'Superstorm') Sandy to devastate parts of New York a week before the election date is agreed by most commentators to have had an effect on the eventual outcome. For Sandy arrived at a time when the incumbent President Barack Obama had performed badly in face-to-face debates with the challenger, Mitt Romney, whose campaign consequently gained momentum. At that point, however, the national emergency caused by the flooding and damage in New York forced both candidates to cease campaigning for several days. Two particular timing effects were evident as a consequence. First, the 'boost' in the opinion polls which Romney had enjoyed as a result of the debates with the President tailed off during the hiatus. Second, Obama had the opportunity to display visible presidential authority by organizing the relief of New York, and visiting the sites of storm damage, only a few days before the voters went to the polls.

Tempo effects arise out of actors' own constructions of the pace of time. In seeking to change political institutions, how long are they prepared to take and how many reversals are they willing to tolerate? Indeed, how do different actors understand 'rapid' and 'slow', and what do they count as 'progress'? In the US, the first 100 days of a presidential term took on symbolic significance from the time of Franklin D. Roosevelt's administration, when the New Deal legislation was pushed swiftly through both Houses of Congress in 1933, setting a standard for action against which all subsequent presidents have been measured. The institutionalized nature of this legacy produces a tempo effect in which all significant actors (the media, the opposition, the public and, not least, the President and his party themselves) have very high expectations of the speed at which policy can be developed, placed on the statute book, and implemented.

By contrast, community-based social movements tend to work with long time horizons in which there is an oscillatory movement between moments of advance and moments of retreat, with successive waves of protest building on past achievements in an extended 'war of position'. New institutions become embedded in the interstices of the mainstream, serving as platforms for further change. Public policy may take a similar approach, extending institutional diversity through 'pilot' and 'beacon' projects, which trial different ways of doing things and allow reformers to both contain resistance and provide bases for further innovation (thus exploiting the strategic benefits of institutional heterogeneity and ambiguity).

The debate between reformism and revolution is, of course, at the heart of many political debates, and is reflected in the theoretical distinction between evolutionary and punctuated equilibrium models that we discussed in Chapter 5. Actors refer to getting a 'big break' or identifying a critical moment and, although these do not always come to fruition, such orientations provide a contrast to programmes of gradual institutional change. Thinking about civil service reform, there is an uneasy coexistence between the impetus for radical reorganization (new structures, new missions, new roles) and reliance upon gradualist programmes (continuous improvement, mentoring and staff development, the 'learning organization'). Being prepared to look 'behind you' as well as 'in front of you' is another aspect of actors' construction of time. The institutional repertoire can be extended through strategies of 'remembering' in which 'dormant' rules, practices and narratives are re-activated in the service of new objectives (Lowndes, 2005). But the privileging of the 'new' remains endemic within much public policy, with 'institutional forgetting' tending to carry a greater political premium (Benington *et al.*, 2006). And constructions of political time – how long, how fast, how sudden – are inevitably contested between different groups, leaving in their wake contingent as well as intentional effects.

An appreciation of temporal contingent effects leads us to caution against any binary treatment of 'old' and 'new' rules. 'Old' and 'new' institutions frequently coexist, often in tension – see, for instance Lowndes (1999) and Newman (2001) on the complex outcomes of waves of Thatcherite and New Labour public service restructuring in the UK. Sometimes old institutions provide bases for resistance, maintained in the face of new arrangements by those who benefit from them or see new rules as hostile to their interests. Old rules may effectively 'co-opt, absorb or deflect new initiatives' (Newman, 2001: 28), thus challenging novel values or ideas embodied in the new rules. Or they may exist in parallel, as an alternative regime. The recognition of the coexistence of old and new institutions brings with it problems. When does a new institution become an old one, and how do we characterize institutions that are currently effective and yet have long historical roots? As with a nuclear half-life, institutions never disappear. Rather, they just reduce in significance at different rates, remaining as part of the environment in which institutional innovation occurs. Rather than any stark contrast between 'old' and 'new', we need a dynamic account of how institutions are 'discovered, invented, suggested, rejected, or for the time being, adopted' (Streeck and Thelen, 2005: 16), which also acknowledges reverse movements in which institutions may be 'forgotten' or 'remembered'.

Spatial contingent effects

Six different levels of analysis for institutional theory are identified by Scott (2001: 83–9, 136–49): the world system, society, the organizational field, the organizational population, the organization itself, and the organizational sub-system. In earlier work, we have shown how the policy impacts upon institutions at different analytical levels, leading to contingent effects which revolve around the disconnections between institutional change in one layer of government and changes being made by actors in other layers. Peripheral actors who operate outside the immediate political space can have an influence on whether and how change occurs. In this way, Lowndes' (2005) UK-based study of institutional change explains why some institutions of English local government appear to have been transformed, while others are 'unmoved'. Forces for continuity and change coexist so that some institutions are faithfully reproduced while others are transformed, adapted or discarded.

In similar vein, criticizing Hay's (2006a) 'dualist' approach to change as theorizing a spurious dichotomy between 'settled times' and 'crisis', David Marsh (2010: 227) argues that consideration of the spatial dimension is essential to understanding institutional change as a mix of processes and effects, some of which preserve stability, and some of which destabilize the status quo. Marsh argues that seemingly radical political agency is often best understood in relation to its links with existing and persistent institutional configurations. Empirically, he argues that Conservative governments under Margaret Thatcher in Britain were able to make major policy innovations in the 1980s principally because they were connected across political space to an enduring 'British political tradition and its discourse of limited democracy'. What looks like change may actually be in part a product of continuity. Correspondingly, looking at constraint and the failure of strategic intent, Marsh argues that New Labour's attempts after 1997 to make far-reaching changes to the British constitution 'were mostly de-radicalised because the attempts at reform occurred within the framework of institutions and processes that were underpinned by the old paradigm' (Marsh, 2010: 229). Marsh argues for a complex appreciation of how stability and change, and similarity and diversity, work together, counselling against any simplistic attempts to separate these out the processes and effects artificially.

Contingent effects arise in relation to the linking of institutions across space, whether within the political domain or between political and non-political domains. So called 'old' or first phase institutionalists were well aware that institutions did not exist in isolation of other institutions, focusing on 'intricate descriptive accounts of interlinked rules, rights, and procedures' (Bill and Hardgrave cited in Scott, 2001: 6). In second phase institutionalism, March and Olsen (1989: 170) first stated that 'political institutions form a complicated ecology of interconnected rules'. From a rational choice perspective, North (1990: 95) concludes: 'In short, the interdependent web of an institutional matrix produces massive increasing returns'. In the same vein, Ostrom (1999: 39) notes that: 'the impact on incentives and behaviour of one type of rules is not independent of the configuration of other rules'. In empirical and comparative study at the international level, historical institutionalists have examined the interconnections between a wide range of public policies and the structures provided by national legislation (Weir and Skocpol, 1985; Hacker, 2002; Pierson and Skocpol, 2002).

Such contingent effects do not always push towards institutional similarity. In his work on institutional complementarities, Colin Crouch (2005: 50) draws our attention to ways in which the 'components of a whole mutually compensate for each other's deficiencies in constituting the whole'. 'Compensatory' effects are definitely *not* created by similar institutions clustering together ('more of the same'), but by the co-existence and co-evolution of diverse institutions. Crouch gives as an example the complementarity of the institutions of the 'free economy and the strong state' (Gamble, 1988) under Thatcherism in the UK. The institutions of the latter are required to keep sectional demands for regulation at bay, thereby allowing the market to operate with a greater degree of freedom. Here then we have two very different patterns of institutional interaction, one which promotes unfettered conduct, and one which promotes centralized state control. As they come together in a particular configuration at a particular point in time, diverse but connected institutional arrangements can compensate for one another's deficiencies, and close down the opportunities for oppositional actors to launch successful resistance. Another example is provided by Rene Mayntz (2004) who shows how, in terrorist organizations, hierarchical and network modes of governance coexist not as a matter of 'design', but as an example of diversity created by contingency. The availability of the two different patterns, and the capacity to switch between them, becomes a matter of survival.

Institutional clustering may have a distinctly territorial character. The term 'institutional thickness' (Amin and Thrift, 1994) has been coined to explain the relative success of economic policy in different regions. Policy that supported institutional development was as important as relative production costs or resource availability. The key to success was locally specific institutional configurations that supported trusting and reciprocal relationships between firms and prioritized knowledge exchange and innovation. Such institutions tended to have deep historical roots and links to familial and community-based resources, as in the common marketing and advisory services of family firms engaged in clothing design and manufacture in Northern Italy, or the strong ties to research groups in local universities of the machine-tool manufacturers of Baden Wurtemberg in South Germany (Coulson and Ferrario, 2007). Research on emerging economies in Asia and elsewhere has suggested that growth will only be sustainable if current 'institutional voids' are filled (e.g. to support credit, innovation and marketing), ideally building on local traditions and resources (Khanna and Palepu, 2010). Locality-specific institutional clustering is important in other policy domains too. We saw in Chapter 3 how different levels of political participation in otherwise similar cities could be explained by the clustering of supportive institutions in both local civil society and the local state (Box 3.3). Although such combinations had developed in the context of long traditions and institutional legacies, we saw that it was possible for local policy makers to support their continued health (and certainly to avoid damaging them), and for those in other areas to seek to address their own 'institutional voids'.

Clearly, understanding contingent effects requires us to consider interconnections between political and non-political institutions, looking at how political rules, practices and narratives interact with those institutions that structure wider social and economic life. Financial institutions, for instance, are deeply implicated in structuring government decision making and behaviour. The UK's fiscal policy seems not just to be influenced but actually led by what are referred to as 'the demands of the market'. In a more dramatic case, the US investment bank Goldman Sachs has been found to have used currency swaps in 2002 to help the Greek government mask the true extent of its deficit, and thus circumvent European Union rules. The swaps will in time mature, benefiting Goldmans hugely and increasing further the Greek deficit. More extreme again, we can consider the case of Zaire (now Democratic Republic of the Congo) which was referred to in the 1970s and 80s as a 'kleptocracy' because political institutions had come to function as no more than vehicles for the financial aggrandizement of officials.

To take a different sort of example, feminist institutionalists have shown how institutionalized practices and narratives about caring responsibilities and women's work in the home, which originate in the domestic arena, have influenced the development and interpretation of political institutions. The case study in Box 6.1 shows how such informal institutions have interacted with other practices and narratives about what makes a 'good' political representative. This 'ideal type' remains a white, male, middle-class professional candidate, even where formal rules eschew any discrimination or even set out to promote 'equality' (Lovenduski and Norris, 1989). As formal political institutions (policies, legislation, rulings) are often shaped by these informal heavily gendered institutions, they serve over time to 're/produce broader social and political gender expectations' (Chappell, 2006: 226).

Actually, we can go so far as to say that there are no clear institutional 'insides' or 'outsides'; rather, such boundaries are subject to strategic action (by both dominant and oppositional actors) and to broader spatial and temporal contingent effects. Such an insight follows from the core new institutionalist achievement of cutting loose the concept of institution from its traditional organizational moorings. If institutions are rules, practices and narratives which exist within, between and around particular organizations (to paraphrase Fox and Miller, 1995: 92), it is a short step to recognize that they interact and co-evolve within and without the political domain. Indeed, change in other domains must be an important source of institutional change – either destabilizing or reinforcing institutions, or providing novel templates for their redesign or adjustment. And the same actors move between different institutional arrangements, bringing with them their values and ideas, and their experience of negotiating institutional constraint in non-political domains. Institutional resistance, as well as redesign, may emerge from these trans-institutional encounters, and

Box 6.1 Gendered institutional change: candidate selection for the Scottish Parliament

Processes of political decentralization in the UK in the late 1990s resulted in the creation of new parliamentary spaces and governance structures, the inclusion of new political actors, and the integration of new concerns and issues on the political agenda. It also brought new opportunities with regards to the candidate selection process, opening up possibilities for change in established selection procedures. Gender equity entrepreneurs framed their demands within these wider reform trajectories, successfully introducing a gendered dimension to Scotland's 'new politics'.

In the run-up to the first elections to the Scottish Parliament in 1999, internal and external pressure was applied to all of the main Scottish political parties with regards to women's representation, particularly Scottish Labour. A record number of women were elected to the first Scottish Parliament (37.2 per cent), largely due to Scottish Labour's use of strong quota-type measures to ensure gender balance in representation. Yet, while the female face of Scottish Labour continues to serve as a powerful symbol of the 'new politics' in Scotland, traditional institutional elements have proved remarkably resilience – resurgent, even.

In a case study constituency, it was found that the new formal job descriptions and person specifications, while technically still in place, were not actually distributed (despite requests from prospective candidates and local party members). Candidate selection criteria continued to carry with them a set of gendered assumptions, for example in relation to what constituted appropriate skills and experience. Female candidates often failed to be selected not because they were less 'qualified', but because of the way in which qualifications for political office were defined. Male-dominated political elites used well-established priorities as narratives to counteract women's increased access and presence in formal decision-making arenas. At the same time, a traditional political masculinity was mobilized through repeatedly highlighting the importance of prospective candidates 'playing the game', being 'well-connected', involved in 'local politicking' and 'knowing the right people'.

Female candidates' experience in community activism (e.g. related to health and childcare) did not carry the same weight as a track record as a councillor or trades union official. Juggling work and caring responsibilities was seen as a liability rather than as evidence of flexibility and connectedness to the daily lives of constituents. Selectors insisted they were looking for a 'local' candidate, but establishing localness was not an objective matter. Instead it relied on gendered assumptions about what constituted significant local links, privileging some and not other aspects of Ostrom's (1999: 39) 'institutional configuration' – for instance, a role in a local business, chamber of commerce, sports club or traditional civic association.

Sources: Kenny and Lowndes (2011); Kenny (2011).

institutional recombination and diversification are the typical outcomes. Political institutions are not insulated from changing gender relations in the home, workplace or civil society. As Mona Lena Krook and Fiona Mackay (2011: 7) note: 'political institutions are themselves constituted by these embodied social practices of "doing gender" on a daily basis. Recognizing these reciprocal relationships, in turn, opens up possibilities for agency and change'.

We are reminded of Chantal Mouffe's (2000: 13) concept of the 'constitutive outside' – that which is excluded in order to make the inside possible. As the case study in Box 6.1 shows, despite attempts to broaden out the process of candidate selection, there remained a gendered process of boundary construction, which sought to determine an institutional 'inside' and 'outside' by privileging certain institutional interconnections over others. It was not a matter of chance when a female candidate's experience was discounted; it had to be discounted in order to establish what *did* count. Colin Crouch (2005: 160) uses the analogy of the spider's web to show how institutions are linked, and how the relative significance of different linkages is the subject of strategic action and political struggle:

> The strands in the centre of the net are thick and clear; as the net extends outwards they become faint, until at a more or less definable point they cease altogether... Where thick strands cluster before a distinct thinning can be perceived, we can talk of a more or less bounded institution... Other institutions will exist at other thick clusters, located at various distances from our original focus... [C]hanges of various kinds can... make previously faint links in the net stronger, and strong ones fainter.

In our case study, the linking of candidate selection to specific political and non-political institutions in the locality, and the delinking from others (women's groups, domestic and caring arrangements), is neither objective nor serendipitous, but the outcome of strategic action on the part of dominant interests. The gendered outcomes that follow are illustrative of the way in which institutional configurations distribute power, but in a dynamic context in which strategic actors seek to influence the articulation of different institutional rules. To deepen our understanding of the 'conflicted institution', we need to problematize institutional boundaries, and (following Crouch, 2005:160) recognize that there is always a continuum between 'internal and external, endogenous and exogenous'. As engaged scholars, we can also highlight strategies which disrupt those institutional interconnections (within and beyond the political domain) that serve to exclude and disempower marginalized actors. Thinking about our case study, political institutions will never realistically be 'de-gendered' but there may be opportunities for their 're-gendering' through the cultivation of new, empowering institutional linkages, alongside the progressive subversion of the established inside/outside boundary.

Conclusion

Consistent with a view of institutions as dynamic processes, rather than static forms, we have used the terms 'similarities' and diversity' not to refer to settled states but to shifting patterns of convergence and divergence. Through our 'vignettes', we showed a movement in third phase institutionalism from reproductive to generative theories, involving a shift in focus from institutional similarity towards institutional diversity. Such a shift runs alongside the growing commitment to 'animate' institutional analysis – to 'bring the actor back in' to theories of both institutional change and stability. Emphasizing the scope for institutional recombination and diversification also serves to highlight opportunities for institutional resistance and reform. But we have also argued against swinging the pendulum too far towards agency, diversity and context, and thereby dislocating institutionalism from its main focus, which must be upon institutions themselves.

Third phase institutionalists are increasingly concerned with the mix between similarity and diversity, rather than with one or the other, and this is illuminating the wider debate on stability and change. In relation to institutions themselves, there is increasing recognition that political institutions are configurations of often disparate elements, connected both within the political domain and through links to institutional elements within the wider economy and society. Recognizing that institutional boundaries are both constructed and contested helps us to understand the dynamism of institutions and appreciate the circumstances of their *relative* stability. Distinctions between the new and the old, the novel and the familiar, may be blurred intentionally by political actors to form and hold together coalitions, but are often a source of conflict and reinterpretation themselves. This brings us to the place of ambiguity in political activity and the way in which actors inherit institutions which contain compromise and conflict and go on to reproduce these tensions in their efforts at institutional reform. Apparent institutional similarities (and continuities over time) may actually disguise ongoing conflict between actors and coalitions. Compromises provide actors with a focus for coalitional activity and a platform from which to defend or attack existing institutional configurations.

In considering the implications for institutionalism as it moves through its third phase, we make one general observation and three more specific points. In general terms, the debate on institutional similarity and diversity underlines our argument that there is little to be gained from constructing further 'new' institutionalisms until the synergy between existing strands has been comprehensively exploited. As Elinor Ostrom (2005: 11) argues, the goal should be a 'cumulative body of knowledge' rather than a 'Tower of Babel' of competing languages about institutions.

In more specific terms, our first point relates to institutions and the need to recognize the tensions incorporated within institutions themselves. Hence we inherit (and construct) a world which is not simply full of institutions of similar and different types, but institutions and institutional configurations which embody power relationships and ongoing contestations. This insight goes beyond arguments about institutional change and diversity and goes to the heart of our understanding of institutions themselves. In this sense, to describe institutionalism as being about rules is unintentionally deceptive, as we tend to have an idealized conception of a rule which implies clarity of meaning, interpretation and legitimacy.

Our second point develops the theme of the oppositional nature of politics. In this chapter we have highlighted the need to regard politics as an activity which takes place within a continuous temporal and spatial sphere, rather than one which is artificially separated into the actors and institutions under consideration, and something called 'the environment'. Evolutionary theory in its various forms has helped us appreciate that actors and institutions do not operate in a vacuum, but has also encouraged the tendency to imagine that 'out there' there is something more powerful and very different which intervenes in politics occasionally. By emphasizing institutional interconnections through time and space, our approach suggests that any given effect can eventually be traced back to human agency, however tortuous or interwoven the route. Metaphorically, we can think of this in the terms of the aphorism that states: 'You aren't stuck in the traffic - you *are* the traffic!'

Third, the chapter has thrown further light on our distinctly institutionalist '5Cs' conception of agency, and the tensions between constraint and empowerment which actors themselves instigate and accommodate. In this way, those who present themselves as outsiders can relatively quickly become insiders and enjoy the privileges, and suffer the constraints, which accompany this change of role. Returning to the Tea Party's intervention in the 2010 mid-term US elections (Box 5.1, p. 132), we can see how the successful candidates from this social movement took up their seats in Congress and became both beneficiaries and subjects of the institutions they proclaimed to despise. Equally, those who successfully reform institutions are then bound to develop strategies to prevent counter-reformation – to make their new institutions 'stick' and continue to constrain actors into the future. In this way, having forced through his health-care legislation, President Obama sought to build a coalition to oppose the reversal of his health-care policies in the House of Representatives, switching rapidly from reforming to conserving strategies. But is it possible for such a coalition to design a set of institutions which are robust enough not to be subverted or replaced further down the line? It is this question of the scope and limitations of institutional design to which we now turn.

Chapter 7

Institutional Design

Given the inevitability of institutional diversity and ambiguity, and the uncertainties inherent in institutional change, this chapter asks whether institutions can be designed in any meaningful sense. Our answer is a qualified yes, based on the book's theorization of the relationship between agency and institutions and our empirical observations of institutional design in the practice of politics. This analysis is also underpinned by our 'engaged' perspective, which recognizes that politics is about a contestation over values. While highly unlikely to achieve all they set out to do, attempts at institutional design are inevitable as political actors seek to make their values 'stick' through institutional mechanisms. Such action does not only include heroic foundational moments (new constitutions, for instance) or fundamental reform programmes, but also many disparate small acts of adjustment undertaken by strategic actors on the ground. If 'design' is emergent rather than planned, this should not lead us to underestimate the importance of intent – as well as accident and evolution – in shaping institutional development.

Through reviewing insights from the main strands of institutionalist scholarship, we identify the challenges faced by institutional designers. First, actors tend to be drawn to changes to formal rules and structures as quick fixes and tend only to pay lip service to the importance of changing interconnected practices and stories. Second, institutional designers often underestimate the strength of opposition which can be mobilized around the existing institutional configuration and the defensive potentials offered by the density of interconnections between institutional modes. Third, once designed, institutions will wither away if they are not constantly and actively maintained. Maintenance serves not only to minimize the gaps in the institutional configuration but also to mitigate against the contingent effects we have discussed in Chapters 5 and 6. So 'design' involves not just institutional creation, but an ongoing commitment to enforce rules, model practices and rehearse stories. As we show in our analysis of 'institutional bricolage', much design is not 'de novo' but more an exercise in the strategic recombination of institutional elements in the immediate and wider environment.

This chapter considers how an understanding of constraints upon institutional design can be translated into a set of principles for good, or good enough, design. Given the realities of institutional embeddedness and ongoing struggles over values, we propose that twin criteria of 'revisability' and 'robustness' are best deployed to evaluate design strategies, or predict conditions for relative success. Through an extended case study, we use these criteria to consider institutional reform strategies in English local governance, while reflecting on the growing interest in 'design' among academics and policy makers alike. We conclude that, in most cases, institutional designers can only hope to displace gradually pre-existing institutional configurations and cannot afford to neglect their new projects once they are in place. Attempts at intentional institutional change remain, with these provisos, worthwhile. However, those who seek to design and redesign institutions are best advised to approach their challenge with a reflexive and ironic cast of mind.

Understanding the scope for design

While first phase, or 'old', institutionalism assumed that institutional design was an activity conducted largely by the state and backed by government's legitimate threat of coercion against non-compliance, second phase institutionalism moved the debate on via its rational choice, historical and sociological variants. As we shall see below, these moves have become the building blocks for more sophisticated, boundary-crossing treatments in institutionalism's third phase.

It is no great surprise that it is rational choice scholars who have put the concept of design centre stage. Indeed, if 'design' refers to the construction of institutional configurations which are intended to achieve a particular purpose, and in which the designers have some continuing interest and involvement, then there are clear resonances with the principal–agent model. Here the emphasis is on creating clear and controlling sets of rules which can be monitored for their effectiveness and adjusted as necessary. In contrast, institutionalists who are more concerned with 'change' than design, tend to focus further down the track on how institutions develop in response to environmental pressures, are reformed in the aftermath of a crisis, and are reinterpreted in the continuity of political struggle. Rational choice theorists anticipate a dramaturgy in which the principal sets in train a relation-ship between agent and institutions and expects to monitor a mix of compliance and defection, where the latter can be managed by a modest redesign of the rules at key stages.

However, just as influential political actors work across boundaries, the same is true of scholarship. Within rational choice theory, more nuanced and 'humanist' approaches have been developed (Crouch, 2005; Ostrom, 2005), in which institutions empower as well as constrain, interconnections between rules are privileged, and where both principals and agents imagine and anticipate institutional impacts, and reciprocity and trust are as important as coercion. In this way, insights from both sociological and historical institutionalism are acknowledged. As Axelrod (1984: 174) suggests, for institutions to stimulate cooperation 'the future must have a sufficiently large shadow'. Or, in Scott's (2001: 108) terms, 'the anticipation of future interaction provides an important stimulus to evoke norms of reci-procity'.

Elinor Ostrom emphasizes that institutions not only delineate what actions are forbidden, but also those which are permitted. In addition to this empowering element, her coining of the term 'rules-in-use' has built in the idea that rule *takers* are able to exercise a degree of agency in putting rules into practice. Indeed, Ostrom is particularly concerned with the ways in which local actors develop their own rules-in-use from the bottom up. This orientation emerges from continuing work on the management of 'common pool resources', within which she includes forests, fisheries, oil fields, grazing lands and irrigation systems. Ostrom has developed an extensive research programme investigating how groups of common pool users have construct practices which are, in many cases, more effective in sustaining the 'commons' than imposed institutional frameworks from outside or above (emanating from government or local regulatory agencies) (see, for example, Ostrom, 1999, 2005, 2007). On the question of design, Ostrom (2007: 18) concludes that 'a series of nested but relatively autonomous, self-organized, resource governance systems may do a better job in policy experimentation than a single central authority'.

Institutional design can thus be seen as a positive sum game from which both rule takers and rule makers can draw significant benefits. However, other rational choice theorists take a less sanguine view of institutional design and its potential to produce positive effects. Indeed, by theorizing even more complex and conflicted processes, Schickler (2001) and Pierson (2004) argue the case for uncertain and potentially damaging effects. Schickler (2001: 5–12), whose pervasive influence we have noted in previous chapters, views the interests of members of the US Congress as being essentially irreconcilable, at both the individual level and through coalitions. In this dystopian environment, institutional design arises as a necessity. But, as an exercise in conflicted compromise, it is doomed to eventual failure. Hence entrepreneurial members build support for reform by framing proposals that appeal to groups motivated by different and radically conflicting interests. These designers create 'common carriers' 'to facilitate cooperative action among legislators who might normally oppose one another'. Schickler (2001: 297, n. 19) argues that 'entrepreneurial leaders exercise influence not chiefly by command of force of personality', but by devising proposals and convincing others that their framing of an issue is more accurate than their opponents' framing. However, the fruits of these labours are, more often than not, 'a never-ending source of dissatisfaction for members and outside observers' alike'.

Borrowing from sociological institutionalism, and taking a longer-term historical perspective, Paul Pierson adopts what might be called a 'monstrous' conception of institutions, which he describes as 'big, slow moving and invisible'. Pierson (2004, 103–32) argues that prospects for institutional design are heavily limited by four factors. First, actors' mixed motivations will always produce multiple effects (as per Schickler). Second, designers may follow logics of appropriateness, rather than logics of consequentiality, privileging the need to legitimize their actions over considerations of effectiveness. Third, political action is short term, and contingent effects are inevitable (see Chapter 6). Fourth, as the external environment changes, weak institutions may become more potent in their shaping effect, and strong institutions may wither.

Pierson also seeks to debunk the conventional wisdom which argues that, if design is flawed at the point of 'institutional selection', processes of competition and learning will come into play further down the line to correct these inadequacies. Pierson (2004: 126–9) argues that, while actors may be competitive, institutions often occupy 'a monopoly over a particular part of the political terrain'. At the same time, 'the complexity and ambiguity of politics create serious problems for learning'. What learning there is comes in the contingent form of trial and error, and hence 'self correction is partial at best'. In conclusion, Pierson stresses that his intention is not to deny that actors find ways of modifying institutions in the light of experience, but to suggest that 'any tendency toward "evolved functionalism", either actor-centred or societal, should be treated as highly variable'.

This scepticism about learning as a significant factor in enhancing the effectiveness of institutional design is also present in Sabatier's extensive work on advocacy coalitions. He argues that 'policy-oriented learning' only produces minor policy change, because deep core beliefs and policy core beliefs are normatively embedded, and not susceptible to factual argument. Major policy change, on the other hand, comes from external perturbations or shocks, which may arise from socio-economic transformations, regime change, outputs from other sub-systems, or even a natural disaster. External shocks are far more likely to lead to the redistribution of both material and political resources, and to shift the balance of power between competing coalitions (Sabatier and Weible, 2007: 199). Hence 'while minority coalitions can seek to improve their relative position through augmenting their resources and "outlearning" their adversaries, their basic hope of gaining power within the subsystem resides in waiting for some *external event* to significantly increase their political resources' (Sabatier 1988: 148–9, original emphasis).

Within historical institutionalism, it is only in the third phase that the question of the intentional design of institutions has begun to emerge, and then in a somewhat fragmented and peripheral fashion. This insouciance to the possibility of design can be attributed to a broader tendency to deal with the coarse grain of institutions and broad span of history at the state level, rather than at the fine level of detail required to consider the process of design. At the same time, historical institutionalism has been characterized by assumptions about the pre-existence of institutions in all aspects of political life, and, therefore, the absence of a blank sheet of paper upon which designs can be committed. Historical institutionalism's focus upon contingent effects has also diverted attention from actors' attempts to direct processes of institutional change.

However, as we saw in Chapter 5, historical institutionalism has sought to bring agency back in to its understanding of institutional change. Mark Blyth adapts the evolutionary model of punctuated equilibrium to argue that there are brief formative periods, which occur as the result of economic crises, and in which actors use ideas as the building bricks for new institutional designs. Looking at the economic crisis in the1930s in the US, Blyth (2002a: 40–1) argues that:

> each solution was predicated on a particular notion as to 'what went wrong' and therefore 'what had to be done'. It is therefore only by reference to the ideas that agents use to interpret their situation that understanding the design of new institutions becomes possible.

Unlike Blyth's brief windows of design opportunity, Vivien Schmidt's actors enjoy high degrees of continuous agency, as they mobilize ideas in pursuit of institutional design. For Schmidt (2009: 533), the practice of politics is 'the product of sentient agents engaged in thinking up new ideas about what to do and how to do it and then engaging in discussions in efforts to persuade others that this is indeed what one needs to do and ought to do'. In his analysis of the UK's current economic crisis, Colin Hay (2012) points to an as yet unresolved 'discursive battleground' in which two accounts are pitted against each other. On the one hand, the discourse of 'Labour's deficit' argues in favour of austerity and blames the crisis on the previous government's profligacy. On the other hand, the discourse of 'Tory cuts' calls for policies to support growth and blames the deepening crisis upon unnecessary and ideologically inspired public spending cuts. Hay argues that such 'alternative understandings of where we are now and how we have got here' are likely to lead to 'different responses', although both accounts point to the collapse of the previous growth model. Like Schmidt he emphasizes that winning over the electorate to one story or the other is a vital precursor to a new round of institutional design (rather than policy prevarication).

Kathleen Thelen's third phase work develops her central theme that it is possible for less powerful groups to 'hijack' the very institutions which have been put in place to subjugate them, by gradually reforming these over time. In this way, actors are seen as always trying to bend institutions and reinterpret the rules which constrain them to fit their interests and goals (Mahoney and Thelen, 2010). Focusing on institutional change but incorporating ideas of creation, institution building and design, Thelen makes three key points. First, 'institutional designers never fully control the uses to which their creations are put'. Second, 'gaps emerge because institutional-building is often a matter of political compromise... institutions and rules are often ambiguous from the beginning, almost *by design*, as a consequence of the particular (often conflicting) coalition of interests that presides over their founding'. And third, institutions distribute power, and for this reason are inevitably contested: 'since the "losers" in these contests do not always go away, it sometimes happens that actors who are not part of the "design coalition" may nonetheless find ways to *occupy and redeploy* institutions not of their own making' (Thelen, 2009: 491, original emphasis). In contrast to Sabatier and Schmidt, who focus on the capacity of elite actors to produce and operationalize their preferred institutional configurations, the emphasis is on the fallibility of the initial design processes and the opportunities for non-elite actors to redesign these through a combination of strategy and opportunism some way down the line.

Through their 'strategic-relational approach', Hay and Jessop (1995) theorize the opportunities for, but also the constraints upon, institutional design (see also Hay, 2002; and Jessop, 2007). Actors 'are presumed to be strategic – to be capable of devising and revising means to realise their intentions'. In addition they inhabit of a world of institutions which is strategically selective; that is to say, the institutional terrain which they negotiate is already shaped, and continues to be shaped, by actors who have gone before and, because of this, favours certain strategies over others. In an iterative process, the actor formulates a strategy within the given institutional context, and then acts upon it. The effects of this strategic action then create two feedback loops. One loop connects the action back to the original institutional terrain, which is impacted by the actor's intervention; another loop links back to the actor in the form of strategic learning. This second loop serves to enhance 'awareness of structures and the constraints/opportunities they impose, providing the basis from which subsequent strategy might be formulated and perhaps prove more successful' (Hay, 2002: 126–34).

At first sight, therefore, these actors appear to have a great deal in common with the calculating actors of a conventional rational choice model. But the processes and effects which are used by, and impinge upon, these actors differentiate the approach in three crucial aspects. First, actors' intentions are conceptualized through a multi-motivational perspective: actors seek to pursue a wide range of perceived interests which are constructed within different spatial and temporal contexts. Hence, as we argued in Chapter 1, in making a single strategic choice, an actor may construct a range of motivations and justifications from fluid perceptions of what seems to be in his or her best interests, what seems to be in their political grouping's best interests, and what seems to be in the best interests of the country or, indeed, the planet.

Second, the approach assumes a level of reflexivity on the part of actors that goes some way beyond the basic capacities of imagination and anticipation which we have observed in third phase rational choice institutionalism. Hay (2002: 131–2) argues that 'in monitoring the consequences (both intended and unintended) of their actions, actors may come to modify, revise and reject their chosen means to realise their intentions as, indeed they may also come to modify, revise or reject their original intentions and the conceptions of interest upon which they were predicated'. Indeed, before they begin on this continuous process of review and revision, actors have projected forward the likely consequences of different strategies in the light of their assessment of the institutional terrain, and made strategic choices on the basis of those projections.

Third, casting a deep shadow over the rational characteristics of this strategic approach are the fallibilities of agency. Hence, actors may 'misread' the institutional terrain, and formulate and project strategies on the basis of inaccurate perceptions of their environment. In addition, as they monitor and review the progress of their strategy, they may attribute progress, or setbacks, to the wrong cause, by fitting the evidence at their disposal to prefabricated perceptions of sources of advantage and disadvantage. In this way, the concept of learning used by Hay and Jessop has no functionalist implication in the sense that policy necessarily improves through the learning process. Further, because their mistaken learning feeds back not only to themselves, but to the continuous shaping of the common institutional terrain, actors' misconceptions may have deleterious consequences for other, often less powerful, parties. And so, using the example of Nazi Germany in the 1930s, the feedback loop may confirm political actors in their violent prejudices against Jews, gypsies and homosexuals, and simultaneously further stack the institutional terrain against these groups.

Within sociological institutionalism, a distinction is drawn between the demand for new institutional designs, which includes the expectation of diversity, and the 'institutionalization' of the supply of design, which tends towards similarity and convergence. As Scott (2001: 109) explains, on the demand side, 'institutions come into existence because players perceive problems requiring new approaches. Participants are motivated by their discomfort in ongoing situations to devise or borrow new and different rules or models'. But their efforts are subject to 'isomorphic' tendencies. DiMaggio and Powell's (1991b) theorization of 'coercive isomorphism' focuses upon the 'environmental' pressures and 'cultural expectations' which are exerted on the organization by other organizations and, as such, implies a reaction to contingent effects, rather than a prospective process of design. However, 'mimetic isomorphism' is theorized as a particular type of response to environmental uncertainty, in which actors intentionally redesign the institutions of their organization along the lines of a similar organization, which seems to be coping with that uncertainty more effectively. 'Normative isomorphism' stems from the process of professionalization of actors within the organization and the wider environment, and again implies that elite actors are, at least in part, actively seeking to remodel the prevailing institutional configurations to comply with a particular set of values and perceived interests.

In a similar vein, Meyer (1994: 42) predicts that more and more arenas of social life are being brought under the 'rubric of ideologies that claim universal applicability'. Such a position is, of course, challenged by social movement scholars who (as we saw in Chapter 5) take a 'bottom-up' approach in which coalitions of rule takers attempt to disrupt the institutional design of rule makers, and substitute or append their own policies (Schneiberg and Lounsbury, 2008). In the oscillating rhythm of the conflict between parties this can best be described as 'design on the run', since there is a marked absence of the punctuations which allow actors to pause and take control of the design process. At the same time, novel institutional designs appear as islands within the traditional institutional landscape and, in turn, provide 'jumping off' points for further reform (as in women's policy agencies in the civil service, for instance, or cooperative housing schemes in the midst of private markets). Just because such outcomes appear haphazard or not completely rational, we should not assume that there were no intentional processes of design at work. Even Cohen, March and Olsen's (1972) famous 'Garbage Can Model' argues that actors opportunistically fit new problems into pre-existing solutions which they have used in the past, employing trusted templates much as dress designers or architects might. This may not be a rational design process, but neither is it a random one. As we shall see below, third phase institutionalism borrows from across the rational, historical and sociological strands to explore how ambiguity, compromise and variety can be resources for, rather than obstacles to, institutional design.

Design as bricolage

As we have emphasized throughout the book, institutions are not 'external' to individuals. It is actors who make and remake institutions on a daily basis. Indeed, we only know that institutions are 'effective' (in the sense of shaping behaviour) through observing patterns of action. Chapter 5 showed how political institutions may change gradually through individuals' efforts to match institutions to changing situations, which includes adapting rules, practices and narratives over time. Chapter 6 showed how political institutions often develop as configurations of disparate elements (with connections to non-political institutions), characterized by ambiguity and compromise. Do such adaptive processes qualify as 'design'? We argue here that design depends critically upon the creative work of multiple institutional entrepreneurs, who seek to expand and recombine their institutional resources as they face new challenges. Such acts may be self-interested, particularly in the context of changing power settlements, but they may also be directed towards some conception of the public good, for instance the remodelling of institutions in order to serve their original purpose, or to express some new set of underpinning values.

The concept of institutional bricolage, which we introduced in the last chapter, captures the inevitability of design through tinkering or patching-together:

> Seldom are institutions created from scratch. Most often they are the outcomes of the recombination and reshuffling of pre-existing components or other institutional materials that happen to be at hand and that, even when depleted, can serve new purposes. (Lanzara, 1998: 27)

Bricolage may actually be the only route to institutional innovation in the face of path dependency, and in a broader context of resource constraint, risk aversion and a generalized lack of trust (Lanzara, 1998: 27). It may also be particularly well suited to a governance environment in which institutions are both more diverse and more entangled. In local governance, for instance, the shape of the institutional matrix emerges as the outcome of action at many different institutional levels (from the EU to national, regional, local and neighbourhood levels) and in different institutional locations (within the political, commercial and civil society domains). Peter John (2001: 132) has argued that institutional arrangements at different levels are becoming 'so embedded in each other's affairs as to make a continuum of networks and interrelationships between overlapping actors'.

The significance of institutional bricolage relates to the growing recognition within third phase institutionalism (documented in Chapter 5) of the importance of *endogenous* sources of institutional change, in contrast to the preoccupation with external shocks that dominated second phase approaches. It also reflects the commitment of third phase institutionalism to *bring the actor back in*. Institutional change does not occur of its own motion; it relies on human agency. We need to be able to theorize the strategies that actors use in shifting institutional arrangements towards new ends. In addition to, or even instead of, grand blueprints and formal plans, institutional design draws upon 'the entrepreneurial discovery of concealed, unacknowledged, or surprising potentialities of the available institutional repertoire' (Crouch and Farrell, 2004: 33). Building on Crouch and Farrell's insights and our previous work (Lowndes, 2005), we can identify four strategies through which institutional entrepreneurship takes place. We term these 'remembering', 'borrowing', 'sharing' and 'forgetting'. The categorization is not intended to be exhaustive, but rather suggestive of a wider range of options. We should not, of course, assume that such strategies are automatically successful, whatever their theoretical resonance. They can only be judged to be effective in as far as they provoke a shift in the rules, practices and narratives that shape actors' day-to-day behaviour, and that remains a matter for empirical enquiry in specific contexts.

Institutional remembering involves the activation of redundant institutional resources in the service of new objectives. Put simply, this means bringing back old ways of working, which have fallen into disuse, to address new problems of situations. 'Dormant' institutional resources are 'potentially accessible to the agent capable of searching into her past repertoire' (Crouch and Farrell, 2004: 18). The retention of redundant capacities may create opportunities for coping with new or changing environments (Crouch and Farrell, 2004: 23). Without the pressures of a commercial 'bottom line', it is possible that the score for institutional remembering may be greater in government and the public sector. Ironically, an insistence on 'best practice' and increased regulation may have squeezed out potentially valuable institutional resources associated with 'redundancy, duplication and slack' (Walsh *et al.*, 1997: 24).

As we saw in Chapter 5, path dependency theory asserts that alternative institutional paths are possible but, due to small events that reinforce initial choices, only one path becomes established. The process of increasing returns then entrenches that path, however arbitrary the initial choice. It is in this context that 'institutional remembering' assumes a particular importance. Searching past repertoires allows institutional entrepreneurs to remember the paths that were feasible but foregone, and to exploit the potentialities of these subordinate paths. In a manner similar to the 'institutional conversion' that Kathleen Thelen observes from a historical perspective, new purposes become attached to old institutions, which are effectively 'redirected' or 'reinterpreted'. At the same time, previously dominant institutions

Box 7.1 'Institutional remembering' in English local government

Mayors

Attempts since 2000 to introduce directly elected mayors in English local government have drawn on the 'memory' of the powerful mayors of the Victorian era. The official point of reference has been US and European mayors, who have executive powers; indeed, care has been taken to explain that new mayors were 'not mayors' in the conventional English sense of 'the social and ceremonial role of first citizen and chair of the council' (Stewart, 2003: 67). But, in effect, designers have attempted to revive, and infuse with new purposes, the dormant institution of the English mayorality which had become essentially redundant in functional terms. The strategy sought to attach to the new role a gravitas not generally associated with the group leader in local government – and hard to cultivate from scratch in a new position. As well as the ceremonial trappings of status, the institution of mayor has historical associations with the type of leadership that Labour and now Coalition governments seek to cultivate. Joseph Chamberlain in Birmingham, Clement Attlee in Stepney and Herbert Morrison in Hackney were charismatic individuals, relatively independent from their party group, who led their community and locality, not just their council. Attempts to introduce elected mayors have actually achieved very little success, showing the limitation of the remembering strategy in the face of a lack of interest or support among the public and opposition from local political interests with a stake in the existing system (notably local authority party groups).

→

come to be 'displaced' as subordinate institutions gain in salience (Mahoney and Thelen, 2010: 15–16). Box 7.1 provides examples of institutional remembering in action.

Institutional borrowing involves the transfer of institutional resources from an adjacent 'action space' (Crouch and Farrell, 2004). The actors most able to exploit this strategy are those who operate within more than one institutional environment. Borrowing is particularly pertinent for 'the complex collective agent, who can simultaneously play different games in its different components' (Crouch and Farrell, 2004: 24). In an environment of multi-actor and multi-level governance, involving multiple rules and multiple players, borrowing provides rich inspiration – and material – for institutional design. To take an example, an unusually high proportion of the new intake of MPs in the British1997 election were also sitting local authority councillors. This enabled extensive processes of institutional borrowing,

Parishes

Remembering has been more successful in terms of attempts to revive the 'parish' as the basis for new neighbourhood-based reforms. The parish council is also an expression of a subordinate institutional path: one which embodied a locality-based conception of local governance and prioritized proximity, community identity and local difference. Over time, this path became subordinate to an institutional path that expressed a professionalized and service-based conception of local governance, which prioritized scale, party allegiance and equality of treatment. The 'local' path has never gone away (there are 9,000 parish councils in England and 75,000 elected councillors); but parish councils are not universal and have no specific duties, their services being entirely discretionary. Sub-local institutions have been a subordinate option in local government, but they are currently being 'remembered' as local authorities seek to make massive spending cuts by integrating a variety of front-line services on a neighbourhood basis, with a focus on 'well-being' in a holistic sense (rather than on service specific performance indicators). Neighbourhood working is also seen as providing a platform for engaging citizens as volunteers and co-producers of services, in the context of the UK coalition government's 'Big Society' agenda. Space for such localist remembering has also opened up as dominant professional and bureaucratic institutions have progressively lost legitimacy and their capacity to shape behaviour and expectations among politicians and public alike. Although there is concern among the public as to whether the 'Big Society' is a cover for cuts, opinion polls do show that citizens aspire to get more involved in practical activities at a very local level. So this remembering strategy may prove more successful than that of the elected mayors.

Sources: Lowndes (2005); Lowndes and Squires (2012).

which operated (with varying success) on a two-way basis – from local councils to parliament (e.g. altering the duration and timing of parliamentary debates to be more similar to conventional working hours) and from parliament to local councils (e.g. designing new local authority 'scrutiny committees' on the model of parliamentary select committees). Interestingly, nearly all the MPs concerned gave up their council seats within a short period of time, thus undermining further opportunities for institutional borrowing of the sort available in political systems (like France) in which the holding of multiple political offices is the norm.

Institutional sharing refers to what Crouch and Farrell (2004: 34) call the 'transfer of experience from other agents through networks of structured relationships'. While 'borrowing' involves the same actor transferring experience between the different arenas in which she acts, 'sharing' provides access to the institutional repertoires of other actors (who operate in different action spaces). If remembering is about looking backwards and borrowing is about looking sideways, then sharing involves looking *outwards* in the search to expand and recombine institutional resources. Conceptually, sharing is of particular interest because it challenges any 'rigid dichotomy between endogeneity and exogeneity as sources of actors' responses' to changing environments (Crouch and Farrell, 2004: 34). As we discussed in Chapter 6, attempts to create institutional 'insides' and 'outsides' are inherently political acts, as are actors' sorties across these boundaries in pursuit of new institutional resources and capacities. The adoption of private sector management techniques by civil servants is a classic example of institutional sharing, which has also led to increasing permeability in the public/private boundary as market reforms created new opportunities for companies to bid for contracts and invest in public/private partnerships, and for business leaders to access high profile and lucrative appointments. Coexisting and ongoing strategies of institutional remembering, borrowing and sharing produce the effect that Kathleen Thelen calls 'institutional layering'. Understanding processes of institutional design is akin to a geologist seeking to split and analyse the sedimented layers of a metamorphic rock.

Because 'effective' institutions are embedded in informal practices and underpinned by supportive narratives, abolishing or cancelling institutions is very difficult. De-institutionalization is every reformer's nightmare. Stopping people doing things the way they are used to doing things is usually more difficult than getting them engaged in new activity. Even when formal requirements are removed from the statute or the rule book, established practices may remain (and the supportive narratives that are used to legitimize them). In addition to institutional persistence, those who perceive their interests to be served by these original institutions are likely to defend them. The promotion of new institutions is also difficult amidst the clutter of not-approved but still-pursued rules and practices. So what options are open to the bricoleur?

Institutional forgetting involves the withdrawal of active maintenance for existing institutions. This is not absentmindedness but strategic forgetting or, in Thelen's words, 'deliberate neglect'. To retain their place at the forefront of political life, institutions require effective cultivation: the provision of information, the allocation of benefits, the enforcement of sanctions, the acting-out of practices, and the rehearsing of supportive narratives. If such maintenance work is neglected, institutions wither on the vine. Old institutions are eventually crowded-out when 'a compromise between old and new' turns gradually into 'defeat of the old' (Mahoney and Thelen, 2010: 15–16). This appears to be the fate of many 'flexible working' and 'family friendly' arrangements within both public and private sector workplaces. While in the 'rule book', they fall into disuse when they are not actively promoted nor role-modelled by senior people, and when those who do seek to use them see their career prospect suffer or face disapproval from their colleagues. Such institutional rules may then be formally dropped on the basis of low take-up or the absence of a compelling 'business case' to retain them. However, while the rules may disappear from the rule book for now, the practices and narratives associated with them are simply submerged, waiting for actors to drag them to the surface and demand reform.

So do institutional bricolage and recombination exhaust the possibilities for institutional design? What are we to make of grand schemes of constitutional engineering and the efforts of heroic champions for institutional reform? We know that every day there are new constitutions written, international treaties prepared, voting systems designed, public services restructured, and social movements re-regulated. Is all this action in vain, with 'real' design only emerging bottom up in the interstices of existing rules, practices and narratives?

We saw earlier in the book that institutionalism has been criticized for stating the obvious – that institutional change is hard to control – and retreating into an 'anything is possible' position. But third phase approaches are responding to this criticism by showing how an understanding of constraints upon institutional reform can be translated into a set of design principles. It is to this issue that we now turn.

The paradox of institutional design

Third phase institutionalism faces a paradox regarding institutional design. Institutional design with a capital 'D' is likely to fail (in the sense of not meeting all of its objectives); but it is also an inevitable – and entirely appropriate – aspiration for political actors. It is clear, not just from research but also from daily life, that attempts at root-and-branch institutional reform rarely satisfy their initiators' intentions. Many of us are familiar with workplace restructurings that amount to no more than a rearrangement of the deckchairs, or to grand policy pronouncements that are watered down during implementation due to resource constraint or opposition. Institutional change is hard to control because of the power relationships inherent in existing institutional arrangements, and because of the embedded or nested nature of political institutions. New institutions are likely to be resisted (or 'hijacked') by those who benefit from existing arrangements or see new rules as hostile to their interests. They are likely to be adapted in ways that suit locally specific institutional environments. Organizations and groups have an immense capacity 'to co-opt, absorb or deflect new initiatives' (Newman, 2001: 28). 'Old' and 'new' institutions frequently coexist, often in tension. Even where new formal rules are put in place, informal practices and narratives may continue to shape political behaviour in old ways.

Yet, despite these obstacles, institutionalists argue that attempts at reform remain enormously important, because they express social values (and reveal struggles over those values) that are generally hidden below the surface of political institutions. Reform attempts provide an opportunity for 'the discovery, clarification and elaboration' of the values that undergird existing and alternative institutional arrangements (March and Olsen, 1989: 90). Institutional reform is a crucial part of the process whereby actors develop 'an understanding of what constitutes a good society, without necessarily being able to achieve it, and how alternative institutions may be imagined to contribute to such a world' (March and Olsen, 1989: 91).

So how should institutional designers proceed, in the knowledge of these practical pitfalls and normative imperatives? In a classic statement of third phase institutionalism, Bob Goodin (1996) argues that the focus should be upon institutional *redesign* rather than design, and upon *indirect* rather than direct mechanisms for securing change. 'Redesign' is important because reformers are inevitably constrained by 'past inheritances'. An 'indirect' approach is important because reformers need to steer or frame the interventions of dispersed political actors, rather than seek to impose a single set of rules. Goodin counsels against 'The Myth of the Intentional Designer':

> Typically, there is no single design or designer. There are just lots of localised attempts at partial design cutting across one another, and any sensible scheme for institutional design has to take account of that fact. Thus... what we should be aiming at is not the design of institutions directly. Rather, we should be aiming at *designing schemes for designing institutions* – schemes which will pay due regard to the multiplicity of designers and to the inevitably cross-

cutting nature of their intentional interventions in the design process. (Goodin,1996: 28, emphasis added)

Third phase institutionalism departs from the assumptions of the first phase that good institutional design is guaranteed by a combination of internal consistency and 'goodness of fit' with the external environment. Good design is actually secured by clear values rather than functional necessities, and by a capacity for learning and adaptation rather than environmental 'fit'. Because institutions inevitably embody values and power relationships, institutional design is inescapably a normative project. There needs to be clarity about the values being promoted (and challenged) within institutional reform programmes. Shifting 'old' values is one reason why institutional change is hard to effect; at the same time, it is this normative dimension that makes institutional design so important. As Rothstein (1996: 138) explains: 'If social norms... vary with the character of political institutions, then we can at least to some extent decide which norms shall prevail in the society in which we live.' In institutional design, guiding values should not only be clear but 'publicly defensible' – that is, legitimate in the eyes of the wider citizenry (Goodin, 1996: 41–2). The values that inform institutional design need to be understood and, preferably, critically debated amongst the citizenry (Luban,1996: 169). Dryzek (1996: 104) argues that: 'No institution can operate without an associated and supportive discourse'. 'Value literacy' may be as important an attribute of institutional design as 'efficiency capacity' (Stoker, 2010).

Hood (1998) counsels against the 'one-best-way reflex' in institutional design and the idea that modernity has a single 'leading edge'. Rather than seeking the universal application of a particular model, or the maximum spread of 'best practice', it is important to sustain a 'variety engine' within institutional design (Hood, 1998: 69). Tolerating, even promoting, variability within institutional design is a way of building in a capacity for innovation and adaptation to changing environments. Thus a value-led 'scheme for designing institutions' can seek to harness, rather than frustrate or override, the local knowledge and creativity of multiple, dispersed institutional entrepreneurs. Goodin (1996: 42) argues that: 'We ought [to] encourage experimentation with different structures in different places; and we ought, furthermore, [to] encourage reflection upon the lessons from elsewhere and a willingness to borrow those lessons where appropriate.' Reflecting upon unintended as well as intended consequences can add further to the store of design variants, and enable

those charged with institutional reform to steer processes of bricolage rather than stumble upon their effects.

Institutions are, of course, associated with stability. The 'point' of
institutions is to stabilize and regularize political behaviour in pursuit
of specific goals, both substantive and procedural. Returning to the
paradox of design, it is the very stability of institutions that makes
reform difficult, but also alluring. Securing institutional change enables
politicians to frame expectations and shape behaviour in new ways.
Rather than having to win the argument on every issue, they can rely
upon a stable institutional configuration that sets the parameters for
debate and action. Institutions prescribe and proscribe certain forms of
behaviour; they establish, in March and Olsen's words, a logic of
appropriateness – what is acceptable and unacceptable, and what is
desirable and undesirable.

Hence the purpose of institutional design is to make rules 'stick'
(however partial the eventual outcome). As Goodin (1996: 40)
explains: 'We want to have the capacity, sometimes, to bind ourselves
to a certain course of action and to ensure that we (or our successors)
resist any temptations to deviate from it'. But the sensibilities of third
phase institutionalism ensure a nuanced approach to making institutions stick. Goodin (1996: 40) argues that political institutions need to
be flexible, but not 'brittle': they should 'be open to alteration where
appropriate' but 'resistant to sheer buffeting by changes in social
circumstances that have no bearing upon their assumptions upon
which those institutions were predicated'. Political institutions need to
be able to *adapt* to new circumstances, without being *destroyed* by
them.

We saw in Chapter 3 that a defining characteristic of institutions is
that they are 'triadic' – that is, 'established and enforced by "third
parties" who are not part of the institutionalised interaction' (Offe,
1996: 203). (In contrast to organizations which are 'diadic', and pure
conventions which are self-enforcing.) In short, the framing effects of
institutions are not accidental; they exist because someone somewhere
cares that they are making a difference. The enforcer may be easily
identified (a professional association or a government department or
the law of the land) but can also take the form of a more amorphous set
of interests (as in the case of 'academic freedom' or, less attractively,
'institutionalized racism'). But in all cases, enforcement is a process
rather than a thing, and rests upon the supply of 'arguments as to why
an institutionalised status order is to be held valid and hence deserves
to be adhered to' (Offe, 1996: 204).

Goodin (1996: 41) argues that institutional design must be 'sensitive to motivational complexity'. The most effective enforcement mechanisms may be those that cultivate trust and embody 'a direct appeal to moral principles', rather than those that seek simply to control the behaviour of actors assumed to be self-interested and prone to 'defection'. He points out: 'by "designing institutions for knaves" such mechanical solutions risk making knaves of potentially more honourable actors'. Such a formulation takes us back to the need for institutional design to be underpinned by a clear, and preferably shared, set of values. The success of institutional design depends as much upon the 'institutional software' of persuasive arguments and convincing discourses, as upon the 'hardware' of rules, rights and operating procedures (Dryzek, 1996: 104).

In summary, we can use Claus Offe's (1996: 219) metaphor of 'institutional gardening' (in contrast to 'institutional engineering') to think about how hardy institutional hybrids might be created and nurtured. In horticulture, techniques of grafting or selective breeding ensure core characteristics are preserved within variants that are able to flourish in specific, and dynamic, conditions. And the environment itself is nurtured to maximize the likelihood of new plants taking root and thriving beyond the first few weeks. The gardener will apply organic and inorganic supplements, erect physical coverings, deter or see off predators, and judiciously remove both weak specimens and alien (or pre-existing) weeds. Clearly the task of designing political institutions is not just a paper exercise. Design also includes the practical work of experimentation and recombination (leading to evaluation and revision); the careful preparation of the political and administrative terrain, through argument and persuasion and the input of physical and human capital; and the active nurturing and protection of juvenile institutions, as they emerge within an already crowded and conflicted institutional space.

Operationalizing design principles

Given the political centrality of institutional design (and in keeping with our 'engaged' perspective), we have argued that third phase institutionalists should not just point out obstacles to institutional design but reflect upon the principles most likely to maximize success, and by which reform programmes may be evaluated. Two key concepts – robustness and revisability – enable us to organize the varied insights

Box 7.2   Institutional design in English local government under New Labour

New Labour launched its programme for local government reform with six consultations, covering issues like community leadership, service quality, financial accountability, and ethical standards. The scale of activity signalled a break from the piecemeal reforms of the Conservative era and a determination to consider local government's fundamental role and purpose. In local government, as elsewhere, New Labour claimed it would secure a shift in values through the redesign of political institutions, insisting that: 'policies flow from values, and not vice versa' (Blair, 1998: 3–4).

In relation to service improvement, the government explained that its flagship policy, Best Value, 'does not depend upon detailed prescriptions from government... [we] will not therefore seek to prescribe a uniform approach or product' (DETR, 1998). In contrast to the previous 'compulsory competitive tendering' regime, Best Value applied to all local authority services and allowed for a wider range of 'tests of competitiveness', and took on board quality, as well as cost, in determining 'value'. Ongoing service improvement, through a rolling programme of service reviews, replaced a specific schedule of tendering procedures for named services. Local authorities were encouraged to develop a wide range of service delivery mechanisms (in-house, partnerships, contracts), providing they complied with four key principles. Local authorities were required to *challenge* themselves as to why and how a particular service was delivered, *compare* their performance with similar authorities, *consult* with service users and other stakeholders on improvement targets, and *compete* effectively with alternative service providers.

Despite the early assumption of revisability, there subsequently developed a high degree of central prescription and pressure towards uniformity. The 'learning by doing' principle was never fully exploited, as the BV legislation was passed long before the pilots could 'yield comprehensive information on the impact of the BV framework or the usefulness of its

→

raised in this chapter, while also expressing the central paradox of institutional design.

Robustness can be operationalized in relation to two criteria:

- first, the clarity of the values informing institutional design; and
- second, the nature and effectiveness of 'third party enforcement'.

Because 'institutionalization' is an ongoing process (institutions are not once-and-for-all creations), it is not sufficient to examine the values and enforcement approach embodied in the original design. We need also to look at the extent to which value clarity is maintained over time, and at the ongoing development of enforcement strategies. By 'enforcement' various parts' (Boyne, 1999: 11). In addition, commitment-based enforcement strategies increasingly gave way to control-oriented approaches. A Best Value Inspectorate came into force in April 2000 to 'review the reviews' (Stewart, 2002: 4). In the first year of the Inspectorate's existence, some 3,000 reviews were completed and 600 inspection reports produced (Audit Commission, 2001). Best Value arrangements on the ground became increasingly uniform. The rationale provided by the government for its change of approach related to poor outcomes on service performance revealed by inspection, alongside low satisfaction levels on the part of services users.

In relation to 'democratic renewal', New Labour set out to restore the public's trust and confidence in elected local government. Consultation with communities was encouraged via a wide variety of different methods (citizens' panels and juries, for instance), and New Labour orchestrated experiments in the conduct of local elections (e.g. postal and electronic ballots). While these developments scored well in terms of revisability, the robustness of new institutional designs was less clear. Surveys showed that many initiatives amounted to 'tick box' exercises only, with little or no influence upon final decision-making (Lowndes *et al.*, 1998). In contrast, New Labour's plans to reform arrangements for political leadership within local authorities moved from an initial focus on pilots and local choice to a requirement (via the Local Government Act 2000) that all councils separated their executive and scrutiny functions via one of three different institutional innovations – leader/cabinet, directly elected mayor, or council manager. The attempt to make new designs stick through compulsion (with a view to clarifying accountability and making leadership more visible) backfired, however, as the vast majority of councils opted for the least radical option (leader/cabinet) which was effectively subsumed within the existing 'rules of the game' (Leach and Lowndes, 2004).

Source: Lowndes and Wilson (2003).

we mean ensuring that new institutional designs 'stick' – that they shape actors' behaviour in desired ways and give rise to new and specific 'logics of appropriateness'. Approaches to enforcement may rely more or less on direct control or on commitment-building among actors.

Revisability can be operationalized in relation to a further two criteria:

- first, flexibility – that is, the capacity within institutional designs for adaptation over time, and for capturing the benefits of 'learning by doing';
- second, variability – that is, the extent to there is tolerance (even encouragement) of different design variants in different locations.

In short, revisability seeks to ensure that institutional arrangements can operate in different local environments and changing circumstances, and that there is a capacity for innovation and learning.

To consider how these principles might fare in practice, we present a case study of English local government reform between 1997 and 2010 (Box 7.2). Dryzek (1996: 121–2) argues that local government provides particularly interesting terrain for institutional innovation because of its distance from the restrictive imperatives of the nation state and because of its capacity to generate critical and imaginative institutional arrangements. Our case study shows that the New Labour government, elected in 1997, started out with a refreshingly different approach to the design of local government institutions, in comparison with what had gone before under the Conservatives. Labour pursued something akin to the 'indirect' approach favoured by third phase institutionalists in their underlining of the constraints upon direct interventions in institutional change. Labour's initial statements on service improvement and democratic renewal recognized that real institutional change would occur only if the efforts of practical 'designers' on the ground were harnessed. New Labour set out demanding design principles, but cultivated a partnership approach towards those responsible for change at the local level, seeking to build commitment through consultation with an extended policy community and the provision of incentives to develop pilot and 'beacon' schemes. Seeking to meet criteria of both robustness and revisability, New Labour was clear about underlying values and enforcement mechanisms, while encouraging experimentation with design variants at the local level.

During Labour's first term, a trade-off started to emerge between criteria of revisability and robustness. In the case of 'Best Value', revisability was increasingly sacrificed in an effort to shore up the robustness of the performance management regime. Was BV delivering institutional arrangements that, in Goodin's phrase, could 'bind' public servants to the goal of service improvement? Was Best Value delivering institutional arrangements that were 'publicly defensible', in the sense of being understood and valued by the wider community? In the case of democratic renewal, New Labour's value base for institutional change grew weaker, and remained contested by those in local government who championed local autonomy *per se*. A formal, structural change was achieved in political leadership arrangements, and a wealth of new citizen participation initiatives were introduced – but there is little evidence of change in the effective rules of local political behaviour. While the government became increasingly prescriptive over time regarding the detail of new systems of political leadership, the robustness of the democratic renewal agenda as a whole was suffering.

Indeed, the 2001 White Paper confirmed the demise of New Labour's distinctive normative blend of service improvement and democratic renewal (Lowndes, 2002). In its second and third term, Labour sought to rebalance design criteria of robustness and revisability through the principle of 'earned autonomy'. On paper, the government recognized that too much central prescription and detailed monitoring could cramp local authorities' creativity and ability to perform. Yet 'comprehensive assessment' and the imposition of national targets came to dominate Labour's approach, with any local freedoms available only to 'high performing' authorities (as judged by central government). Freedoms were limited to modes of service delivery and not to greater democratic or financial autonomy. The trajectory of local government reform ultimately reflected longer-term institutional legacies of centralization and 'control freakery' (Wilson, 2003) inherited from the Conservatives.

That New Labour achieved so little of its original vision for local government can be explained with reference to our design criteria. On robustness, the distinctive value blend of service improvement and democratic renewal became compromised over time; at the same time, a sophisticated enforcement strategy involving hard and soft means was progressively replaced by a top-down approach characterized by Wilson and Game (2011) as 'carrots and Semtex'. On revisability, while variation and flexibility were initially encouraged, the government became increasingly impatient to tie-down its preferred institutional designs and legislative timetables and squeezed out any meaningful 'learning by doing'. The partnership approach was undermined by the imposition of more and more central targets, a burdensome inspection regime, and the threat of direct government intervention in running 'failing' local authorities. Crude enforcement mechanisms ('designed for knaves') led to widespread game-playing on the part of local authorities aiming to maximize inspection outcomes at all costs. As Bevan and Hood (2006: 517) point out: 'Governance by targets rests on the assumption that targets change the behaviour of individuals and organizations, but that "gaming" can be kept to some acceptably low level'. Gaming can be defined as reactive subversion, such as 'hitting the target and missing the point', or reducing performance where targets do not apply. Bevan and Hood (2006: 517) are scathing in their assessment:

In the 2000s, governments in the UK, particularly in England, developed a system of governance of public services that combined targets with an element of terror. This has obvious parallels with the Soviet regime, which was initially successful but then collapsed.

In New Labour's defence, their modernization agenda confronted opposition at the local level, and institutional inertia. In seeking tighter control over the institutional reform process, the government claimed to be acting to further the public's interest against the 'forces of conservatism' within local governance and the public sector more generally. At the time, Stoker (1999: 35) expressed the government's dilemma thus: 'There is a danger that the reform programme is seen as external and imposed. Equally there are considerable vested interests that make a wholly bottom-up approach unviable'. Later, reflecting upon New Labour's unfolding strategy, Stoker detects what he calls a 'fatalist' approach, which takes a step further our insights regarding institutional design and contingency. Stoker (2002: 417) argues that there was a deliberate strategy to destabilize existing institutional configurations and exploit existing ambiguities:

> New Labour's response... resembles that of a strategy based on the principles of a lottery. The strategy has allowed a plethora of decentralization units and reform initiatives to find favour but none to dominate... The key point is not that New Labour's policies have been *ad hoc* or even that they have been confused. Rather its policies are a chosen course of action aimed at searching for the right reform formula and creating a dynamic for change by encouraging instability but also space for innovation among the institutions of devolved governance... The adoption of the strategy in addition, reflects political contingencies. Moreover, the lottery strategy has helped New Labour sustain its coalition of supporters and manage tensions between different reform approaches.

As such, New Labour put its faith in institutional emergence and, in line with the analyses of Schickler, Pierson and Thelen that we discussed earlier, *intentionally* blurred (rather than clarified) its value base, with the aim of holding together the restless coalition of MPs, local government politicians, public service managers, and business leaders who occupied the 'Big Tent'. The approach could be described as anti-design, in the sense of accepting the likelihood of failure, but pro-change, in the sense of intervening to unsettle the status quo and provoke entrepreneurship and institutional recombination.

Within policy studies there has been a resurgence of interest in issues of design and, interestingly, many British local authorities and public service bodies are now re-naming their policy sections 'design units'. Does this amount to any novel engagement with the challenges of institutional design? Policy statements actually read very much like manifestos for third phase institutionalism. For example, we can easily map the main claims of the UK's 'Public Services Lab' on to three propositions arising from third phase institutionalism:

- Design as expressing values: 'there is no such thing as neutral design... the way that public services are organized inevitably influences the outcomes they achieve'.
- Design as constituted through (embedded) agency: 'design in public services is about engaging people – the users, citizens and professionals working at the front line. It starts with their lived experience...'.
- Design as bricolage: 'experimenting with the concept of prototyping... trying lots of things, failing quickly at low cost, iterating and learning' (Colligan, 2011).

'Design thinking' is prescribed by US business school consultants as a vehicle for 'social innovation', with a particular emphasis on tackling complex, intransigent problems that have not responded to conventional public service responses. There is an emphasis on moving from mechanical images of rational design (pulling levers, causes and effects) towards an approach that is 'deeply human' and builds upon designers' 'ability to be intuitive, to recognise patterns, to construct ideas that have emotional meaning as well as being functional' (Brown and Wyatt, 2010: 33). The consultants recommend that designers spend time 'in the field' and draw inspiration from people's actual practices, looking out particularly for cases of 'positive deviance' (for example, poor families with healthy children) in order to study – in effect – rules of the game that have developed 'on the margins' and may form the basis for new prototypes that can be refined, piloted and scaled in the form of major social programmes. That design is an ongoing project is recognized in a three stage model of inspiration, ideation and implementation (Brown and Wyatt, 2010).

Gerry Stoker has argued that the take-up of these insights among policy advisers and practitioners underlines the need for political science itself to develop a 'design arm'. This requires an intellectual reorientation away from 'identifying problems' towards 'designing solutions'. It has the potential to add to the mix an 'essentially political' conception of the design process. Recognizing that design is about 'the play of power' need not consign the political scientist to the sideline. Both contingency and partisanship may be inevitable in final outcomes, but the expertise of the political scientist should, in Stoker's (2010: 83) words, be 'at the service of democracy, not above it'. Drawing on the insights of Laswell and Dryzek regarding the 'science of democracy', Stoker (2010: 81) recommends that:

> the overarching framework for design in political science is set within a commitment to open democratic debate and the presence of a real politics of open deliberation and exchange. The designer is signing up to support that process of democratic politics rather than support every product of that process.

Practically, a commitment to a design arm for political science would involve institutionalists in the co-production, evaluation and improvement of a repertoire of design alternatives. 'Design experiments' provide one such avenue. John, Smith and Stoker (2009) have used such a method to compare and contrast the 'nudge' strategy which has been embraced by US Democrats and UK Conservatives aiming to secure behaviour change among citizens, on the one hand, and the 'think' strategy, which emerges from the deliberative turn that has dominated how academics have theorized democracy from the 1990s onwards, on the other. The nudge concept originates from behavioural economic and psychology, and works on the basis that politicians and managers can offer citizens a 'choice architecture' that encourages them to act in ways which benefit themselves and others. The 'think' strategy originates from political theory and sociology, and 'holds that citizens, given the right context and framing, can think themselves collectively towards a better understanding of problems and more effective collective solutions, avoiding thereby a narrow focus on their short term self interest' (John *et al.*, 2009: 361). Indeed, the two strategies can work together and 'no government should want to get rid of either tool'. In terms of institutional design, nudge practitioners need to 'give more attention to the way collective and institutional settings help determine the success or failure of a nudge' (John *et al.*, 2009: 369). While advocates of think need to consider how the rules which apply to the deliberative process can reduce power asymmetries and encourage the disadvantaged to find their individual and collective voices.

Conclusion

In second phase institutionalism, Schotter (1986: 118) questioned whether institutions could be 'pre-designed' and argued that they should be theorized as 'unplanned and unintended regularities (social conventions) that emerge "organically"'. In third phase institutionalism, few, if any, scholars now take this radically evolutionary perspective. The turn to agency in explaining institutional change has convinced most theorists that there are points in the policy cycle when political actors will engage in attempts at purposive design. As we have seen above, the causes of scholars' divergence originate from how much control they envisage their actors will be able to exercise over the longer-term processes and effects of designs as they are implemented.

Hence, theorists such as Pierson and Schickler do not doubt actors' capacity to engage in institutional design, but are highly sceptical about the possibilities for achieving satisfactory outcomes. Blyth, Hay and Jessop see moments of crisis as formative periods in which political actors can redesign institutions from the ideas to hand, in conditions of conflict and contestation, and with unpredictable outcomes. Schmidt, on the other hand, sees state actors as having much more control over processes and effects, as they bring together ideas through the coordinative discourse and the communicative discourse to manipulate the polity's perception of economic conditions. Ostrom argues that actors much further down the hierarchy can design institutions at a local level, and predicts that these will be more effective in preserving common pool resources than rules designed centrally. In a positive sum game, both rule makers and rule takers can control processes and effects to the greater public good. While sociological institutionalists emphasize the bounded nature of actors' rationality, they do not deny that actors are purposeful and creative in seeking to shape political institutions in circumstances of both uncertainty and struggle.

We have argued throughout this book that institutionalists must place institutions at the heart of their theorizing, and that the key characteristics of institutions are to be found in the interconnections which create enduring configurations – between rules, practices and supporting narratives. In addition to attempting to exploit gaps and ambiguities within these configurations, actors also dedicate a great deal of energy to the maintenance and defence of existing institutions (and their interconnections), spurred on by multi-motivational constructions of their interests. This is why institutional configurations tend to be relatively stable, with relatively predictable processes and effects. This is not to argue that institutions simply work in a mechanistic cause-and-effect manner; rather it is to affirm that, if the rules of the game matter, they must be theorized as constraining and empowering actors in ways which we can confidently project into the future, at least, in broad terms. And we conclude from this basic theoretical point that it is therefore possible for actors to design institutions which take forward (if not fully achieve) their desired objectives in line with such broad projections.

Attempts at institutional design, as we have shown in this chapter, are at the heart of politics (democratic and otherwise). Institutional design presents an opportunity for actors to bind themselves and others to certain courses of action (which in turn express particular values and power settlements). Design is the attempt to create and maintain institutional rules that are sufficiently robust and revisable to ensure a high degree of 'stickability' in the face of continually changing environments. Typically, grand blueprints for change will be interpreted and implemented via dispersed yet strategic acts of bricolage, which together feed processes of institutional emergence. The aspiration to institutional design is inevitable, but success is not. Paraphrasing Bob Jessop's (2000: 31) remarks on governance, we believe that institutional design requires 'a self-reflexive irony, in the sense that participants must recognise the likelihood of failure but proceed as if success were possible'.

Chapter 8

Conclusion

This book set out to show 'why institutions matter'. It has argued for the centrality of institutions to an understanding of political behaviour and political outcomes, not just for the purpose of post-hoc explanation but to anticipate the shape and dynamics of ongoing political projects. The explosion of new institutional forms (linked, for instance, to globalization and the information revolution) has simply increased the need for sophisticated concepts and imaginative methods to inform research. The book proposes a new periodization of institutionalist thought. It departs from the conventional distinction between 'old' and 'new' institutionalism, and takes issue with the splintering of new institutionalism into many different, competing, variants. Instead, we have sought to identify the heart of the institutionalist project – in both theory and practice – and to specify a common core of concepts. We insist that institutionalist explanations should start with institutions themselves, regarding them and not other phenomena as the chief object of analysis and, indeed, the variable that explains most of political life. Too many 'institutionalists' have drifted away from this position, using the label as no more than a 'flag of convenience' within wider academic debates. We argue for a focus on what is specific to institutionalism, rather than on spawning sub-varieties in which the term may be used as no more than a legitimating suffix. The researcher claiming an 'institutionalist' approach needs to be sure that they are privileging institutions over other possible explanations of political behaviour, and indeed that they are able to identify clearly the institutions in question.

We have sought to address such fundamental issues, and to link theoretical concerns with methodological strategies. We have elaborated our arguments in relation to a wide range of case studies, seeking to check that concepts can be operationalized in research, while also resonating with the worlds of policy, practice and political struggle. Our claim for a common core to institutionalism does not, however, imply a settled state, or a monolithic enterprise. As well as specifying the common conceptual core, we have identified the key theoretical and methodological dilemmas faced by institutionalists. Despite the second phase divergence of institutionalisms, we detect significant convergence regarding the challenges ahead and argue that the greatest traction is to be gained by borrowing across different strands. The remainder of this chapter offer a reprise of the main argument, in the context of a forward agenda for institutionalist research.

The institutionalist trajectory

We propose that the trajectory of institutionalist thought is best captured in terms of three phases. We begin with 'Phase 1 – Exploration and Rediscovery', which combines the so-called 'old institutionalism' and the subsequent emergence of the 'new institutionalism'. Next comes 'Phase 2 – Divergence and Division', which sees the new institutionalism growing rapidly through three main schools – rational choice, sociological and historical institutionalism – while also spinning off newcomers such as discursive and feminist institutionalisms. We have now entered 'Phase 3 – Convergence and Consolidation', which sees an effective coming together across different schools of institutionalism around a set of core concepts and key dilemmas (although such schools may continue to emphasize their differences rather than similarities). The book argues that, through a series of consolidatory moves, a shared picture is emerging of how political institutions work which can be summarized as follows: they shape actors' behaviour through informal as well as formal means; they exhibit dynamism as well as stability; they distribute power and are inevitably contested; they take a messy and differentiated form; and they are mutually constitutive with the political actors whom they influence, and by whom they are influenced.

Rules, practices and narratives

Recognizing the tendency towards conceptual stretching within institutionalism, we explore these characteristics in depth. We attempt to pin down how it is that political institutions do their work. We propose that institutions shape political behaviour in three different ways: through rules, practices and narratives. These we term modes of constraint. In each case, we draw on insights from rational choice, historical and sociological institutionalism to establish points of convergence and consolidation, while also identifying key dilemmas and forward research agendas. Our key conclusion is that, while rules, practices and narratives constrain actors in their own right, it is when they work together that they are most effective. The way in which these different modes of constraint are combined (or not) in practice is an empirical rather than an ontological matter. Rejecting a search for ontological purity, we do not privilege *a priori* one type of constraint over another. We argue that actors construct the world according to mixed motivations, and that the institutions they encounter are themselves the outcome of mixed motivational constructions. We gain a deeper understanding of how institutions work (and how they can be reformed or resisted), if we accept that actors may be constrained simultaneously by rules, practices and narratives. Separating out these different modes is important not just analytically but methodologically, as it provides a guide as to what to look for in research on political institutions (whether this involves analysing historical documents, interviewing political actors, or undertaking lab studies or policy experiments).

Having specified a common conceptual core for third phase institutionalism, we went on to identify, and address, the shared dilemmas with which institutionalists of different hues are currently grappling. These centre on how to conceptualize power and agency, institutional change and diversity, and prospects for intentional institutional design.

Power and agency

Allowing actors a distinctly institutional form of agency, we do not assume that they will comply with the precepts of the institutions they encounter. The character of enforcement varies across modes of constraint, from formal sanctions to normative disapproval and cognitive dissonance. The effectiveness of institutional enforcement depends upon the power, resources and strategic action of (individual or collective) actors. Through case studies, we have shown how constraint can be strengthened through the articulation of rules, practices and narratives, but also how rules are broken, dominant practices resisted and authoritative narratives disrupted. And, just as institutions seek to constrain, they also empower. Applying our three-fold model of rules, practices and narratives, we examine how institutions directly empower through visible, recorded mechanisms such as laws, rights and licences; how they indirectly empower through informal and unwritten mechanisms such as gender norms or the privileges associated with nepotism or patronage; and how the narrative accounts of individual and group actors legitimize their authority and pre-empt challenge. Conceptualizing the constraint/empowerment dialectic is a key challenge for third phase institutionalism, which we address through our '5Cs' model of agency. Institutions shape actors' behaviour but are themselves the creations of human agency; they both embody and serve to reproduce specific power settlements. Institutionalism is able to illuminate how inequality and injustice are 'built in' to political systems, while also having the potential to inform the bottom-up institutional building of those who seek to resist such constraints.

Institutional change

First and second phase institutionalists have been routinely criticized for an inability to provide a convincing account of how political institutions change. First phase institutionalism undoubtedly focused upon explaining stability and predictability in politics. Second phase institutionalism was interested in institutional change but explained this in stop/go terms, identifying long periods of path dependence punctuated by critical junctures, the origins of which lay outside the institution itself. We argue that, from a range of different perspectives, third phase institutionalism has succeeded in breaking out of this restrictive model. Drawing on insights from rational choice, historical and sociological institutionalism, we show how gradual institutional change may have transformative effects, and how significant change may result from internal as well as external drivers. Using case studies, we show how institutions' stability over time is actually the outcome of a contested process of institutional maintenance, reflecting shifting power relationships and an ongoing 'war of position' over ideas and values.

Institutional diversity

Institutions change over time through processes of recombination, through the articulation of old and new institutional elements and shifts in the configuration of rules, practices and narratives. While first and second phase scholarship was preoccupied with institutional convergence, third phase institutionalism helps us identify widespread institutional diversity within and across political systems. Through a series of vignettes we show how the interconnections between political and non-political institutions spawn diversity (as in 'varieties of capitalism', for instance), and how the demarcation of what is considered inside and outside the political realm is itself a subject of political contestation. Institutional hybridity arises also out of ambiguities which are built in at foundational moments (and tend to expand over time), reflecting both political compromise and the enduring legacy of former arrangements. It is hard to predict the trajectory of institutional change because of such contingent effects, which have both temporal and spatial dimensions. But what is clear is that institutional change is inevitably contested and context-dependent, while also being driven by agents who are themselves constrained by wider institutional configurations.

Institutional design

In this context, one of the most vexed questions for third phase institutionalism is whether it is possible actually to design political institutions. We argue that political actors will always seek to design political institutions as they endeavour to bind others, over time, to particular courses of action that reflect their ideas and values. While highly unlikely to achieve all it sets out to do, the impulse to institutional design is both an inevitable and an appropriate aspect of political life. At the same time, resistance to particular institutional regimes is to be expected from those actors disadvantaged by their precepts, or seeking to establish alternative arrangements. We argue that design does not only include those heroic foundational moments in which constitutions are written or fundamental reforms launched, but also the many disparate acts of 'institutional bricolage' undertaken by strategic actors on the ground who respond to changing environments and shifting power relations. For these actors, ambiguity, compromise and variety can actually become resources for, rather than obstacles to, institutional design. We explore how an understanding of the constraints on institutional design can be translated into a set of principles for good, or good enough, design. Given the realities of institutional embeddedness and ongoing struggles over values, we propose that criteria of 'robustness' and 'revisability' are best deployed to assess design strategies, or predict conditions for relative success. Indeed, engaged institutionalists within the academy are well placed to contribute to the co-production, trialling, evaluation and improvement of design alternatives.

Looking forward

The book has argued that an institutionalist canon is emerging around the recognition that diverse modes of constraint (rules, practices, narratives) coexist and interact, that institutions and actors are mutually constitutive, and that institutional change and stability are governed by the same mechanisms. As such we feel it is time to move on from those modest knowledge claims which have described institutionalism as an 'organizing perspective' (Lowndes, 2002) or the 'new pretender' (Hay, 2002). Thinking back to our argument in Chapter 2 about what makes a 'good' theory, we can conclude that institutionalism now meets this benchmark. In this context, such a theory need not set out essential and constant laws of conduct. Rather, it should establish a credible base of interlocking concepts which enables scholarship to move forward, and provides resonant heuristics for practitioners. Equally a good theory does not stifle dissent but raises questions and dilemmas to stimulate inquiry and practice.

Moving forward, the importance of understanding political institutions cannot be underestimated – how they are designed, how they shape behaviour, how they confer power, how they vary over time and space, and how their strictures are enforced but also resisted. In confronting the big political challenges of the twenty-first century – like financial regulation, human rights, environmental sustainability, racism and gender equality, access to health provision and good governance – political institutions constitute both a threat and an opportunity. Because they are so tenacious, established political institutions may present powerful obstacles to political change. But, at the same time, the possibility, and, as we argue, the inevitability, of institutional design offers creative political actors the chance to destabilize enduring power relationships and reshape these using alternative rules, practices and narratives. This book argues in favour of an 'engaged' perspective on institutions that recognizes their role in distributing power within politics, society and economy. Institutionalism enables us not just to understand better how political institutions work, but also to generate strategies for institutional resistance and reform in the interests of social justice.

References

Acosta, A. M. (2006) 'Crafting Legislative Ghost Coalitions in Ecuador: Informal Institutions and Economic Reform in an Unlikely Case', in G. Helmke and S. Levitsky (eds) *Informal Institutions and Democracy* (Baltimore: Johns Hopkins University Press).

Aglietta, M. (1979) *A Theory of Capitalist Regulation* (London: Verso).

Amin, A. and Thrift, N. (1994) *Globalisation, Institutions and Regional Development in Europe* (Oxford: Oxford University Press).

Aoki, M. (2001) *Towards a Comparative Institutional Analysis* (Cambridge, MA: MIT Press).

Aoki, M. (2010) *Corporations in Evolving Diversity: Cognition, Governance and Institutions* (Oxford: Oxford University Press).

Arrow, K. (1951) *Social Choice and Individual Values* (New York: Wiley).

Audit Commission (2001) *Changing Gear: Best Value Annual Statement 2001* (London: Audit Commission).

Axelrod, R. (1984) *The Evolution of Cooperation* (New York: Basic Books).

Bagehot, W. (1867) *The English Constitution* (London: Chapman & Hall).

Bannister, D. and F. Fransella (1971) *Inquiring Man* (Harmondsworth: Penguin Books).

Barnes, M., Newman, J. and Sullivan, H. (2007) *Power, Participation and Political Renewal: Case Studies in Public Participation* (Bristol: Policy Press).

Baumgartner, F. R. and Jones, B. D (1993) *Agendas and Instability in American Politics* (Chicago: University of Chicago Press).

Bell, F. and Feng, H. (2009) 'Reforming the Chinese Stock Market: Institutional Change Chinese Style', *Political Studies*, 57 (1) 117–40.

Benington, J., de Groot, L. and Foot J. (eds) (2006) *Lest We Forget: Democracy, Neighbourhoods and Government* (London: SOLACE Foundation Imprints).

Berger, P. and Luckman, T. (1967) *The Social Construction of Reality* (New York: Anchor Books).

Bevan, G. and Hood, C. (2006) 'What's Measured is What Matters:

Targets and Gaming in the English Public Health Care System', *Public Administration*, 84 (3) 517–38.

Bevir, M. and Rhodes, R. (2008) 'The Differentiated Polity in Narrative', *British Journal of Politics and International Relations*, 10, 729–34.

Bill, J. and Hardgrave, R. (1981) *Comparative Politics: The Quest for Theory* (Boston: University Press of America).

Blair, T. (1998) *The Third Way: New Politics for the New Century* (London: Fabian Society).

Blyth, M. (2002a) *Great Transformations: Economic Ideas And Political Change In The Twentieth Century* (Cambridge: Cambridge University Press).

Blyth, M. (2002b) 'Institutions and Ideas in Marxism', in G. Stoker and D. Marsh (eds) *Theories and Methods in Political Science* (2nd edn) (Basingstoke: Palgrave Macmillan) pp. 292–310.

Blyth, M. (2007) 'Powering, Puzzling, or Persuading? The Mechanisms of Building Institutional Orders', *International Studies Quarterly*, 51, 761–77.

Boyer, R. and Saillard, Y. (eds) (2002) *Regulation Theory: The State of the Art* (London: Routledge).

Brinks, D. (2006) 'The Rule of (Non) Law. Prosecuting Police Killings in Brazil and Argentina', in G. Helmke and S. Levitsky (eds) *Informal Institutions and Democracy* (Baltimore: Johns Hopkins University Press).

Brown, T. and Wyatt, J. (2010) 'Design Thinking for Social Innovation', *Stanford Social Innovation Review*, http://www.ssire view.org/articles/entry/design_thinking_for_social_innovation/.

Boyne, G. (ed.) (1999) *Managing Local Services: from CCT to Best Value* (London: Frank Cass).

Bulmer, S. (2009) 'Politics in Time Meets the Politics of Time: Historical Institutionalism and the EU Timescape', *Journal of European Public Policy*, 16 (2) 307–24.

Cairney, P. (2012) *Understanding Public Policy* (Basingstoke: Palgrave Macmillan).

Calvert, R. (1995) 'The Rational Choice Theory of Social Institutions: Co-operation, Co-ordination and Communication', in J. Banks and E. Hanushek (eds) *Modern Political Economy* (Cambridge: Cambridge University Press).

Carey, J. (2006) 'Legislative Organization', in R. Rhodes, S. Binder and B. Rockman (eds) *The Oxford Handbook of Political Institutions* (Oxford: Oxford University Press).

Chandler, A. (1977) *The Visible Hand: The Managerial Revolution in American Business* (Cambridge, MA: Harvard University Press).

Chappell, L. (2006) 'Comparing Political Institutions: Revealing the

Gendered "Logic of Appropriateness"', *Politics and Gender*, 2 (2) 223–34.

Clarke, J. (2005) 'New Labour's Citizens: Activated, Empowered, Responsibilised, Abandoned', *Critical Social Policy*, 25 (4) 447–63.

Clarke, J. and Newman, J. (1997) *The Managerial State* (London: Sage).

Clegg, S. (1990) *Modern Organizations* (London: Sage).

Clemens, E. (1997) *The People's Lobby: Organizational Innovation and the Rise of Interest Group Politics in the United States 1980–1925* (Chicago: The University of Chicago Press).

Coase, R. H. (1937) 'The Nature of the Firm', *Economica*, 4 (16) 386–405.

Cohen, M., March, J. and Olsen, J. (1972) 'A Garbage Can Model of Organizational Choice', *Administrative Science Quarterly*, 17 (1) 1–25.

Collier, R. B. and Collier, D. (1991) *Shaping the Political Arena* (Princeton, NJ: Princeton University Press).

Colligan, P. (2011) 'What Does it Mean to Design Public Services?', *Guardian*, 01.09.2011, http://www.guardian.co.uk/public-leaders-network/blog/2011/sep/01/design-public-services.

Coulson, A, and Ferrario, C. (2007) '"Institutional Thickness": Local Governance and Economic Development in Birmingham, England', *International Journal of Urban and Regional Research*, 31 (3), 591–615.

Crouch, C. (2005) *Capitalist Diversity and Change: Recombinant Governance and Institutional Entrepreneurs* (Oxford: Oxford University Press).

Crouch, C. and Farrell, H. (2004) 'Breaking the Path of Institutional Development? Alternatives to New Determinism', *Rationality and Society*, 16 (1) 5–43.

Crouch, C. and Keune, M. (2005) 'Changing Dominant Practice: Making use of Institutional Diversity in Hungary and the United Kingdom', in W. Streeck and K. Thelen (eds) *Beyond Continuity: Institutional Change in Advanced Political Economies* (Oxford: Oxford University Press).

DETR (1998) *Modern Local Government: In Touch with the People* (London: Department of the Environment, Transport and the Regions).

David, P. (1985) 'Clio and the Economics of QWERTY', *American Economic Review*, 75, 332–7.

Davies, Y., Nutley, S. and Smith, P. (eds) (2000) *What Works? Evidence-based Policy and Practice in Public Services* (Bristol: Policy Press).

Davis, G. F. and Thompson, T. (1994) 'A Social Movement Perspective on Corporate Control', *Administrative Science Quarterly*, 39, 141–73.

Dean, M. (2010) *Governmentality: Power and Rule in Modern Society* (2nd edn) (London: Sage).

Derrida, J. (1982) 'Différance', *Margins of Philosophy*, trans A. Bass (Chicago and London: University of Chicago Press).

DiMaggio, P. J. and Powell, W. (1991a) 'Introduction', in W. Powell and P. J DiMaggio (eds) *The New Institutionalism in Organizational Analysis* (Chicago: Chicago University Press) 1–30.

DiMaggio, P. J. and Powell, W. (1991b) 'The Iron Cage Revisited: Institutional Isomorphism and Collective Rationality in Organizational Fields', in W. Powell and P. J DiMaggio (eds) *The New Institutionalism in Organizational Analysis* (Chicago: Chicago University Press) 63–82.

Dionne, E. J. (2010) 'Explaining the Tea Party's Radicalism and Venom', *The Seattle Times*, 11.02.2010 http://seattletimes.nwsource.com/html/opinion/2011049825_dionne12.html.

Douglas, M. (1987) *How Institutions Think* (London: Routledge & Kegan Paul).

Drum, K. (2010) 'Tea Party: Old Whine in New Bottles' at http://motherjones.com/politics/2010/08/history-of-the-tea-party accessed 23.3.2012.

Dryzek, J. (1996) 'The Informal Logic of Institutional Design', in R. Goodin (ed.) *The Theory of Institutional Design* (Cambridge: Cambridge University Press).

Dunleavy, P. (1991) *Democracy, Bureaucracy and Public Choice* (London: Harvester Wheatsheaf).

Dunleavy, P. and O'Leary, B. (1987) *Theories of the State: The Politics of Liberal Democracy* (New York: The Meredith Press).

Eckstein, H. (1963) 'A Perspective on Comparative Politics: Past and Present', in H. Eckstein and D. E. Apter (eds) *Comparative Politics: A Reader* (Glencoe, IL: Free Press).

Eckstein, H. (1979) 'On the "Science" of the State', *Daedalus*, 108 (4) 1–20.

Eggertsson, T. (1996) 'A Note on the Economics of Institutions', in L. J. Alston, T. Eggertsson and D. C. North (eds) *Empirical Studies in Institutional Change* (Cambridge: Cambridge University Press).

Elkin, S. (1986) 'Regulation and Regime: A Comparative Analysis', *Journal of Public Policy*, 6, 49–71.

Evans, M. (2006) 'Elitism', in C. Hay, M. Lister and D. Marsh (eds) *The State: Theories and Issues* (Basingstoke: Palgrave Macmillan).

Feldman, M. S., Skoldberg, K., Brown, R. N. and Horner, D. (2004) 'Making Sense of Stories: A Rhetorical Approach to Narrative

Analysis', *Journal of Public Administration Research and Theory,* 14 (2) 147–70.

Finer, H. (1932) *The Theory and Practice of Modern Government* (London: Methuen).

Finlayson, A. and Martin, J. (2006) 'Poststructuralism', in C. Hay, M. Lister and M. Marsh (eds) *The State: Theories And Issues* (Basingstoke: Palgrave Macmillan).

Foley, M. (1999) *The Politics of the British Constitution* (Manchester: Manchester University Press).

Fox, C. and Miller, H. (1995) *Postmodern Public Administration* (Thousand Oaks, CA: Sage).

Freidenvall, L. and Krook, M. L. (2011) 'Discursive Strategies for Institutional Reform: Gender Quotas in Sweden and France', in M. L. Krook and F. Mackay (eds) *Gender, Politics and Institutions: Towards a Feminist Institutionalism* (Basingstoke: Palgrave Macmillan).

Froese, M. (2009) *Towards a Narrative Theory of Political Agency,* downloaded from http://www.cpsa-acsp.ca/papers-2009/froese.pdf accessed 23.3.2012.

Gamble, A. (1988) *The Free Economy and the Strong State: the politics of Thatcherism* (Basingstoke: Palgrave Macmillan).

Garfinkel, H. (1974) 'On the Origins of the Term Ethnomethodology', in R. Turner (ed.) *Ethnomethodology* (Harmondsworth: Penguin).

Gibbs, D. (1996) 'Integrating Sustainable Development and Economic Restructuring: a Role for Regulation Theory?', *Geoforum,* 27 (I) l–10.

Giddens, A. (1979) *Central Problems in Social Theory: Action, Structure and Contradiction in Social Analysis* (Basingstoke: Palgrave Macmillan).

Giddens, A. (1999) 'Elements of the Theory of Structuration', in A. Elliott (ed.) *Contemporary Social Theory* (Oxford: Blackwell).

Goldstein, G. and Keohane, R. O.(eds) (1993) *Ideas and Foreign Policy: Beliefs, Institutions and Policy Change* (Ithaca, NY: Cornell Press).

Goodin, R. E. (ed.) (1996) *The Theory of Institutional Design* (Cambridge: Cambridge University Press).

Goodin, R. E. and Klingemann, H. (eds) (1996) *A New Handbook of Political Science* (Oxford: Oxford University Press).

Gorges, M. J. (2001) 'New Institutionalist Explanations for Institutional Change: A Note of Caution', *Politics,* 21 (2) 137–45.

Grafstein, R. (1988) 'The Problem of Institutional Constraint', *Journal of Politics,* 50, 577–99.

Granovetter, M. (1992) 'Economic Institutional as Social

Constructions: A Framework for Analysis', *Acta Sociologica*, 35 (1) 3–11.

Hacker, J. (1998) 'The Historical Logic of National Health Insurance: Structure and Sequence in the Development of British, Canadian, and U.S. Medical Policy', *Studies in American Political Development*, 12, 57–130.

Hacker, J. (2002) *The Divided Welfare State: The Battle over Public and Private Social Benefits in the United States* (New York: Cambridge University Press).

Hacker, J. (2004) 'Privatizing Risk without Privatizing the Welfare State: The Hidden Politics of Social Policy Retrenchment in the United States', *American Political Science Review*, 98 (2) 243–60.

Hall, P. (1986) *Governing The Economy: The Politics of Intervention In Britain And France* (Cambridge: Polity Press).

Hall, P. (1989) *The Power of Economic Ideas* (Princeton: Princeton University Press).

Hall, P. (1993) 'Policy Paradigms, Social Learning, and the State: The Case of Economic Policymaking in Britain', *Comparative Politics*, 25 (3) 275–96.

Hall, P. (1998) *Cities in Civilisation* (London: Weidenfeld & Nicolson).

Hall, P. (2009) 'Historical Institutionalism in Rationalist and Sociological Perspective', in J. Mahoney and K. Thelen (eds) *Explaining Institutional Change: Ambiguity, Agency, and Power* (Cambridge: Cambridge University Press).

Hall, P. and Taylor, R. (1996) 'Political Science and Three New Institutionalisms', *Political Studies*, 44, 936–57.

Hall, P. and Taylor, R. (1998) 'The Potential of Historical Institutionalism: a Response to Hay and Wincott', *Political Studies*, 46 (5) 958–62.

Hall, P. and Thelen, K. (2008) 'Institutional Change in Varieties of Capitalism', *Socio-Economic Review* (2009) 7, 7–34, advance access publication 14.10.2008.

Hardin, G. (1963) 'The Cybernetics of Competition: A Biologist's View of Society', *Perspectives in Biology and Medicine*, 7, 58–84.

Hardin, G. (1968) 'The Tragedy of the Commons', *Science*, 162, 1243–8.

Hawkesworth, M. (2005) 'Engendering Political Science: An Immodest Proposal', *Politics and Gender*, 1 (1) 141–56.

Hay, C. (1997) 'Divided by a Common Language: Political theory and the Concept of Power', *Politics* 17 (1) 45–52.

Hay, C. (2001) 'The "Crisis" of Keynesianism and the Rise of Neo-Liberalism in Britain: An Ideational Institutionalist Approach', in J. L. Campbell and O. K. Pedersen (eds) *The Second*

Movement in Institutional Analysis (Princeton, NJ: Princeton University Press).

Hay, C. (2002) *Political Analysis: A Critical Introduction* (Basingstoke: Palgrave Macmillan).

Hay, C. (2006a) 'Constructivist Institutionalism', in R. A. W. Rhodes, S. A. Binder and B. A. Rockman (eds) *The Oxford Handbook Of Political Institutions* (Oxford: Oxford University Press).

Hay, C. (2006b) '(What's Marxist About) Marxist State Theory?', in C. Hay, M. Lister and M. Marsh (eds) *The State: Theories And Issues* (Basingstoke: Palgrave Macmillan).

Hay, C. (2010) 'Constructivist Institutionalism... Or, Why Ideas into interests Don't Go', in D. Béland and R. Cox (eds) *Ideas and Politics in Social Science Research* (Princeton, NJ: Princeton University Press).

Hay, C. (2012) 'Treating the Symptom Not the Condition: Crisis Definition, Deficit Reduction and the Search for a New British Growth Model', *British Journal of Politics and International Relations*, early online view, accessed 5/9/12 at http://onlinelibrary.wiley.com/doi/10.1111/j.1467-856X.2012.00515.x/full.

Hay, C. and Jessop, B. (1995) 'The Governance of Local Economic Development and the Development of Local Economic Governance', paper presented to the annual meeting of the American Political Science Association, Chicago, September 1995.

Hay, C. and Wincott, D. (1998) 'Structure, Agency, and Historical Institutionalism', *Political Studies*, 46, 951–7.

Healey, P. (2007) 'The New Institutionalism and the Transformative Goals of Planning', in N. Verma (ed.) *Institutions and Planning* (Oxford: Elsevier).

Heclo, H. (1974) *Modern Social Policies in Britain and Sweden: From Relief to Income Maintenance* (New Haven: Yale University Press).

Heclo, H. (2006) 'Thinking Institutionally', in B. A Rockman, S. A. Binder and R. A. W. Rhodes (eds) *The Oxford Handbook of Political Institutions* (Oxford: Open University Press).

Heclo, H. and Wildavsky, A. (1974) *The Private Government of Public Money: Community and Policy Inside British politics* (Basingstoke: Palgrave Macmillan).

Heffernan, R. (2003) 'Prime Ministerial Predominance? Core Executive Politics in the UK', *British Journal of Politics and International Relations*, 5 (3) 347–72.

Held, D. and Leftwich, A. (1984) 'A Discipline of Politics?', in A. Leftwich (ed.) *What is Politics? The Activity and its Study* (Oxford: Basil Blackwell).

Held, D. and Kaya, A. (eds) (2006) *Global Inequality: Patterns and Explanations* (Cambridge: Polity).

Helmke, G. and Levitsky, S. (2006) 'Introduction', in G. Helmke and S. Levitsky (eds) *Informal Institutions and Democracy: Lessons from Latin America* (Baltimore: Johns Hopkins University Press).

Heywood, A. (2011) *Global Politics* (Basingstoke: Palgrave Macmillan).

Hindmoor, A. (2010) 'Rational Choice', in G. Stoker and D. Marsh (eds) *Theory and Methods in Political Science* (3rd edn) (Basingstoke: Palgrave Macmillan).

Hochschild, J. and Birch, T. (2004) '(Purposes + Unintended Consequences) X 2 Policy Changes = Large Effects: Contingency and Intention in American Racial and Ethnic Categories', in papers to the Conference in Honour of Robert Dahl, *Contingency in the Study of Politics*, Yale University, 3–4 December 2004.

Hood, C. (1998) *The Art of the State* (Oxford: The Clarendon Press).

Hughes, E. (1936) 'The Ecological Aspects of Institutions', *American Sociological Review,* 1, 180–9.

Hughes, E. (1958) *Men and Their Work* (Glencoe, IL: Free Press).

Huntington, S. (1968) *Political Order in Changing Societies* (New Haven, CT: Yale University Press).

Immergut, E. (1992) *Health Politics: Interests and Institutions in Western Europe* (New York: Cambridge University Press).

Jackson, P. J. (2006) 'Making Sense of Making Sense: Configurational Analysis and the Double Hermeneutic', in D. Yanow and P. Schwartz-Shea (eds) *Interpretation and Method- Empirical Research Methods and the Interpretive Turn* (New York: M.E. Sharpe).

James, T. (2009) 'Whatever Happened to Regulation Theory? The Regulation Approach and Local Government Revisited', *Policy Studies*, 30 (2) 181–201.

Jessop, B. (1990) *State Theory: Putting Capitalist States In Their Place* (Pennsylvania: Pennsylvania State University Press).

Jessop, B. (2000) 'Governance Failure', in G. Stoker (ed.) *The New Politics of British Local Governance* (Basingstoke: Palgrave Macmillan).

Jessop, B. (2007) *State Power: A Strategic-relational Approach* (Cambridge: Polity).

Jessop, B. (2010) 'The "Return" of the National State in the Current Crisis of the World Market', *Capital & Class,* 34, 38–43.

John, P. (1998) *Analysing Public Policy* (London: Continuum).

John, P. (2001) *Local Governance in Western Europe* (London: Sage).

John, P. and Margetts, H. (2003) 'Policy Punctuations in the UK: Fluctuations and Equilibria in Central Government Expenditure since 1951', *Public Administration*, 81 (3) 411–32.

John, P., Smith, G. and Stoker, G. (2009) 'Nudge Nudge, Think Think: Two Strategies for Changing Civic Behaviour', *Political Quarterly*, 80 (3) 361–70.

Johnson, N. (1975) 'The Place of Institutions in the Study of Politics', *Political Studies*, 23, 271–83.

Jordan, G. (1990) 'Policy Community Realism versus "New" Institutional Ambiguity', *Political Studies*, 38 (3) 470–84.

Kathlene, L. (1995) 'Position Power versus Gender Power: Who Holds the Floor?', in G. Duerst- Lahti and R. M. Kelly (eds) *Gender Power, Leadership and Governance* (Ann Arbor, MI: University of Michigan Press) 167–93.

Katzenstein, P. (ed.) (1978) *Between Power and Plenty: Foreign Economic Policies of Advanced Industrial States* (Madison, WI: University of Wisconsin Press).

Keck, M. E. and Sikkink, K. (1998) *Activists Beyond Borders* (New York: Cornell University Press).

Kenny, M. (2007) 'Gender, Institutions and Power: A Critical Review', *Politics*, 27 (2) 445–66.

Kenny, M. (2011) 'Gender and Institutions of Political Recruitment: Candidate Selection in Post-Devolution Scotland', in M. L. Krook and F. Mackay (eds) *Gender, Politics and Institutions* (Basingstoke: Palgrave Macmillan) 21–41.

Kenny, M. and Lowndes, V. (2011) 'Rule-Making and Rule-Breaking: Understanding the Gendered Dynamics of Institutional Reform', paper presented at the Political Studies Association Annual Conference, London, 19–21 April 2011.

Khanna, T and Palepu, K. (2010) *Winning in Emerging Markets* (Cambridge, MA: Harvard Business School Press).

Kiser, L. L. and Ostrom, E. (1982) 'The Three Worlds of Action: A Metatheoretical Synthesis of Institutional Approaches', in E. Ostrom (ed.) *Strategies of Political Enquiry* (London: Sage).

Klijn, E.-H. (2001) 'Rules As Institutional Context For Decision Making In Networks: The Approach to Post-War Housing Districts in Two Cities', *Administration and Society*, 33 (2) 133–64.

Knight, F. H. (1921) *Risk, Uncertainty, and Profit*. Hart, Schaffner, and Marx Prize Essays, no. 31 (Boston and New York: Houghton Mifflin).

Knight, J. (1992) *Institutions and Social Conflict* (Cambridge: Cambridge University Press).

Krasner, S. D. (1980) *The Politics of the International Economy* (Berkeley, CA: University of California Press).

Krasner, S. D. (1984) 'Approaches to the State: Alternative Conceptions and Historical Dynamics', *Comparative Politics*, 16 (2) 223–46.

Krasner, S. D. (1988) 'Sovereignty: An Institutional Perspective', *Comparative Political Studies*, 21 (1) 66–94.

Krook, M. L. and Mackay, F. (2011) 'Introduction: Gender, Politics and Institutions', in M.L. Krook and F. Mackay (eds) *Gender, Politics and Institutions: Towards a Feminist Institutionalism* (Basingstoke: Palgrave Macmillan).

Laclau, E. and Mouffe, C. (1985) *Hegemony and the Socialist Strategy: Towards A Radical Democratic Politics* (London: Verso).

Langston, J. (2006) 'The Birth and Transformation of the Dedazo in Mexico', in G. Helmke and S. Levitsky (eds) *Informal Institutions and Democracy: Lessons from Latin America* (Baltimore: Johns Hopkins University Press).

Lanzara, G. (1998) 'Self-Destructive Processes In Institutional Building And Some Modest Countervailing Mechanisms', *European Journal of Political Research*, 33, 1–39.

Laraña, E., Johnston, H. and Gusfield, J. R. (eds) (1994) *New Social Movements: From Ideology to Identity* (Philadelphia: Temple University Press).

Leach, S. (1995) 'The Strange Case Of Local Government Review', in J. Stewart and G. Stoker (eds) *Local Government In The 1990s* (Basingstoke: Macmillan).

Leach, S. and Lowndes, V. (2004) 'Understanding Local Political Leadership: Constitutions, Contexts and Capabilities', *Local Government Studies*, 30 (4) 557–75.

Leach, S. and Lowndes, V. (2007) 'Of Roles and Rules: Analysing the Changing Relationship between Political Leaders and Chief Executives in Local Government', *Public Policy and Administration*, 22 (2) 183–200.

Lemarchand, R. (1981) 'Comparative Political Clientelism: Structure, Process and Optic', in S. N. Eisenstadt and R. Lemarchand (eds) *Political Clientelism, Patronage and Development* (Beverly Hills, CA: Sage).

Lichbach, M. I. (1998) *The Rebel's Dilemma* (Ann Arbor, MI: University of Michigan Press).

Lijphart, A. (1999) *Patterns of Democracy* (New Haven, CT: Yale University Press).

Linde, C. (2001) 'The Acquisition of a Speaker by a Story: How History Becomes Memory and Identity', *Ethos*, 28 (4) 608–32.

Lovenduski, J. and P. Norris (1989) 'Selecting Women Candidates: Obstacles to the Feminisation of the House of Commons', *European Journal of Political Research*, 17, 533–62.

Lowndes, V. (1996) 'Varieties of New Institutionalism: A Critical Appraisal', *Public Administration*, 74, 181–97.

Lowndes, V. (1999) 'Management Change in Local Governance', in G. Stoker (ed.) *The New Management of British Local Governance* (Basingstoke: Macmillan).

Lowndes, V. (2002) 'Institutionalism', in D. Marsh and G. Stoker (eds) *Theory And Methods In Political Science*, (2nd edn) (Basingstoke: Palgrave Macmillan).

Lowndes, V. (2005) 'Something Old, Something New, Something Borrowed ... How Institutions Change (And Stay The Same) In Local Governance', *Policy Studies*, 26, 291–309.

Lowndes, V. (2010) 'The Institutional Approach', in D. Marsh and G. Stoker (eds) *Theory and Methods in Political Science* (3rd edn) (Basingstoke: Palgrave Macmillan).

Lowndes, V. and Pratchett, L. (2008) 'Public Policy and Social Capital: Creating, Redistributing or Liquidating?' in D. Castiglione, J. van Deth and G. Wolle (eds) *The Handbook of Social Capital* (Oxford: Oxford University Press) pp, 677–707.

Lowndes, V. and Squires, S. (2012) 'Cuts, Collaboration and Creativity', *Public Money and Management*, 32 (6), 401–8.

Lowndes, V. and Wilson, D. (2001) 'Social Capital and Local Governance: Exploring the Institutional Design Variable', *Political Studies*, 49 (4), 628–47.

Lowndes, V. and Wilson, D. (2003) 'Balancing Revisability and Robustness?: A New Institutionalist Perspective on Local Government Modernisation', *Public Administration*, 81 (2) 275–98.

Lowndes, V., Pratchett, L. and Stoker, G. (2006) 'Local Political Participation: The Impact of Rules-In-Use', *Public Administration*, 84 (3) 539–61.

Lowndes, V., Stoker, G. and Pratchett, L. (1998) *Enhancing Public Participation in Local Government* (London: DETR).

Luban, D. (1996) 'The Publicity Principle', in R. Goodin (ed.) *The Theory of Institutional Design* (Cambridge: Cambridge University Press).

Lupia, A. and McCubbins, M. D. (1994) 'Learning from Oversight: Fire Alarms and Police Patrols Reconstructed', *Journal of Law, Economics and Organisation*, 10, 96–125.

Maguire, D. (2010) 'Marxism', in G. Stoker and D. Marsh (eds) *Theories and Methods in Political Science* (3rd edn) (Basingstoke: Palgrave Macmillan) pp. 136–55.

Mahoney, J. and Thelen, K. (2010) 'A Theory of Gradual Institutional Change', in J. Mahoney and K. Thelen (eds) *Explaining Institutional Change: Ambiguity, Agency and Power* (Cambridge: Cambridge University Press).

March, J. G. and Olsen, J. P. (1984) 'The New Institutionalism:

Organisational Factors in Political Life', *American Political Science Review*, 78, 738–49.

March, J. G. and Olsen, J. P. (1989) *Rediscovering Institutions* (New York: Free Press).

March, J. G. and Olsen, J. P. (2004) 'The Logic of Appropriateness', *Arena Working Papers*, Centre for European Studies, University of Oslo, 17/07/2007, www.arena.uio.no/publications/working-papers 2004/papers/wp04_9.pdf.

March, J. G. and Olsen, J. P. (2009) 'The Logic of Appropriateness' Arena Working Papers WP 04/09 Arena Centre for European Studies University of Oslo.

Marr, A. (2007) *A History Of Modern Britain* (Basingstoke: Palgrave Macmillan).

Marsh, D. (2002) 'Marxism', in D. Marsh and G. Stoker (eds) (2nd edn) *Theory and Methods in Political Science* (Basingstoke: Palgrave Macmillan).

Marsh, D. (2008) 'Understanding British Politics: Analysing Competing Models', *The British Journal of Politics and International Relations*, 10 (2) 251–68.

Marsh, D. (2010) 'Meta-Theoretical Issues', in D. Marsh and G. Stoker (eds) (3rd edn) *Theory and Methods in Political Science* (Basingstoke: Palgrave Macmillan).

Marsh, D. and Rhodes, R. A. W. (1992) *New Directions in the Study of Policy Networks* (Dordrecht: Kluwer).

Mayntz, R. (2004) 'Organisational Forms of Terrorism: Hierarchy, Network or a Type *Sui Generis*', MPIfG Discussion Paper 04/4 (Cologne: Max-Plank Institut fur Gessellschaftsforschung).

Mayntz, R. and Scharpf, F. W. (1995) 'Der Ansatz des akteurzentrierten Institutionalismus', in R. Mayntz and F. W. Scharpf (eds) *Gesellschaftliche Selbstregelung und politische Steuerung* (Frankfurt: Campus).

Mayr, E. (1963) *Animal Species and Evolution* (Cambridge, MA: Harvard University Press).

McAdam, D. (1988) *Freedom Summer* (Oxford: Oxford University Press).

McAnulla, S. (2006) *British Politics: A Critical Introduction* (London: Continuum).

Merelman, R. M. (2003) *Pluralism at Yale: The Culture of Political Science in America* (Madison, WI: University of Wisconsin Press).

Meyer, J. W. (1994) 'Rationalised Eenvironments', in W. R. Scott and J. W. Meyer (eds) *Institutional Environments and Organizations: Structural Complexity and Individualism* (Thousand Oaks, CA: Sage).

Meyer, J. and Rowan, B. (1977) 'Institutional Organizations: Formal

Structure as Myth and Ceremony', *American Journal of Sociology*, 83 (2) 340–63.

Mills, C. Wright (1956) *The Power Elite* (Oxford: Oxford University Press).

Moon, D. (2012) 'Towards a Post-structuralist Institutionalism', Unpublished paper.

Morris, E. (2010) 'The Tea Party Last Time', *New York Times*, 31/10/2010.

Mossberger, K. and Stoker, G. (2001) 'The Evolution of Urban Regime Theory: The Challenge of Conceptualization', *Urban Affairs Review*, 36 (6) 810–35.

Mouffe, C. (2000) *The Democratic Paradox* (London: Verso).

Newman, J. (2001) *Modernising Governance: New Labour, Policy and Society* (London: Sage).

Newman, J. (2005) 'Enter the Transformational Leader: Network Governance and the Micro-Politics of Modernization', *Sociology*, 39 (4) 717–34.

Niskanen, W. (1971) *Bureaucracy and Representative Government* (New York: Aldine- Atherton).

Niskanen, W. (1973) *Bureaucracy: Servant or Master?* (London: Institute of Economic Affairs).

North, D. C. (1990) *Institutions, Institutional Change And Economic Performance* (Cambridge: Cambridge University Press).

North, D. and Thomas, R. (1973) *The Rise of the Western World: A New Economic History* (Cambridge: Cambridge University Press).

Nye, J. (2008) *The Powers to Lead: Soft, Hard, and Smart* (New York: Oxford University Press).

Offe, C. (1996) 'Designing Institutions in East European Transitions', in R. Goodin (ed.) *TheTheory of Institutional Design* (Cambridge: Cambridge University Press).

Offe, C. (2009) 'Governance an Empty Signifier?', *Constellations*, 16 (4) 550–62.

Ohmae, K. (1995) *The End of the Nation State* (New York: Free Press).

Orren, K. and Skowronek, S. (2002) 'American Political Development', in I. Katznelson and H. Milner (eds) *Political Science: The State of the Discipline* (New York: Norton).

Ostrom, E. (1986) 'An Agenda for the Study of Institutions', *Public Choice*, 48, 3–25.

Ostrom, E. (1999) 'Institutional Rational Choice: An Assessment of The Institutional Analysis and Development Framework', in P. Sabatier (ed.) *Theories of the Public Policy Process* (Oxford: Westview Press).

Ostrom, E. (2005) *Understanding Institutional Diversity* (Princeton and Oxford: Princeton University Press).

Ostrom, E. (2007) *The Challenge of Crafting Rules to Change Open Access Resources into Managed Resources*, paper presented at the International Economic Association round table on the Sustainability of Economic Growth, Beijing, China, 13–14 July 2007.

Ostrom, E. and Cardenas, J/ (2004) 'What do People Bring into the Game: Experiments in the Field about Cooperation in the Commons, *Agricultural Systems*, 82, 307–26.

Ostrom, E., Gardner, R. and Walker, J. (1994) *Rules, Games, and Common Pool Resources* (Ann Arbor, MI: University of Michigan Press).

Painter, J. (1995) *Politics, Geography and Political Geography: A Critical Perspective* (London: Arnold).

Parsons, D. (2010) 'Constructivism and Interpretive Theory', in D. Marsh and G. Stoker (eds) *Theory and Methods in Political Science* (Basingstoke: Palgrave Macmillan).

Parsons, T. (1951) *The Social System* (Glencoe, IL: Free Press).

Perrow, C. (1987) *Complex Organizations: A Critical Essay* (New York: McGraw-Hill).

Peters, B. G. (1996) 'Institutionalism Old and New', in R. E. Goodin and H. Klingenmann (eds) *A New Handbook of Political Science* (Oxford: Oxford University Press).

Peters, B. G. (1999) *Institutional Theory in Political Science: The New Institutionalism* (London: Pinter).

Peters, B. G. (2005) *Institutional Theory in Political Science: The 'New Institutionalism'*, (2nd edn) (London: Continuum).

Peters, B. G. and Hogwood, B. W. (1991) 'Applying Population Ecology Models to Public Organizations', *Research in Public Administration*, 1, 79–108.

Peters, B. G. and Pierre, J. (1998) 'Institutions and Time: Problems of Conceptualisation and Explanation', *Journal of Public Administration Research and Theory*, 4, 565–83.

Pierson, P. (1996) 'The Path to European Integration: A Historical Institutionalist Analysis', *Comparative Political Studies*, 29 (2) 123–63.

Pierson, P. (2000) 'Increasing Returns, Path Dependence, and the Study of Politics', *American Political Science Review*, 94 (2) 251–67.

Pierson, P. (2003) 'Big, Slow-moving and... Invisible: Macrosocial Process in the Study of Comparative Politics', in J. Mahoney and D. Rueschemeyer (eds) *Comparative Historical Analysis in the Social Sciences* (Cambridge: Cambridge University Press).

Pierson, P. (2004) *Politics In Time* (Princeton, NJ: Princeton University Press).

Pierson, P. and Skocpol, T. (2002) 'Historical Institutionalism in Contemporary Political Science', in I. Katznelson and H. V. Milner (eds) *Political Science: The State of the Discipline* (New York: W.W. Norton).

Polanyi, K. (1992) 'The Economy as Instituted Process', in M. Granovetter and R. Swedberg (eds) *The Sociology of Economic Life* (Boulder, CO: Westview Press).

Polsby, N W. (1975) 'Legislatures', in F. Greenstein and F. Polsby (eds) *A Handbook of Political Science* (Reading, MA: Addison-Wesley).

Premfors, R. (2004) 'The Contingency of Democratization: Scandinavia in Comparative Perspective', in papers to the Conference in Honour of Robert Dahl, *Contingency In The Study Of Politics*, Yale University, 3–4 December 2004.

Putnam, R. (1993) *Making Democracy Work: Civic Traditions in Modern Italy* (Princeton: Princeton University Press).

Putnam, R. (2000) *Bowling Alone: The Collapse and Revival of American Community* (New York: Simon & Schuster).

Rawnsley A. (2010) *The End of the Party: The Rise and Fall of New Labour* (London: Viking).

Reich, R. B. (1990) *The Power of Public Ideas* (Cambridge, MA: Harvard University Press).

Rhodes, R. A. W. (1988) *Beyond Westminster and Whitehall: The Sub-central Governments of Britain* (London: Unwin Hyman).

Rhodes, R. A. W. (1995) 'The Institutional Approach', in M. Marsh and G. Stoker (eds) *Theory and Methods in Political Science* (Basingstoke: Macmillan).

Rhodes, R. A. W. (1997) *Understanding Governance: Policy Networks, Governance, Reflexivity and Accountability* (London: Open University Press).

Rhodes, R. A. W. (2006) 'Old Institutionalisms', in R. A. W. Rhodes, S. A. Binder and B. A. Rockman (eds) *The Oxford Handbook of Political Institutions* (Oxford: Oxford University Press).

Rhodes, R. A. W., Binder, S. A. and Rockman, B. A. (2006) *The Oxford Handbook of Political Institutions* (Oxford: Oxford University Press).

Richardson, J. and Jordan, G. (1979) *Governing Under Pressure. The Policy Process in a Post Parliamentary Democracy* (Oxford: Martin Robertson).

Riker, W. H. (1980) 'Implications from the Disequilibrium of Majority Rule for the Study of Institutions', *American Political Science Review,* 74, 432–46.

Riker, W. H. (1982) *Liberalism Against Populism: A Confrontation Between the Theory of Democracy and the Theory of Social Choice* (San Francisco: W.H. Freeman).

Ringen, S. (2005: 5) *The Powerlessness of Powerful Government* (Oxford: Oxford University Press).

Rittberger, V. (1993) *Regime Theory and International Relations* (Oxford: Clarendon Press).

Roberts, M. (2008) 'Bringing the Actor Back In: Agency as the Engine of Collaborative Public Governance', unpublished PhD thesis, INLOGOV, School of Public Policy, University of Birmingham.

Robson, W. A. (1960) *Nationalized Industry and Public Ownership* (London: Allen & Unwin).

Rose, N. S. (1999) *Powers of Freedom Reframing Political Thought* (Cambridge: Cambridge University Press).

Rothstein, B. (1996) 'Political Institutions – An Overview', in R. E. Goodin and H. D. Klingemann (eds) *A New Handbook for Political Science* (Oxford: Oxford University Press).

Sabatier, P. (1988) 'An Advocacy Coalition Framework of Policy Change and the Role of Policy-oriented Learning Therein', *Policy Sciences,* 21, 129–68.

Sabatier, P. (2007) *Theories of the Policy Process* (Boulder, CO: Westview Press).

Sabatier, P. and Weible, C. M. (2007) 'The Advocacy Coalition Framework: Innovations and Clarifications', in P. Sabatier (ed.) *Theories of the Policy Process* (Boulder, CO: Westview Press).

Sanders, D. (2010) 'Behavioural Analysis', in D. Marsh and G. Stoker (eds) *Theories and Methods in Political Science* (3rd edn) (Basingstoke: Palgrave Macmillan).

Scharpf, F. W. (1997) *Games Real Actors Play: Actor-Centred Institutionalism In Policy Research* (Boulder, CO: Westview Press).

Schickler, E. (2001) *Disjointed Pluralism: Institutional Innovation and the Development of the U.S. Congress* (Princeton, NJ: Princeton University Press).

Schmidt, V. (2006) 'Institutionalism', in C. Hay, M. Lister and D. Marsh (eds) *The State: Theories and Issues* (Basingstoke: Palgrave Macmillan).

Schmidt, V. (2008) 'Discursive Institutionalism: The Explanatory Power of Ideas', *Annual Review of Political Science*, 11, 1, 303–26.

Schmidt, V. (2009) 'Putting Political Back into the Political Economy by Bringing the State Back in Yet Again', *World Politics,* 61 (3) 516–46.

Schmidt, V. (2010) 'Taking Ideas and Discourse Seriously: Explaining Change Through Discursive Institutionalism as the Fourth "New Institutionalism"', *European Political Science Review,* 2, (1) 1–25.

Schneiberg, M. and Clemens, E. (2006) 'The Typical Tools For The Job: Research Strategies In Institutional Analysis', *Sociological Theory*, 3, 195–227.

Schneiberg, M. and Lounsbury, M. (2008) 'Social Movements and Neo-institutional Theory: Analyzing Path Creation and Change', in

R. Greenwood, C. Oliver, S. Sahlin-Andersson and R. Suddaby (eds) *Handbook of Institutional Theory* (Thousand Oaks, CA: Sage).

Schotter, A. (1986) *The Economic Theory of Social Institutions* (Cambridge: Cambridge University Press).

Scott, W. R. (2001) *Institutions and Organizations* (2nd edn) (Thousand Oaks, CA: Sage).

Scott, W. R. (2008) *Institutions and Organizations: Ideas and Interests* (3rd edn) (Thousand Oaks, CA: Sage).

Scott, W. R., Ruef, M., Mendel, P. and Caronna, C. (2000) *Institutional Change and Organizations: Transformation of a Healthcare Field* (Chicago: University of Chicago Press).

Selznick, P. (1949) *TVA and the Grass Roots: A Study in the Sociology of Formal Organization* (Berkeley, CA: University of California Press).

Selznick, P. (1957) *Leadership in Administration; a Sociological Interpretation* (Evanston, IL: Row, Peterson).

Shepsle, K. (1986) 'Institutional Equilibrium and Equilibrium Institutions', in H. Weisberg (ed.) *Political Science: The Science of Politics* (New York: Agathon).

Shepsle, K. (1989) 'Studying Institutions: Some Lessons from the Rational Choice Approach', *Journal of Theoretical politics*, 1, 131–47.

Silverman, D. (1971) *The Theory of Organizations: A Sociological Framework* (New York: Basic Books).

Skocpol, T. (1979) *States and Social Revolutions: A Comparative Analysis of France, Russia, and China* (Cambridge: Cambridge University Press).

Skocpol, T. (1985) 'Bringing the State Back In: Strategies of Analysis in Current Research', in P. Evans, D. Rueschemeyer and T. Skocpol (eds) *Bringing the State Back In* (Cambridge: Cambridge University Press).

Skowronek, S. (1982) *Building a New American State: The Expansion of National Administrative Capacities, 1877–1920* (Cambridge: Cambridge University Press).

Smith, M. (2006) 'Pluralism', in C. Hay, M. Lister and D. Marsh (eds) *The State: Theories and Issues* (Basingstoke: Palgrave Macmillan).

Sørenson, E. and Torfing, J. (2008) 'Theoretical Approaches to Governance Network Dynamics', in E. Sørenson and J. Torfing (eds) *Theories of Democratic Network Governance* (Basingstoke: Palgrave Macmillan).

Steinmo, S., Thelen, K. and Longstreth, F. (eds) (1992) *Structuring Politics Historical Institutionalism in Comparative Analysis* (Cambridge: Cambridge University Press).

Stewart, J. (2000) *The Nature of British Local Government* (Basingstoke: Palgrave Macmillan).

Stewart, J. (2002) 'Will Best Value Survive?', *Public Money and Management*, 22 (2) 4–5.

Stewart, J. (2003) *Modernising British Local Government: An Assessment of Labour's Reform Programme* (Basingstoke: Palgrave Macmillan).

Stinchcombe, A. L. (1997) 'On the Virtues of the Old Institutionalism', *Annual Review of Sociology*, 23, 1–18.

Stoker, G. (1995) 'Regime Theory and Urban Politics', in D. Judge, G. Stoker and H. Wolman (eds) *Theories of Urban Politics* (London: Sage).

Stoker, G. (1999) 'Remaking Local Democracy: Lessons from the New Labour Reform Strategy', paper presented at Department of Government, University of Manchester, Golden Jubilee Celebrations.

Stoker, G. (2002) 'Life is a Lottery: New Labour's Strategy for the Reform of Devolved Governance', *Public Administration*, 80 (3) 417–34.

Stoker, G. (2010) 'Blockages on the Road to Relevance: Why has Political Relevance Failed to Deliver?', *European Political Science*, 9, 72–84.

Stoker, G. and Mossberger, K. (1995) 'The Post-Fordist Local State', in J. Stewart and G. Stoker (eds) *Local Government in the 1990s* (London: Macmillan).

Stone,C. (1989) *Regime Politics: Governing Atlanta 1946–1988* (Lawrence: University Press of Kansas).

Strang, D. and Meyer, J. (1993) 'Institutional Conditions for Diffusion', *Theory and Society*, 22, 487–512.

Streek, W. (2001) 'Introduction: Explorations into the Origins of Nonliberal Capitalism in Germany and Japan', in W. Streek and K. Yamamura (eds) *The Origins of Nonliberal Capitalism: Germany and Japan* (New York: Cornell University Press).

Streek, W. and Thelen, K. (eds) (2005) *Beyond Continuity: Institutional Change in Advanced Political Economies* (Oxford: Oxford University Press).

Sullivan, H. and Skelcher, C. (2002) *Working Across Boundaries* (Basingstoke: Palgrave Macmillan).

Sumner, W. G. (1906) *Folkways, a Study of the Sociological Importance of Usages, Manners, Customs, Mores, and Morals* (Boston, MA: Ginn).

Thelen, K. (2004) *How Institutions Evolve. The Political Economy of Skills in Germany, Britain, the United States and Japan* (Cambridge: Cambridge University Press).

Thelen, K. (2009) 'Institutional Change in Advanced Political Economies', *British Journal of Industrial Relations*, 47 (3) 471–98.

Thelen, K. and Steinmo, S. (1992) 'Historical Institutionalism in Comparative Politics', in S. Steinmo, K. Thelen and F. Longstreth (eds) *Structuring Politics: Historical Institutionalism In Comparative Analysis* (Cambridge: Cambridge University Press).

True, J. L., Jones, B. D. and Baumgartner, F. R. (1999) 'Punctuated-Equilibrium Theory: Explaining Stability And Change In Public Policymaking', in P. Sabatier (ed.) *Theories of the Policy Process* (Colorado: Westview Press).

Verba, S., Schlozman, K. and Brady, H. (1995) *Voice and Equality: Civic Voluntarism in American Politics* (Cambridge, MA: Harvard University Press).

Walker, J. and Ostrom, E. (2007) 'Trust and Reciprocity as Foundations for Cooperation: Individuals, Institutions, and Context', Paper presented at the Capstone Meeting of the RSF Trust Initiative at the Russell Sage Foundation in May 2007, http://www.iew.uzh.ch/static/seminars/downloads/Walker-Ostrom-v6-4-06-07.pdf, accessed 30.3.2012.

Walsh, K., Deakin, N., Smith, P., Spurgeon P. and Thomas, N. (1997) *Contracting for Change* (Oxford: Oxford University Press).

Ward, H. (2002) 'Rational Choice', in D. Marsh and G. Stoker (eds) *Theory and Methods in Political Science* (Basingstoke: Macmillan).

Waylen, G. (2011) 'Gendered Institutionalist Analysis: Understanding democratic transitions', in M. L. Krook and F. Mackay (eds) *Gender, Politics and Institutions: Towards a Feminist Institutionalism* (Basingstoke: Palgrave Macmillan).

Weingast, B. (1996) 'Political Institutions: Rational Choice Perspectives', in R. Goodin and H.-D. Klingemann (eds) *A New Handbook of Political Science* (Oxford: Oxford University Press).

Weir, M. and Skocpol, T. (1983) 'State Structures and Social Keynesianism: Responses to the Great Depression in Sweden and the United States', *International Journal of Comparative Sociology*, 24, 4–29.

Weir, M. and Skocpol, T. (1985) *Bringing the State Back In* (Cambridge: Cambridge University Press).

Wendt, A. (1999) *Social Theory of International Politics* (Cambridge: Cambridge University Press).

Williams, R. (1983) *Keywords: A Vocabulary of Culture and Society* (Oxford: Oxford University Press).

Williamson, O. E. (1985) *The Economic Institutions of Capitalism: Firms, Markets, Relational Contracting* (New York: Free Press).

Wilson, D. (2003) 'Unravelling Control Freakery: Redefining Central–Local Government Relations', *British Journal of Politics and International Relations*, 5 (3) 317–46.

Wilson, D. and Game, C. (2011) *Local Government in the United Kingdom* (5th edn) (Basingstoke: Palgrave Macmillan).

Wilson, W. (1956) *Congressional Government: A Study in American Politics* (Cleveland: World Publishing).

Wood, D. (2001) *The Deconstruction of Time* (Evanston, IL: North Western University Press).

Zucker, L. G. (1977) 'The Role of Institutionalization in Cultural Persistence', *American Sociological Review*, 42, 726–43.

Zucker, L. G. (1991) 'The Role of Institutionalization in Cultural Persistence', in W.W. Powell and P.J. DiMaggio (eds) *The New Institutionalism in Organizational Analysis* (Chicago: University of Chicago Press).

Author Index

Subject Index

POLITICAL ANALYSIS

Series Editors: B. Guy Peters, Jon Pierre and Gerry Stoker

POLITICAL ANALYSIS

Series Editors: B. Guy Peters, Jon Pierre and Gerry Stoker

Political science today is a dynamic discipline. Its substance, theory and methods have all changed radically in recent decades. It is much expanded in range and scope and in the variety of new perspectives – and new variants of old ones – that it encompasses. The sheer volume of work being published, and the increasing degree of its specialization, however, make it difficult for political scientists to maintain a clear grasp of the state of debate beyond their own particular subdisciplines.

The *Political Analysis* series is intended to provide a channel for different parts of the discipline to talk to one another and to new generations of students. Our aim is to publish books that provide introductions to, and exemplars of, the best work in various areas of the discipline. Written in an accessible style, they provide a 'launching-pad' for students and others seeking a clear grasp of the key methodological, theoretical and empirical issues, and the main areas of debate, in the complex and fragmented world of political science.

A particular priority is to facilitate intellectual exchange between academic communities in different parts of the world. Although frequently addressing the same intellectual issues, research agendas and literatures in North America, Europe and elsewhere have often tended to develop in relative isolation from one another. This series is designed to provide a framework for dialogue and debate which, rather than advocacy of one regional approach or another, is the key to progress.

The series reflects our view that the core values of political science should be coherent and logically constructed theory, matched by carefully constructed and exhaustive empirical investigation. The key challenge is to ensure quality and integrity in what is produced rather than to constrain diversity in methods and approaches. The series is intended as a showcase for the best of political science in all its variety, and demonstrates how nurturing that variety can further improve the discipline.

Political Analysis Series
Series Standing Order
ISBN 9780333786949 Hardback
ISBN 9780333945063 Paperback
ISBN 9780230585386 Electronic Book Text
(outside North American only)

You can receive future titles in this series as they are published by placing a standing order. Please contact your bookseller or, in the case of difficulty, write to us at the address below with your name and address, the title of the series and one of the ISBNs quoted above.

Customer Services Department, Macmillan Distribution Ltd
Houndmills, Basingstoke, Hampshire RG21 6XS, England, UK